ISRAEL'S GONE
GLOBAL

EXPLORING BIBLICAL SALVATION

- 3 -

Steve H Hakes

Israel's Gone Global

Exploring Biblical Salvation

~

Steve H Hakes

Paperback ISBN: 978-0-9957013-5-9
Hardback ISBN: 979-8-4485317-8-1
Kindle ISBN: 978-0-9957013-4-2

V251128163800

Scripture quotations marked...

ALT are taken from the Analytical-Literal Translation of the New Testament Devotional Version, copyright © 2007 by Gary F Zeolla, of Darkness to Light ministry (www.dtl.org). Used by permission.

CEB are taken from The Common English Bible © 2012. Used by permission.

CEV are from the Contemporary English Version Copyright © 1991, 1992, 1995 by American Bible Society, Used by permission.

CJB are taken from the Complete Jewish Bible, copyright © 1998 by David H Stern. Published by Jewish New Testament Publications, Inc. www.messianicjewish.net/jntp. Distributed by Messianic Jewish Resources. www.messianicjewish.net. All rights reserved. Used by permission.

GNB are from the Good News Bible © 1994 published by the Bible Societies/HarperCollins Publishers Ltd UK, Good News Bible © American Bible Society 1966, 1971, 1976, 1992. Used with permission.

EJB are taken from the Jubilee Bible, copyright © 2000, 2001, 2010, 2013 by Life Sentence Publishing, Inc. Used by permission of Life Sentence Publishing, Inc., Abbotsford, Wisconsin. All rights reserved.

ERV are taken from the Holy Bible: Easy-To-Read Version © 2014 by Bible League International, and used by permission.

HCSB are taken from the Holman Christian Standard Bible®, Copyright © 1999, 2000, 2002, 2003, 2009 by Holman Bible Publishers. Used by permission. Holman Christian Standard Bible®, Holman CSB®, and HCSB® are federally registered trademarks of Holman Bible Publishers.

ISV are taken from the Holy Bible: International Standard Version® Release 2.0. Copyright © 1996-2012 by the ISV Foundation. Used by permission of Davidson Press, LLC. All rights reserved internationally.

NCV are taken from the New Century Version®. Copyright © 2005 by Thomas Nelson, Inc. Used by permission.

NIV are taken from the Holy Bible, New International Version® NIV®. Copyright © 1973, 1978, 1984, 2011 by Biblica, Inc.® Used by permission of Biblica, Inc.® All rights reserved worldwide.

NJB are from The New Jerusalem Bible, copyright © 1985 by Darton, Longman & Todd, Ltd. and Doubleday, a division of Random House, Inc. Used by permission.

NKJV are taken from the New King James Version®. Copyright © 1982 by Thomas Nelson, Inc. Used by permission.

NLT are taken from the Holy Bible, New Living Translation, copyright © 1996, 2004. Used by permission of Tyndale House Publishers, Inc., Wheaton, Illinois 60189. All rights reserved.

Thanks...

- to Anne my wife, for her patient endurance.
- to the Salvation Army, for getting Christ into me, and for what in those days was called the Christian Revival Crusade (Australia), for getting me into Christ.
- to C S Lewis, whose works helped ground me in Christianity.
- to my daughter Charlotte (BA), for painstakingly going through the draft version—any imperfections remain mine.
- to all who have with good heart interacted with me, socially and spiritually. Some I should have heeded more. Some I should have heeded less. Some heeded have taught me well. Good life is listening, discriminating, adjusting in Christ.

Real life is a life of gratitude.

Dedicated to the memory of
Dr. David Allen
my former tutor at Mattersey Hall
in church history and doctrines

Contents

Biblical Abbreviations

Ac. *Acts*
Am. *Amos*
Chr. *Chronicles*
Col. *Colossians*
Cor. *Corinthians*
Dan. *Daniel*
Dt. *Deuteronomy*
Ec. *Ecclesiastes*
Eph. *Ephesians*
Est. *Esther*
Ex. *Exodus*
Ezk. *Ezekiel*
Ezr. *Ezra*
Gal. *Galatians*
Gen. *Genesis*
Hab. *Habakkuk*
Heb. *Hebrews*
Hg. *Haggai*
Hos. *Hosea*

Is. *Isaiah*
Jas. *James*
Jg. *Judges*
Jhn. *John*
Jl. *Joel*
Jnh. *Jonah*
Job *Job*
Jos. *Joshua*
Jr. *Jeremiah*
Jude *Jude*
Kg. *Kings*
Lk. *Luke*
Lm. *Lamentations*
Lv. *Leviticus*
Mic. *Micah*
Mk. *Mark*
Ml. *Malachi*
Mt. *Matthew*
Nah. *Nahum*

Nb. *Numbers*
Neh. *Nehemiah*
Ob. *Obadiah*
Phm. *Philemon*
Php. *Philippians*
Pr. *Proverbs*
Ps(s). *Psalm(s)*
Pt. *Peter*
Rm. *Romans*
Ruth *Ruth*
Rv. *Revelation*
Sam. *Samuel*
Sg. *Song of Songs*
Ths. *Thessalonians*
Tm. *Timothy*
Tts. *Titus*
Zc. *Zechariah*
Zp. *Zephaniah*

Grades[1]

Percent	100-95	94-90	89-85	84-80	79-75	74-70	69-65	
Letter	A+	A	A-	B+	B	B-	C+	
Point	4.3	4	3.7	3.3	3	2.7	2.3	
Percent	64-60	59-55	54-50	49-45	44-40	39-27	26-14	13-00
Letter	C	C-	D+	D	D-	U+	U	U-
Point	2	1.7	1.3	1	0.7	0	0	0

---

[1]   For handier sorting in tables, I advise using A1/A2/A3 and B1/B2/B3, etc, for grade letters. I have put these here in the more familiar forms of, eg, A+/A/A- and B+/B/B-. For grade points, I round final totals to the nearest 0.5 points.

Preface

In Jane Austen's *Pride and Prejudice*, Elizabeth bluntly tells Mr Darcy that he's a disgrace to the human race and has ruined major life-journeys of two good people. He replied by letter, begging for open-mindedness. She knew he could not justify his actions, but with a second more reflective reading, she wavered on one point. A third closer reading, and she reluctantly dropped her opposition—as regards Darcy's treatment of Wickham. Then the other offence, closer to home, also seemed to melt away. My journey so far has turned from some roads I once held dear. Opposition to some scandalous ideas has, with rereading, melted away. I have done an Elizabeth, and challenge with the challenges I have faced. You think me wrong? Like Elizabeth, re-read me, yet you might be right.

Over some 60 years as a Christian, I have come to think that seeking to systemise the facts of sin and salvation, are at best human reflections on heavenly data. Christian systems have arisen to resolve various issues and to attain a cohesive framework as a platform. Augustine confessed he hadn't achieved "a satisfactory and worthy explanation". No agreed framework exists throughout the church, since none are perfect. Here I but add my own rough framework of inexclusivism, a work in progress.

Questions there are aplenty. Was there a heavenly road before Sinai? Did Sinai become the only road, excluding any earlier? Has the gospel become the only road, excluding Sinai? If not, do the ethnic-Jewish people have a special road of salvation? If so, does all humanity have a road all people can travel to heaven? Do the unborn have special dispensation, or disaster? Is heaven based on our conscious choice in our mortal years? Can heaven be based on our conscious choice after our mortal years? Is there any unfairness whatsoever in final destinations? Is there deific salvation before death?

For Bible texts, my main English versions (MEVV) are the CEB/CEV/ERV/ LEB/NABRE/NCV/NIV/NKJV/NLT/NRSV. For grading, the best will be A+, and the worst D-: none shall fail. In quotes, I often amend [the LORD] to [Yahweh], and remove false capitals from nouns and pronouns. I sometimes take liberties when quoting generally: for example, updating gender style, adjusting tenses, standardising abbreviations, and simplifying bibliographies intext.

Steve H Hakes (2025) mallon.detc@gmail.com

Prologue

In Brooklyn, New York, David Wilkerson was on the loose. So too were the dreaded Mau Mau gang. Switchblades were in; rumbles were the name of the game. Spiritual enlightened, gang president Israel Narvaez, said "Look! I'm in the Bible. Here's my name all over the place. See? Israel. That's me. I'm famous."[2] Well, it's his famous name which is my focus as I go through levels of Israel and levels of salvation.

Chapters 1–3 look at the basic idea of covenant, using the prism of marriage, a common covenant. Have all biblical covenants explicitly or implicitly allowed for annulment? If so, has the Sinai Covenant been annulled, or does it remain valid, and its people and land remain as God's exclusive or parallel covenant people and land? This opens up ideas about whether all of Sinai commands were all for all peoples and all times, so has ethical implications.

I look at four levels of the salvation-term, *Israel*. If asked whether we should support Israel, let us be clear what both question and answer mean. Does Israel support us? Is the messianic community true Israel of true Israel? What is the true holy land? Did the Sinai road lead to the Golgotha road, and are both still special to God? I look at some key texts behind the idea that ethnic-Israel is still as such under a racial covenant with Yahweh. What do the texts say?

Chapters 4–6 look at whether salvation under Sinai was the same as salvation under Golgotha. Was the non-Jewish Moses *born anew*, *indwelt* by God's spirit? What do these terms actually mean? Did the cross open up a new relationship to God, and in what way or ways can people be children of God, when even Adam was a child of his?

Do attempts to argue a Sinaitic mission from a so-called Great Commission of Exodus 19, the psalms, and from Intertestamental Jewish writings, get past Eckhard Schnabel's *Early Christian Mission* (2004)? Was Mt.23:15 simply about turning God-fearers into full proselytes (Scot McKnight: Themelios 2007:32.2.64)? Was Sinai good news?

Who has been able to enter heaven? Did Yahweh then hold back everlasting life from all except under Sinai? Does he now hold back everlasting life from all who do not hear the gospel? Why did Naomi

---

[2]   http://runbabyrun.ovh.org/books/run_baby_run.pdf, p84

try to turn her daughters-in-law away from Sinai, if Sinai was a road necessary for life with God after death? And why for its first 10 years, did the church not bother about evangelising ethnic-Gentiles, if Golgotha was a road necessary for life with God after death? Has God been able to speak life beyond the specific covenants he has set up of Sinai and Golgotha? Are there levels of his salvation which people can enjoy before death, but are not needed for true life beyond death?

James called Global Christianity, a religion. We might not say that other world religions give life with God, but do we wonder whether sub-Christian humanity can have some level of life with God, and wonder whether the other world religions were created by people seeking him? Have they created their own roads, instilling them with their limited yet somewhat helpful wisdom, roads not fully of God nor roads to God, but roads of the godly and followers? Do such roads show traces of spiritual desire to please and to touch deity?

Chapters 7–8 look at the question of infant death. Various suggestions have been made is seeking an answer based on God's goodness and on the seriousness of sinful nature. If a Hindu baby dies, does it go to heaven? If a Hindu parent dies, do they go to hell? Do all people who die in or before infancy, end up in hell? Is hell something that will exist beyond Christ's return, or will it be either swallowed up in heaven or wiped from existence? Is there some intermediate dimension for those who haven't personally repented of their sinfulness but who haven't personally sinned? Are all heaven-bound at death?

Is there some action, such as parental belief, or water-baptism, which applies salvation only to some who die before birth? If salvation was thus guaranteed before adult years, but not within adult years, it might even give those who died younger an advantage over those who die older. If the giving of the gift of everlasting life, unfair? Or might it be that people ultimately divide between those who are conceived with a core orientation towards or away from God, irrespective of at what age they die?

Chapters 9–10 look at the delights of salvation now, specifically knowing God through christ, and the delights that await us beyond death. In C S Lewis' *That Hideous Strength* (7.2), the Pendragon is about to turn from the deep to the delightful. His masters arrive.

Under their weight of glory—hugeness—Jane shrinks. Grace invites her to focus on the basics of obedience. But I think we have the leisure to turn to joyful matters. Joy is the serious business of heaven, and looking at what we can enjoy, and into the future as to what we might enjoy, is all part of exploring salvation. God wishes joy for all.

Chapter 11 looks back to various covenants, picking up names such as Adam, Noah, Abraham, Isaac, Jacob, and Moses. In short, it rounds off by a backwards look. This chapter has dispensationalism—in which circles I was raised but no longer dwell—in mind. It disturbs me that many who claim Ps.122:6 for ethno-Zionism, neither pray for the apostle Paul (2 Ths.3:1) nor advocate the physical circumcision of boys (Lv.12:3). Paul asked the Thessalonians, not us, to pray for him. The psalmist asked Sinaites, not us, to pray for social peace for their then social capital. Yahweh commanded Sinaite males, not us, to be physically circumcised. Bound to Sinai, Peter rebuked God (Ac.10:13-6); having annulled Sinai, God rebuked Peter. Some commands have simply fallen by the fulfilment of symbolic prophecy by the cross. A spiritual Jerusalem of the spiritually circumcised, has arisen, which we can enjoy now as we await the final level of Jerusalem to arrive.

Chapter 1   A Test Bed for Covenant

Defining Marriage

What it isn't

Marriage is foundationally instituted by God for humanity, so forget political craze terms such as *Gay Marriage, Homosexual Marriage, Same Sex Marriage* (SSM). These terms lack reality. Our talk should not imply otherwise. *If* God alone truly defines marriage, and *if* he has not defined marriage as other than heterosexual, then *per force* the concept cannot move beyond fantasy (subreality) into reality.

Before I forget, you might like to know that my government is asking us to vote on whether unicorns should live in zoos. Should I vote No, because Yes is unloving to unicorns? After all, unicorns should run free. Or should I vote Yes, because No is unsafe to humans? After all, unicorns running free could endanger humans. Are you in favour of free-unicorns, or zoo-unicorns? Or is the government asking the wrong question, because there are no unicorns save in imagination?

But if I vote Yes, I am affirming the idea that unicorns exist in reality. And if I vote No, I am affirming the idea that unicorns exist in reality. But unicorns don't exist in reality. A bit like the old question, Are you still beating up your granny? If you have a granny who's never been beaten up, Yes or No don't work. The question is wrongly put.

By debating *whether* 'same sex marriage' should or should not exist, many good Christians imply that such *can* exist, implying that society can create marriage. If it can, I'd better become an atheist, since I have ruled out objective reality to the concept, God, at least as defined along the lines of Abrahamic religions. But then atheism doesn't give a hoot about voting Yes or No in any caring way, since it doesn't care: human life is random, meaningless; all life and nonlife is random, meaningless, and morality is at most whatever we individually wish it to be. Of course, atheists can care. But then, they unknowingly remain in God's image of care, even if they reckon the idea, God, to belong only to imagination.

Marriage is of heavenly origin, so heaven alone does define it as it is. Human redefinitions are but fantasy. Origins matter. Jesus, prepared to die, asked whether John's baptism was of heavenly or human origin

(Mk.11:30). It matters. Western Christians should be ready to die for loyalty to God, even as Jesus was. We must not think human law the benchmark. It can deceive. Our feelings are irrelevant.

Biblically, the term *homosexual marriage*, lacks intrinsic reality. It is illogical, a mirage into reality, at most a legal illusion that no more creates a reality than legislating that the earth is flat would create a flat earth, even if some folk will tenderly claim they're flat earthers. Such pretence can be called reality, but isn't. Human law can be made to satisfy any police force's itch to prosecute and persecute any who deny it's real. But SSM can never be real.

If it could be and God is, I would enthusiastically support it since God would have defined it. If it is real without deific support, then deity is a concept without reality. This is the core weakness of the concept SSM—it must either dismiss God or assume that he considers homosexuality normal yet was unfit for purpose in that he overlooked providing marriage for that form of normality.[3]

To debate 'homosexual marriage' as if it's a *valid* term, conceptually concedes the point, since logically to ask 'should it be?' presupposes that the 'can it be?' has been accurately answered in as 'yes'. Can it exist, or does merely the concept exist? To merely present it clearly as an invalid term, to debate the *concept*, 'homosexual marriage' (and square circles), does not lend it credence. I can love homosexuals (even paedophiles), but not homosexualism.[4]

What it is

Having defined what marriage is not, let us briefly examine marriage in relation to covenant. By the way, let's be clear that we're not talking about agreements or contracts, but about covenants. Let's conform our ideas to the Bible. With covenants, the inner relationship is about parties, not produce and not performance. And strictly speaking, the

---

[3]   I mean 'normal' as befitting humanity, not 'normal to sinfulness'.

[4]   John White's challenging book, *Eros Defiled*, touches on his own journey into homosexualism and reorientation into heterosexuality. He wrote as a Christian, as having been an associate professor in psychiatry, and as one who in private practice professionally and lovingly counselled practicing homosexuals. He seemed to conclude (*Eros Redeemed*) that homosexualism was generally too deeply an orientation for mere psychiatry to overcome.

vassal/subservient party could not break their covenant, though they could violate it, permitting the suzerain (overlord) to annul, terminate, the covenant.[5]

A deviation into homosexualism can help underline the basic fact that the institution, *marriage*, was established by God, and so understanding it is best based on Scripture, not on society.

God's perfect institution can be abused. A perfect mansion can house abusive people. Leadership is good, and our word *anarchy* comes from the Greek for *leaderless*. But human tyranny is not good leadership. Roads are good, but road carnage is not. Food is good; gluttony is not. Many are unhappy within marriage by marriage. Far more are unhappy by not being married and happy by being married.

Marriage should be a sensible goal for most people, and selection of spouse should be a matter of serious reflection—lest the old adage, *marry in haste, repent at leisure*, rings true after the wedding bells have fallen silent. God can be an active and background part of each marriage, helping the spouses to succeed as spouses. How many cop out by saying that *the marriage*, that imaginary third-party thing— heaven forbid not they themselves—*failed*?

Much woolly thinking has crept into church thinking, perhaps partly due to the idea of marriage being a sacrament. On the one hand it's right to restrict it to biblical parameters, and on the other hand it's right to include all who are within those parameters. But any idea that tends to limit fully fledged marriage to a human institution, whether that institution be church, mosque, state, temple, whatever, will obscure the concept, *marriage*.

Indeed, even benignly said, church leaders who speak of marrying couples, undermine the concept, *marriage*. In 1997 (stardate 50975.2), *Deep Space 9*, a mixture of harmful vice-based philosophy and some happier themes, had a fun line where Rom a Ferengi nervously asked the captain, "Would you marry me, I mean us, I mean, would you

---

5   This difference isn't always clear in English translations. For hitting the right spots, both by calling covenants *covenants*, and indicating that vassals couldn't break covenants, the LEB/NABRE/NIV/NKJV/NRSV gain an A+, followed by CEB/NLT (A-), ERV (D), and the CEV/NCV (D-).

perform our wedding ceremony?" (5.26). Rom had finally stumbled out the right words, without realising it.

Truth is, each marriage is a covenant created purely between the couple, never by a third-party. Such mutual personal commitment, the point of no return, the taking the plunge, can be before or during third-party witness, that is, before or at the wedding. Biblically, a third-party should witness the covenant, but does not create the covenant witnessed. Has not the idea that the witness creates the marriage, led to the idea that if the witness can be state or temple *instead* of church, then *states* can create marriages, and indeed that what one creates, one can redefine as creator?[6]

Biblically there is a distinction between marriage and wedding, the former being the substance, the inner core, the latter being the public declaration of lifelong commitment of person-to-person. Biblically there is a distinction between betrothal (covenant) and engagement (contract). The former being the pre-sexual stage of marriage, and the latter being the pre-sexual stage before marriage.

There is scope within bureaucratic societies for marriages to be recorded, and to bestow benefits in line with recognition. For marriage is a pivotal blessing to human society, even if governments adulterate it. Ideally, through marriage sexuality is channelled into lifelong loyalty, and children develop well with committed parents modelling well their children's future lifelong loyalties.

We mustn't marry the idea of marriage being covenant, with the idea of marriage being social contract. The idea that marriage has always required a *legal contract*, and has then been fully open to legal termination of contact, all too easily obscures both what marriage is and what besides death, if anything, can end it.[7]

---

6   And if priesthood is needed to marry and if all Christians are priests, then any Christian can marry couples if marriage comes from God through a sacrament. If it comes from the state, then only those permitted by the state can marry couples, and if state forbade priests to marry couples, then priests could not. Does the NT indicate that marrying couples was a function of the church?

7   Those who trick-questioned Jesus, besides not understanding resurrection, also failed to understand death (Mt.22:28; Rm.7:2). Admittedly even for the

A third-party such as parents, might command couples to marry. If they comply, the couple covenant together. The covenant unity of Yahweh and Israel was symbolised as husband and wife (eg *Hosea*; Jr.3), but no one married them! On the human level, this covenant is a *companionship thing*: it was not good for the man[8] to live alone (Gen.2:18). Pr.2:17 and Mal.2:14 speak of companionship, which some Bible versions show clearly.[9]

Marriage is a life pattern *set up by God* but *entered* by couples, not begun or activated by some officiating agency. Here it may be said

---

Pharisees the hope of resurrection had only appeared at the frontiers of the Tanak, so the Sadducees had some excuse for scepticism.

[8] Poetically put, *man* as male (*ish*), needed to be told of his need for companionship more than women have needed telling. It is subsequently taught that woman (*ishah*) needs man, see for example the Christ/Church analogy of Eph.5.

[9] After the meaning of *partner* narrowed into the morally unacceptable, social engineering morphed it to engulf the distinct concept, marriage. Correctivism's mantra: if healthy and unhealthy all live under the same hospital roof, then there is no sickness (illusion, don't disillusion); if all are *partners*, there is no distinction between the wedded marriage partners and the unwedded partners, between covenant and convenience. Libertarianism asks, 'Why make our choice and settle down, when we can never make a choice and never settle down?' In the light of the antimarriage barrage, Bible versions should avoid *partner* (forced onto society by government and commerce) like the plague—the way to the dark side that is. For *'allûp* (Pr.2:17) avoid CEB/LEB/NIV/NRSV, prefer CEV/ERV/NABRE/NCV/NKJV/NLT; for *ḥᵃberet* (Mal.2:14), I have ignored [wife] in Mal.2:14.a—all rightly have it. I have also ignored footnotes. However, contaminant in Mal.2:14.b sows evil seed. The worst offenders (CEV/NCV) throw in unqualified *partner*, compounded by loss of covenant—mere broken promises/agreement: a partner is not a spouse precisely because they have an agreement, not a covenant. The next three (CEB/NIV/NLT) also introduce the unqualified *partner*, but at least immediately define as wife by marriage covenant/vows. The remaining five (ERV/LEB/NABRE (and worthwhile footnote)/NKJV/NRSV) are all acceptable, though the ERV adds a foreign idea about girlfriends becoming wives. *Marriage partner* (LEB) reverts to an age of moral contrast to a mere partner, a qualifier levelled nowadays by Correctivism in the interests of immorality. The CEB/NIV failed to make the grade on both texts. Christians "in particular would be wary of any moral consensus of an ungodly society in a fallen world" (Holmes 60).

that Ancient Near Eastern covenant language (such as the Bible endorsed by usage) spoke strongly of third-party witnessing of covenants, and them rewarding loyalty and rebuking disloyalty. Biblically "marriage is a covenant motif (eg Jr.2:1-3; 3:1-2; Ezk.16)" (Motyer 1993:397).

Marriage, Sinai, Sin, and Divorce

So, marriage is a God-created institution for humanity, existing only within its intrinsic parameters, without happiness guaranteed, opted into by couples and ideally publicly witnessed within the covenant motif of loyalty for life (wedded-marriage). It should be a case social customs fitting this model, not this model fitting social customs.

Let's examine marriage and divorce, allowing that marriage is framed as permanent, and that the Sinaitic Covenant was likewise framed as permanent. Now, if it is biblically justified to say that the permanence of marriage has an implicit option to annul, *ipso facto* did the Sinaitic Covenant begin with at least an implicit option to annul? That is, let us examine the possibility of covenant annulment, divorce, from the lens of marriage.

We should not learn from societal ideas on divorce. Society did not create marriage, so cannot create divorce. So, society can broadly record marriage, so can broadly record divorce. It may also offer benefits and blames, and exert due pressure to heal marriages, for by healthy marriages society is healthy. It is the biblical teaching on marriage and divorce we should learn, accepting as decisive its definition of marriage. I recommend Jay Adams' *Marriage, Divorce and Remarriage*, 1980, as a solid primer. But it underplayed covenant. Thus, I reject his idea that because of Dt.24:4, remarrying someone you've divorced is sin. I reject the idea that Dt.24 had validity beyond the Sinai Covenant, though it still offers wisdom.[10]

---

[10]   Palingamy was precluded to prevent men from selfish divorced, by disallowing an option to claim her back if her subsequent husband had died (Daniel Bock: Thomas A Noble *et al*, *Marriage, Family and Relationships*, 2017:27).

King Henry 8 on marriage and divorce

Roman Catholicism holds the idea that a consummated sacramental marriage (*holy* matrimony)[11] is indissoluble, rejecting the [absolute] divorce idea, though if the relationship falls short of marriage it may be annulled.[12] This approach has had some interesting outcomes. For instance, have you seen the film where Richard Burton played King Henry 8 in *Anne of the Thousand Days* (1969), or listened to Herman's Hermits' recording of the 1910 "I'm Henery the Eighth I Am" spoof? That was an interesting time in global politics, replete with assassinations at high places—and did the film commit its own character assassination of Anne Boleyn? Let's review the saga.

Catherine as never Arthur's wife: denial justifies marriage

Aged sixteen, Spanish princess Catherine married the healthy fifteen-year-old Arthur, son of English king, Henry 7, the first Tudor monarch. Possibly they never had HSI (human sexual intercourse) in their wedded months before Arthur died. An assumption was that without HSI there is no marriage. She was then set aside to marry Henry's little Henry once he turned fourteen.

Leviticus should not have been invoked, since its covenant died at the cross. But Rome invoked it. Still, England replied that Catherine's *wedding* had not been consummated into marriage. Seven years later, she wed seventeen-year-old Henry, now Henry 8. Henry's sexual promiscuity gave her ground to divorce him, and her not birthing a boy—which he believed necessary to keeping the country united

---

[11]   "Most people, including most Roman Catholics, do not realize that the ministers of the sacrament are the spouses themselves": https://www.thoughtco.com/the-sacrament-of-marriage-542134. This site states that sacramental marriage is heterosexual covenanted (the site says *contracted*, but I suspect in the sense of *undertaken*) union for life between two baptised believers (even Protestant), requiring neither priest nor licence.

[12]   Annulment is sometimes used shorthand for a *Declaration of Nullity*. Technically some take nullity as not to end marriage but to formally end what never was marriage: *void ab initio*. Nullity is a doctrine which might find more uptake now that the West has bought into the conflicting idea that the concept, *homosexual marriage*, exists, and assumes that backtracking would mean divorcing real marriages, rather than declaring an error of judgment which never led to actual marriage, ie Declaration of Nullity.

under an undisputed male monarch—determined him to divorce her. And Catherine seemed too old to have children. Enter Anne Boleyn. I suspect that she was sexually pure, seriously wished to save sex for marriage, and had her wish. She inclined to Protestantism.

<u>Catherine as never Henry's wife: denial justifies divorce</u>

All that stood between Henry and dynasty was Catherine. How could a married man marry in a monogamous society? Divorce? But the Defender of the [Roman] Faith was permitted neither divorce nor polygamy. Henry had a brainwave: resurface Lv.20:21 and have the pope agree that Catherine had been Arthur's true wife after all, so in God's eyes had never been Henry's.[13]

Rome didn't want Henry to have eaten his cake only to hand it back for a new one. Of two contemporaries, William Tyndale took a Lutheran position and concluded that Henry and Catherine truly married, with no biblical grounds for Henry to divorce. On the other hand, Thomas Cranmer, whose position has become the Anglican norm, backed up Henry—~~divorce~~ annulment by denying marriage, was deemed OK. Later Henry and Catherine's daughter Mary, became Queen Mary 1 of England, and got revenge on old Cranmer!

Not permitted by Rome to divorce, and fertile time running out, Henry reluctantly ditched Rome, wife Catherine, and daughter Mary, and pressured his people to legitimise him to both oust Catherine and marry the vivacious Anne. He asked Canterbury to allow what Rome did not. He rightly said that biblical authority exceeded papal authority, and wrongly said that English authority exceeded Roman authority. He affirmed the legend that Jesus' feet in ancient time walked upon England's mountains green, prior to Petrine authority: Glastonbury-Canterbury before Rome! This unintended unhooking from papal power encouraged England to become Protestant in spite of Henry's English Catholicism. A church divorce?

---

[13] *Lāqaḥ* (lit. *take*) may mean marriage (CEB/CEV/LEB/NCV/NIV/NLT)—would mere cohabitation or affair not already be covered under the basic idea of fornication? If marriage occurred, then Lv.20:21 affirmed it as marriage (let no pope put asunder) to be continued as childless, possibly meaning that any children were to be treated as illegitimate: had he had had an extant son, Henry would not have delegitimised him!

Anne as Henry's unfaithful wife: adultery justifies divorce

Anne bore Elizabeth, later Queen Elizabeth 1, but failed during her short innings to produce a son. Frustrated, Henry sought to marry Jane Seymour for a son. Anne was trapped, probably by false charges of being adulterous and executed for high treason—divorce by death, so to speak.[14]

Some say that King Henry 8, / to three wives he was wedded. / One died, one survived, / two annulled, two beheaded. That works on the false idea that Catherine of Aragon, Anne Boleyn, and later Anne of Cleves, had simply cohabited under the guise of marriage, or at the most as substandard, noncanonical, marriage. No, King Henry 8, / to six wives he was wedded. / One died, one survived, / two divorced, two beheaded. Mary had succeeded Edward 6 by her father's will though officially a bastard, Elizabeth succeeded her as his legitimate heir.

Chess king sacrifices four queens

Catherine and Anne were truly wives of Henry. Edward, later King Edward 6, was his son by Marriage 3. Protestant King Edward 6 soon died, and Mary 1 (*Bloody Mary*) of Marriage 1, took over for 5 years, reverting England to Roman Catholicism. After she died, Protestant Elizabeth 1 (Marriage 2) took over for forty-four years. Ought Protestants to thank God? What shall I say?

- One, that the Levitical law was specific to Ethnic-Israel, not a global command, so was irrelevant to the discussion.
- Two, in line with Tyndale, that Catherine of Aragon had truly married Henry, and he was truly wrong to divorce her and to delegitimize Mary.
- Three, that there shouldn't have been an Elizabeth 1, since there shouldn't have been a divorce. If Rome had continued to

---

[14] The CEV suggests that we're talking about *illicit marriage* based on *Leviticus*: that would no longer apply. Perhaps for reasons of dogmatic theology the NABRE actually adds into the text *porneia* as *illicit marriage* in Mt.5:32/19:9, but in a context where it speaks of singleness it rightly translates as *immorality* (1 Cor.7:2). Since the type of immorality is sexual, most MEVV say *sexual immorality*, and the Modern English Version may be justified to pin it down in *Matthew* to *marital unfaithfulness*.

dominate England *via* Mary, unimpeded by Protestant claimants to the English throne, tough.

- Four, that we should not take the line that God ordained a divorce in order to transfer Britain into a Protestant nation to free the world from Rome. Would God have ordained Henry's *sinful* divorce from Catherine, and subsequent *adulterous* marriage with Anne?

It's all too easy for victorious sides to claim that God was on their side, that God backs the biggest gun, and that they can read history. C S Lewis warned about historicism, for as readers we're too immature and have far too few texts to read history as God's story. I suspect that only the metanarrative, the big picture, is by God who fits human and diabolical narratives into his master plan. History is co-authored.

As with any human institution, monarchy has gone through evil twists and turns, but let us neither thank nor blame God for its sins. It's the history of our own lives that is our privilege to create, under the obligation of the Ought, the moral imperative. For God's help, let us give thanks. Henry's agenda had some merit, but his means to achieve success were devious and reprehensible.

Desiderius Erasmus and the Bible

I'll use the term annulment to cover both commonly overlapping concepts of wedding *and* marriage, dispensing with any ecclesiastical distinction between the idea of sacred and secular marriage. Marriage is marriage; marriage is covenant; covenant can be annulled. I like the line taken by the C15-6 Christian Humanist, Desiderius Erasmus.[15] Essentially, he divided divorce between sinless and sinful. The sinless is based on either one or two sins, namely porneia, and/or a non-Christian rejecting their Christian spouse. That is, though most divorces stem from direct sin,[16] divorce, and remarriage, can be sinless.

---

[15]   For his role in Bible translation, see such as my *The Word's Gone Global*.

[16]   For example, subjectively sinless are both they who discovered theirs was a consanguineous 'marriage', and they who had been polygamists in a polygamist culture, who subsequently obeyed their belief in God's disapproval and divorced. So, no direct sin of attitude. However, if Adam hadn't sinned, divorce would be unknown, so every divorce has indirect sin as causal.

Incidentally don't discard the *Humanist* tag. Some good terms get stolen; some get scorned. C16 Humanists were those who "taught, or learned, or at least strongly favoured, Greek and the new kind of Latin" and Puritans were those who "wished to abolish episcopacy and remodel the Church of England on the lines which Calvin had laid down for Geneva" (Lewis 1954:17-8). Christian Humanists were simply Christian scholars who dug back to source—*ad fontes*.

Erasmus questioned Rome's position, particularly in the light of NT scripture. That's one reason he dug back into the NT Latin and Greek text. He argued two possible biblical grounds for divorce—for annulment of the covenant called marriage. As a sequel, remarriage is too big a topic to be fully thrashed out here. But every biblical divorce truly demolishes the bridge between the former couple, leaving both parties (whether guilty or guiltless) free to build new bridges.

Paul, and I think he was envious of marriage, favoured remarriage for those biblically divorced, who were thus free from residual obligation to either lifelong celibacy or to marital reunion. Theologically, might it be that if the new Yeshuic covenant supersedes the old Sinaitic Covenant, as marriage after divorce supersedes the marriage before divorce,[17] then residual obligations to the former covenant might be zero?[18] Covenant establishes a relational bridge, as in marriage.

The early church did some serious homework on this subject. It never achieved one mind in this, and had it done so it might have had the wrong mind. But we shouldn't reject old positions as if all ideas become dotards, only fit to give way to younger ideas—that's chronological snobbery. The early church was simply the people like you and I of long years ago, who had different glasses of approach. Glasses keep changing, and real gains go alongside real losses.

The question is, did they get the Eternal's perspective, and if so in what ways? I have long reflected on this, but so have some I disagree with. We approach these things with presuppositions, hermeneutical glasses often picked up from churches we have been in or are in.

---

[17]   I am not saying that obligations might not remain *vis-à-vis* co-produced children, both financially and with regard to some measure of parenting.

[18]   This is not to deny that liabilities of care might be justified to avoid leaving former parties in the lurch.

Every church causes some network interference, distorts God's message in some ways and in some degrees. The more parochial we are, the more parochial blackspots we will suffer from. My approach here is by no means a comprehensive study, though it is based on one I have done.

I will limit it to Erasmus' two arguably *biblical* grounds for divorce. Some speaking for *laissez-faire* marriage/divorce, presume an imperfect Bible produced by imperfect man.[19] Some speaking for divorceless marriage, presume perfect church teachers of long yore, as if church theology is the same as, or better than, biblical theology. The whole subject is profoundly important, and is relevant to the question of whether the Sinaitic Covenant was open to annulment, if indeed covenants not explicitly affirming annulment can be annulled.

On a point of pastoral theology, let it be said that some are too slow to discourage divorce (But he cheated on me) and some are too quick to encourage it (Well she burnt my toast). In pictorial terms, we can use ancient Greco-Roman words about man/woman romantic love, speaking as if the goddess Aphroditē-Venus was cause and effect. Picture Venus as a fickle goddess who demands loyalty—we marry by her whim and just as easily divorce when we 'fall out' of love with our spouse, and 'fall in' love with someone else. Laws of romantic feeling include fornication and divorce—simply obligations to Venus who justifies, even celebrates our antics. Yet obedience to her, if disobedience to God, is idolatry.

Marriage, like it or lump it, is a real bind that's not to be unbound. To a friend who sadly claimed his marriage had been a mistake, I suggested that divorce might be a bigger one—and I fear that it was. Joshua's careless covenanting with the Gibeonites wasn't sorted by Saul contemptibly killing off that covenant (2 Sam.21:2). *'Till death do us part*, does not mean the death of romance, and does not justify undermining the covenant or covenant-party. In ancient mythology, Venus' son Cupid married a mortal, Psychē. In English, we often translate psychē as 'Soul': she was his soulmate. But we are neither

---

[19]   Many books might be recommended on Bible authority. Craig Blomberg's *Can We Still Believe the Bible?* (2014), answering with a strong affirmative.

obliged nor allowed to divorce simply because we think someone else to be our true soulmate: that is mere paganism.[20]

There is a glue in life we are simply, well, stuck with. The glue of our sworn word, of honesty, even of stoicism in pain and depression. And those who bow to neither God, nor the concept of gods and goddesses, in effect deify themselves—laws unto themselves, which equates to being lawless, anomic, having denied the absolute.

Jesus and Covenant Violation

As said, marriage is a covenant which does not explicitly rule in divorce, but obviously assumes death as a terminator. Paul agreed that residual obligations did not exist after death (Rm.7:2), which is not to say that divorce does not act as death. Paul had been married to Sinai. Neither party were viewed here as divorcing due to sin, but merely separating by death, a simplified illustration to picture a death to Sinai and a new life to Golgotha, based on spiritual identification with messiah's death and resurrection. Some Christians still held things like weekly sabbath, physical circumcision, and kosher laws, to be residual obligations, but Paul did not, at least not for Christians.

But other than physical death, are there biblical grounds for ending marriage? Let's look first at the Matthean Exception, the dominical 'except' that only *Matthew* records (*viz* Mt.5:32; 19:9—except for...).

But firstly, what or who had God joined together (19:6)? Historically, much of the church has taught the sacerdotal idea that it, and only it, could spiritually join folk together. That any other sexual cohabitation was at best honourable as 'natural marriage' (that is, not joined together by a priest to God).

We still speak of getting *married* in church, or of the 'minister' *marrying* folk, as if that spiritually joins the couple. But it is better to speak merely about the minister *conducting a wedding*. It is better to

---

[20] Scripture never indicates that humanity, or part thereof, is God's *soulmate* bride. Even Eph.5 is within the framework that Christ's bride is relatively unattractive until made attractive by him. Redemption is based on the twin ideas of us being unattractive but capable of being made attractive, cleaned up, glorified. Putting it in pictorial terms, we are to be his spiritual (pneumatic, not psychic) 'bride'.

take *joined by God*, as meaning an overall deific sanction on marriage, applicable for Atheists, Christians, Eskimos, Hindus, Polygamists, in fact any couple who *covenant* interpersonal sexual relations (if viable and permissible) with each other.

For remember, a covenant is not a contract: it is for life, and loyal commitment is basic. God requires each couple who have entered into his institution of marriage (into his binding, his envelope) to keep faith with the other. God is seldom matchmaker. He does not take each couple into the land of marriage, but he does grant free citizenship to each couple who mutually enter, a citizenship with privileges and obligations. The institution is by him; individuals plug into it for better or worse.

Incidentally, the background in *Matthew* goes back to Adam, not just Moses, indicating a relevancy beyond the limits of Sinai, both as regards the framework of marriage and the framework of divorce. The aetiology (Adam)[21] also indicates that Jesus' teaching here belonged to Christian couples, indeed any couple, and not just to Intertestamental Jewish Religion.

To illustrate, if I put my teaching material onto the web, as public domain rather than as copyright, some may access it and be taught. Thus, I have taught them without specifically enrolling them. Likewise, 'Whom God has joined', means that God plays the foundational role, not by deific selection, nor by a limitation of some priestly third-party, but by establishing the marriage model into which couples may enrol themselves. Their choice comes into his jurisdiction, and thus they are joined by him. No third-party is to remove them from their covenant, and if they divorce unbiblically, they are judged by God adulterous whether they affirm him or not.

Is divorce for adultery adulterous?

What is the exception in the Matthean Exception? The answer in the Greek is *porneia*, which in this context I roughly define as disloyal human sexual intercourse (HSI) in line with the biblical analogy of Ethnic-Israel cheating on Yahweh.[22] Western ideas can misinterpret

---

[21]   A motif for humanity's beginning.

[22]   Similarly, Paul urged spiritual fidelity to Christ (2 Cor.11:2).

Scripture, and some have a long way to backtrack. Some, translating porneia as *fornication*, take *fornication* to be HSI sin only by an unmarried person, and *adultery* to be HSI sin only by a married person. Combined with the Western idea of *engagement* as a step before marriage, they might conclude that Jesus only allowed pre-married couples to break off their engagement if either party had committed HSI with another, perhaps only if within the engagement.

It is all too easy to begin where we are and read our culture into the Bible, rather than reading its words in its culture. On this, more formal Bible versions are less prone to confuse and more prone to challenge. For instance, the NKJV's less functional approach avoids squeezing Joseph and Mary either into a sacerdotal or a Secular Humanist framework of marriage, which looks either to the 'church' or 'state' to create.

Too often Westernism thinks that marriage is a contract made at a wedding, and calls the stage before *engagement*—as breathing space to renege or ratify one's tentative pledge. Questions about the ethics of this approach, and how our ignorance interacts with the biblical reality and excuses sin, are too wide to be treated here. Sufficient to say that too easily translators, if so conditioned, misrepresent biblical teaching, preferring foreign terms to biblico-historical particularity.

Catering for this foreign approach, the NLT straightforwardly says that "Joseph, [Mary's] fiancé," decided to "break the engagement" (Mt.1:19). A one-world-our-world picture. It's pretty consisten—consistently wrong. The NIV complicates it, telling us that no, he was simply "pledged to be married" (18), yet *was* "her husband" and "had in mind to divorce her" (19), sadly mixing 50/50 two mentalities. As a breath of fresh air, the NKJV almost seamlessly shows us a society that deemed marriage to be a covenant begun before wedlock. A one-world-their-world picture. The RSV is even better.

In Spenser's *The Faerie Queene*, "the foes to Chastity that she encounters are superficial passion, boorish sexuality, wimpish fear of femininity, manipulative flirtation, and the underlying cruelty of the mannered, sophisticated upperclass dalliance that literary historians have called 'courtly love'. Spenser's allegory is not a preachment, but the portrayal of sexual virtue as an adventure" (Martin 2000:91). In biblical culture, you didn't 'sleep with' your *betrothed*, yet they were your unwedded spouse, so divorce was an option.

Sadly, the NIV's "take Mary as your wife" (20) also falls below par by suggesting that his *already* wife (biblical thinking) should *become* his wife (Western thinking)—drop the 'as'. The Roman Catholic NABRE, the Eastern Orthodox Bible, and some earlier Protestant versions do better for v20. From an African perspective, "the Bemba say Nkobekela: te cupo ['an engagement is not a marriage'], but the Israelites would have insisted that Nkobekela: cupo ['betrothal is marriage']" (Adeyemo 1109). Joseph, a righteous man, considered *divorce*.

"The equivalence of betrothal and marriage is...reflected in Mt.1:18,20, 24-5, which shows that Mary's betrothal to Joseph made her his wife, even though they did not have sexual relations until after the birth of Jesus" (VanGemeren H829 ['*aras*]). Bible versions are not always consistent in quality. Take for instance the NKJV, commended above. On Rv.19:7 it misleads us by speaking of the messianic *marriage* being future, whereas only the *wedding* was future, for his bride is his wife.

Happily, most of the Bible versions rightly strained out this gnat, even though they swallowed the camel above. We shouldn't redraft the biblical approach into Western thinking.

Thus, before their public statement and celebration (wedding), Joseph and Mary were *unwedded* husband and wife, so hadn't had HSI together. As her loving husband, believing her adulterous he considered the options, then opted for divorce, then discovered it was righteous to *wed* her since she hadn't done the dirty (Mt.1:18-20). Some months later, husband and wife went to Bethlehem—possibly to his disappointed parents, but not to a village pub facing the Christmas Rush—where they probably had a family wedding.

To understand biblical teaching on divorce, we need to read the Bible in its terms, and only then apply it to ours. Having looked a little at Joseph and Mary, let's see what their son taught.

The key word, *porneia*, "refers to sexual sin...; adultery is unfaithfulness toward one's spouse" (Adams 53). *Adultery* speaks of a covenant-violation; *porneia* specifies how it is violated. Jr.3:1-2,8 speaks of Yahweh's *wife* committing *porneia* (sexual sin, fornication). "The word-group *pornē* in the Greek OT, generally stands for the Heb. *zānâh*—to commit fornication—whereas *moicheuō*—to commit adultery—

regularly represents *nā'ap̄*. Both word-groups are therefore to be clearly separated" (Brown 1.498). A later Jewish writing has the phrase, *en porneia emoicheuse* = adultery by sexual sin (Sirach 23:23).

Let's look at the picture of Yahweh as betrayed by Israel's fornication. Be aware that though bigamy wasn't a naughty word, Jr.3 no more means that Yahweh was a bigamist than it means that one wife divided into two wives—though the *wives* were divided enough! Poetically, *Jeremiah* illustrates marriage as being righteously annulled after the sin of *porneia*. Yahweh was a divorcee, but not an adulterer, a point Yeshua made clear!

The covenant between Yahweh and the people, had long divided into the kingdoms of Israel and Judah, had been violated by both kingdoms. The people of Israel (the North Kingdom) had been sent away, as if divorced for the sin of *porneia*, and the people of Judah (the South Kingdom) soon became even worse. It might seem that the call to Israel to return, implied that Yahweh wouldn't divorce Judah so felt obliged to remarry the less offensive Israel. Yet it can be argued that since Israel, as the North Kingdom, never returned, eventually Yahweh has divorced Judah, the South Kingdom, *she* having long commandeered the title *Israel* by that time.

My immediate point is that if Yahweh was justified in divorcing any wife, then any human husband is likewise justified in divorcing any wife who like Israel has committed *porneia*. I hold this principle to extend to wives divorcing their husbands for similar sins against them, but let's leave that for now.

When Yahweh said it was okay for him to divorce on the ground of *porneia*, he said was okay for us to divorce on the same ground, which is what we find in *Matthew*. When we read about Joseph being commended by God for planning to divorce Mary because he believed she had violated their marriage by *porneia*, we're reading about godly divorce, just as in Jr.3:8. Fortunately Joseph soon realised her purity, forgot about divorce, and the rest is history. His attitude fits into his son's teachings of godly divorce permitted in cases of *porneia*, a teaching some call the Matthean Exception. The flip side of the dominical coin was that where *porneia* wasn't the ground for divorce, then it opened up adultery (*moicheia*) for both parties.[23]

<u>What is adultery?</u>

Let's consider 1# marriage as covenantal, 2# Jr.3 as likening the breach of covenant by Israel to Yahweh, as being like a covenant breach by sexual sin of a wife, and 3# an earlier Jewish writing which has as a then common idea, *en porneia emoicheuse* = adultery by sexual sin (Sirach 23:23). If we divest our minds of adultery (Gk. *moicheia*) being a synonym for fornication, I think we can better approach the NT texts on moicheia/adultery as being in breach of covenant obligation, whether ongoing or residual, and a contamination.

Excluding the *pericope adulterae*, the 17 NT texts are...

1–6   Mt.5:27-8,32; 15:19; 19:9,18: In a setting where one or both parties are married, seeking to seduce a woman (so Carson 2010:380, and I presume that the converse would apply) would be an inner breach of the ongoing obligation of covenant-loyalty, a breach God has forbidden (Mt.5:27-8). Unless a husband had biblically divorced his wife, being divorced she lives in breach of residual obligation, and if any other man marries her, he shares her guilt, and indeed seals off the way back to reunion (5:32). Covenant breach is an evil idea (15:19). If a man unbiblically divorces his wife and marries another, he should realise that being divorced he lives in breach of residual obligation (19:9). Covenant-breach against a spouse is one of many sins (19:18).

7–10   Mk.7:22; 10:11-2,19: Covenant breach against a spouse is one of many sins (7:22; 10:19). Any unbiblical divorce from your spouse commits a covenant-breach which adversely affects you too (10:11-2), and gender equality is underlined, a two-way street.

11–2   Lk.16:18; 18:20: Any unbiblical divorce from your spouse commits a covenant-breach, and any who marry the former spouse marries into the sin of adultery (16:18). Covenant-breach against a spouse is one of many sins (18:20).

13–4   Rm.2:22; 13:9: Covenant-breach against a spouse is one of many sins, falling below loving your neighbour as yourself (2:22; 13:9).

---

[23]   A mere *partner* cannot commit adultery; a mere *partner* has a mere contract.

15   Jas.2:11: Covenant-breach against a spouse is one of many sins, falling below the law of loving your neighbour as yourself.

16   2 Pt.2:14: Covenant-breach is a common sin for some.

17   Rv.2:22: If Christians commit covenant-breach against Christ, they will be punished unless they repent.

So how should we define adultery? We tend to mean cheating on one's spouse, whereas Jesus spoke of sinful divorce as cheating on one's immediately *former* spouse. Did he not imply that adultery can be a sinful (abnormal) state begun by sinful divorce (divorce *unless*: Matthew), sealed by a sinful act of a replacement marriage[24] finally cutting off the moral option of remarriage to the divorced ex-spouse and thereby showing explicit commitment to adultery (*Mark/Luke*)? Adultery is living in breach of obligation, whether ongoing or residual, but healing often is possible.

Divorce is a very serious thing. "The commitment to marry is a commitment to stay married" (Bock 426). The covenant attitude of lifelong loyalty, is paramount. Even passive adultery can be transmitted by marriage. Other than a sinless divorce...

- any man who divorces commits adultery if he marries a replacement (Mk.10:11/Lk.16:18), she shares his guilt;
- any woman[25] who divorces commits adultery if she marries a replacement (Mk.10:12), he shares her guilt (Mt.5:32/Lk.16:18);
- a divorced wife plays her part in adultery, perhaps by simply living with residual unmet obligation to the prior covenant (Mt.5:32).[26]

---

[24]   Jesus' teaching was weighed against polygamy, where an additional wife does not replace another.

[25]   I think there is biblical ground to extend the principle to both genders.

[26]   An assumption of her *marrying another*, in line with the verb *moicheuō* which bespeaks something she does or has done unto herself, may be implied, since the second part is of another husband, and seems to parallel Mk.10:11, where "for a man to divorce his wife and marry another was an act of adultery against his first wife" (Stein 701).

In God's sight, they who shoot down the albatross wear it around their neck and can even share it with new and former spouse. Sinful covenant annulment is possible but shameful.

Literal reading of the texts throws up some puzzles, but the stress on replacement marriage is that that level of adultery kills off the last chance to get back to whoever was wrongly divorced. One puzzle is this: if Ken wrongly divorced Kathy, then replaces her with Jo, how does Kathy commit adultery by marrying James the next year, since Ken was closed history? Another is why divorcing Kathy (Matthew's emphasis) makes her commit adultery, and subsequently infects James *if* they marry—it's less puzzling if remarriage was assumed.

These puzzles may exist because on the one hand we are too Aristotelian, and on the other hand because we do not make adjustments for the cultural setting (*sitz im leben*). Moreover, when a bit is said about a woman after a bit about a man, it's not clear that she had been *his* wife—Wycliffe's "the *wijf*" (Lk.16:18) is doubtful. So it's not clear that she remains guilty if remarrying after he remarries. What we have are two general principles closely joined. Both principles are open to mitigating circumstances, as Jesus taught. Take Lk.16:18: such a man commits adultery *unless* (as Matthew reminded us) she had cheated on him; marrying a wrongly divorced woman spreads adultery and she and her new husband have committed adultery by together sealing the door against rightful reunion.[27] However, she is precluded from remarrying her former spouse, by him having sealed-off that option by adulterous union with another, she would no longer be in adultery.

This I think is what the lord taught, and what Paul alluded to when he spoke of separation (*infra*) as nonadulterous, and of death as permitting rightful remarriage, in the sense that all spiritually crucified life is as such post-Sinai life, though mere desertion would be spiritual adultery (Rm.7:1-6). Rightful divorce severs like death.

Factoring in data such as Lv.20:10/Jr.3:8/Mt.5:28,[28] we can see that the wider meaning of adultery is an antimarital dimension in life, a

---

[27] Real repentance of adultery brings real forgiveness and blessing by God.

[28] The latter has the idea of deliberately harbouring a desire for an illicit relationship (Keener 189).

dimension that we ought not to even daydream about, an ought-not-to-be-but-is, which can dishonour others. Adultery as a real or imaginary sexual relationship (positive or negative) existing outside of virtue, can exist in or after marriage, and has markers such as porneia, divorce, and remarriage. It conflicts with a right attitude towards marriage. "Be faithful to your own wife and give your love to her alone" (GNB: Pr.5:15). Covenant life should be committed life.

Marital Separation

Each Evangelist marshalled material and translation to highlight their own themes. It's a legitimate process called redaction. The aims of Mark and Luke did not require any exception to be noted, but the more Jewish-ecclesiastical aim of Matthew did. Therefore Mk.10 and Lk.16 serve less for a systematic treatment on divorce than does Mt.5/19. Except, that is, to reinforce the point that divorce is an ethically serious step, not the termination of a contract that has outlived its usefulness and/or pleasure to one or both.

Enough has perhaps been said to my task, which is not a counselling one, but it is good to add some true flesh to marriage, divorce, and remarriage. Ought one to divorce a sexually wayward spouse? Ought one to not divorce a sexually wayward spouse who professes repentance? Good questions, but not answered here.

On the preceding issue, in Mt.19:3 Jesus touched on *Deuteronomy's erwath dabar*, hotly debated by those under Sinai. Adams argued that Rabbi Yeshua agreed with Rabbi Hillel against Rabbi Shammai, that it meant *petty dislikes*, not *sexual disloyalty*. But that disagreeing with both rabbis, Rabbi Yeshua taught that *erwath dabar* didn't justify divorce. Hillel was right that it meant *petty dislikes*; Shammai was right that only sexual disloyalty justified separation by divorce. There is also separation without divorce, an option some disdain (Adams 42).

In 1 Cor.7:10 Paul spoke of oppugnant spouses where neither faith nor infidelity divided. He underlined that Jesus highlighted that marriage was for life. To render *parangellō* as *command* is perhaps too strong, but it makes good sense when seen as part of v11. I think that The Message interprets quite well: "...if you are married, stay married. This is the master's command, not mine. If a wife should leave her husband, she must either remain single or else come back and make things right with him."[29]

In short, separation isn't ideal but isn't the real objection. The real objection is replacement-marriage killing off any chance or reunion. After all, after *parangellō* Paul said that remaining separate was an acceptable alternative to reunion. 1 Cor.7:11 falls short of divorce. And if the wife walked out (*chōrizō*), the husband mustn't divorce (*aphiēmi*) her. In line with Mk.10:12, Paul was not reflecting a Jewish norm that only husbands could divorce, since a sentence or so on he said that wives were not to divorce (13: *aphiēmi*).

Paul was egalitarian here, using a simple illustration to highlight that while separation wasn't ideal (even if justified for such as for brutality), neither separated party ought to trash the idea of repairing (if separated) or rebuilding (if divorced) the bridge that should unite them. Until sorting out that bridge, neither side would have what we call marital 'rights', living as if unmarried (single but not free: *agamos*). The minimum ask in such situations was that no other bridge be built while the old was repairable (1 Cor.7:11), covenant obligations on hold. But if they united with someone else, it would justify divorce after the event: porneia *ex post facto*. An innocent party would be free from the shame. Both parties would have unimpeded access to fresh marriages 'in the sight of God'. For covenant is dissoluble for gross disloyalty.

Paul and Covenants Rejection

Paul's words fit in with Jesus' public position on marriage, divorce, and remarriage. It's not about a different hymn sheet but about a different part of the hymn. As said, in general, divorces for general dislikes were common but sinful, and the general biblical principle was that *sinful* divorces lacked deific approval, so obligated both parties (technically, single again/*agamos*) to remain open to covenant reunion, a residual obligation (1 Cor.7:10-1).

Paul used the common terms of his day, with each having their common meaning. *Aphiēmi* has the idea of leaving, divorcing, sending away (12-3). *Chōrizō* has the idea of leaving of setting free (by divorce)

---

29   And yes, she might have genuine grievances he should make right with her.

(15). Both hit the same target. Thus, he did not need to explain them to new converts.

Jesus' death had introduced a new scenario that Paul addressed. Those committed to God's true road could be urged off the path by their still pagan spouses—whether ethnic-Gentile or ethnic-Jewish. God authorised both Jesus and Paul. The contrast between the lord's words and Paul's words is one of prior public record, not of authority levels (10,12). God, through the lord, gave his general disapproval of selfish divorces, anything short of *porneia*. God, through Paul, covered fresh ground. Paul, to underline to sceptics (1:10-2) that he and Christ were singing from the same hymn sheet, underlined points made by citing the christ. Through Paul, God equally gave his specific approval of faith-based divorces as extreme choices.

Praying about spouses being fundamentally rejected because they were Christian, God revealed to Paul what is sometimes called the Pauline Privilege (*Privilegium Paulinum*). Roman Catholicism accepts it, but categorises 'marriages' into ① pseudo/invalid (requiring annulment), ② valid as secular (one or neither party a Christian = natural, dissoluble), or ③ valid as sacramental.

The first we have queried when reviewing cases of Henry 8's queens. Within Roman Catholicism, the second alone allows the Pauline Privilege only if one of two non-Christians becomes a Christian, and the other party rejects both them and Christ. If only one party was already a Christian and their 'natural marriage' becomes insufferable, Rome occasionally offers a Petrine Privilege *via* the pope (deemed Peter's heir), citing Ezr.10:1-14 and Mt.16:18-9 as biblical rationale. In the third scenario, if one apostatises, separation is permitted (1 Cor.7:10-11) but divorce is deemed invalid (one cannot dissolve the indissoluble)—social divorce would not be spiritual divorce.

Was Peter licensed to divorce?

I have neither the wish nor the wit to defend the idea of a Petrine Privilege. Its very branding implies that a three-pronged defence would be needed: ① a defence of papacy as carrying unique Petrine authority; ② an exegesis that affirms Ezra's mandate in Ezra's time; and ③ a hermeneutic that transfers Sinai into Golgotha. Biblically, it might be easier to rebrand it the Ezraic Privilege or Ezraic Command.

But if Ezra was justified, was it a one-off situation, or an ecclesiastical principle? Mine isn't to pontificate.

Was Paul privileged to divorce?

The term *Pauline Privilege* can carry the ideas that such divorce is a privilege, rather than a sad even if needful event, and that its ultimate authority links to Paul, not to God. *Pauline Prerogative* might be nearer the mark: divorce was sad yet, within stated conditions, a permitted and recommended choice. It is biblical to heed Paul.

He has always been attacked, inside and outside of the church. One church he founded even excommunicated him for political incorrectivism; later the Roman emperor cut off his head—Jeremiah might have had a sinking feeling at the bottom of a well, but never got as low as Paul! Paul was the apostolic founder *par excellence*. As someone once said, following ancient methods of attack, the West attacks the king (Jesus) by first undermining his chief minister (Paul).[30]

But some would happily push Paul out of the divorce equation, one way or the other. Either that no divorce is biblical (thus Paul's *privilege* to divorce was in error), or that divorce is mandatory (thus Paul's *privilege* not to divorce was in error). Paul was a canonical messenger of God.

I prefer to speak of the *Pauline Exception*, twinned with the *Matthean Exception*. That is, divorce would be adultery *except* if based *either* on what Matthew recorded in the earlier context of same-faith-marriage, *or* on what Paul proclaimed for a mixed-Christian-marriage context.

But does Paul's point justify, say, Hindus divorcing, if they find their spouses reject them and their faith? Equality might say Yes, but I suspect that the true answer is No. I do not see that whatever God allows for Christian covenant living, must be allowed for non-Christian covenant living. Equality that bows not to God is demonic; marital peace is not divine and sometimes disharmony must be borne. Paul was an oracle of God. Matthew recorded, not made, the *Matthean Exception*. Paul recorded, not made, the *Pauline Exception*.

---

[30]   And the spirit of the age affects our thinking, too. Eg: for pastoral concerns Steve Chalke rejected the Pastorals as human thinking so errant, enthroning his thinking as inerrant.

Jesus recorded, not made, the *Matthean Exception*. God made both. Jesus and Paul spoke as canonical apostles of God.

Whatever caused the marital rift, divorce is recommended where the antichrist[31] party insists on it. Some arrogantly assume that if Paul could make an exception, so can they. I am uneasy when others, based on subjectivity (what their hearts say) rather than objectivity (what God says), go beyond biblical allowances, even if they claim that that is where the biblical trajectory was headed, assuming it was evolving and that they are the cells through whom evolution flows. God calls us to bravery. Spousal abuse may permit separation from bed and board, but does not permit divorce. That can sound unkind. So is telling a soldier that they must remain in the battle, or a parent that they must keep their child. We have no right to happiness.

For Paul, there was no ground for believers to initiate a divorce—*even if the believer was the husband!* Paul, like Jesus, put genders on an equal footing: full equality without full interchangeability. Many mechanical tasks can be equally performed, but a basic masculine/feminine distinction remains at the psychological level. John Gray's *Men Are From Mars, Women Are From Venus*, has had a mixed reception. Yet it remains true that gender, as well as the sexual distinction, requires differing approaches and adaptability, especially in marriage.

For instance, no wife should treat her spouse as a woman, and no husband should treat his spouse as a man. Elaine Storkey's *What's Right with Feminism*, which classifies different types of feminism (including Christian), remains an intelligent read. This said, some argue that the Sinaitic gender specifics are irrelevant, and that the Yeshuic specifics are either read into interpretation, or are culturally plastic. This is an observation, not an argument that I will pursue here. Suffice to say that there is good argument that Jesus and Paul were both philogynists—there is no valid evidence that either was a misogynist—and that the Bible is philanthropic.

---

[31]   A strong term, justified I think by Paul's context of a nonbeliever who seems to be in genuine conflict with Christ, thus causing the spiritual conflict with shalom (1 Cor.7:15).

Being squeezed into the world's mould, the cosmic *zeitgeist* (Rm.12:2), includes negatively misreading Scripture and is deadly to critical thinking. "She would say that, she's a fundamentalist", "he would say that, he's a heretic", and "they would say that 2+2=4, they're mathematicians", must all bow to the question, "are they right in what they say?" Critical re-examination of scepticism is much needed.

Child protection

In Paul's days, men usually had more so-called *rights*, and sometimes women weren't allowed to divorce. The New Testament (NT) neither teaches divorce as a willy-nilly 'right', nor unfairly treats the sexes *un*equally. A mixed-faith marriage wasn't recommended (1 Cor. 7:39— why ask for spiritual conflict?). It wasn't a sin, but it was spiritually risky.

Indeed, in a scenario sometimes taken to dissuade from divorce, marriage to a nonbeliever could be spiritually positive, since the nonbeliever's closeness to the believer 'sanctified' him/her and any children, in some limited way (14). A spiritual child protection. Let's look at the Greek word *hagios*, usually put as 'sanctified', 'holy', or 'towards God'.

Here it simply means that the nonbelieving spouse and any children, have a privileged closeness to the gospel through a live-in witness. That it gives them ultimate salvation, any guarantee of such, or preferential treatment after death whatsoever, is a myth (1 Cor.7:16). Yet it is common misinterpretation that if a married person receives Christ, their spouse/children will gain ultimate life.[32] Well, where there's life, there's hope, so 'keep on praying' is good advice, so long as the desired result isn't taken for granted.

What may be said is that other things being equal, having a Christian as spouse/parent puts their spouse/children in a better position to receive Christ and so get into salvation now. Ac.16:31 was either a specific prophecy about the jailer's family who would also hear the gospel, or given to assure the jailer—probably a believer in Mithraism, a religion that taught that salvation was for men only—

---

[32]   Throughout this book I shall use two contrasting terms for eternal life, namely *immediate* life, and *ultimate* life, both aspects of spiritual salvation. The ultimate belongs to consummated eschatology, life beyond death with God.

---

that salvation was also for women and children who could believe (that is, welcome) Christ and be saved in the now.

Likewise, all Israelites were *sanctified* under Sinai, which offered sub-Christian Sinai-level salvation. But not all took up that advantage to get close to Yahweh and thus become true Sinaites (eg Mt.8:11-2; Jhn.8:44-5). Mixed-Christian-marriage gives light to family members, but members offered light must choose whether to welcome it.

For the relevant passage, 1 Cor.7:12-6, I grade the CEV (A+); NCV (3+); NABRE/NIV (C+); CEB (C-); ERV/LEB/NRSV (D); NKJV/NLT (D-). Paul's words neither proscribe nor prescribe divorce, nor guarantee that non-divorce would help the other parties. His focus was not here about the well-being of children—covered elsewhere—but was the basic understanding of the admissibility and advisability of divorce in certain situations Christians would have to take it from there, possibly trying marriage counselling, yet in some cases speeding up the divorce—soonest ended soonest mended.

Marriage is dissoluble

So, marriage is a covenant and, while not originally traced for grounds for annulment, we see that there were biblical grounds to annul. What such grounds were was debated, as was shown by the debate between rabbis Hillel & Shammai, into which Yeshua was drawn in God's will. I have been hurt indirectly by sinful divorce by siblings. This is a sensitive area, and as such I have added in some pastoral implications within the brief space permitted for this book.

There was strong belief in the early church that Jesus prohibited divorce, and many today cite Mal.2:16. But Malachi's context makes it more akin to divorce by the *erwath dabar* (unhappiness) of social ladder climbing types, ditching Jewish wives for pagan ones, so was compounded covenant violation, extremely hateful.

That said, proper translation depends on proper text, and the current text might be damaged. Malachi *either* said that any husband who hated and sinfully divorced their wife, committed covenant violence and treachery (NIV), or in context he said that Yahweh hated sinful divorces (NLT). Both are true. Neither forbade divorce. I'd *hate* amputation, but it might save my life. Nowadays the NIV reading would in principle apply to any wife who hated and sinfully divorced their husband, as committing covenant violence and treachery. I sadly know a few cases of the latter.

Remember that Yahweh took the step of covenant-annulment (by the suzerain), following covenant-violation by the vassal (Jr.3:8). Like it or loathe it, sometimes it is right to do what we hate, even as it can sometimes be wrong to do what we love.

We move from proof texting, to understanding Scripture. Regaining an understanding of biblical Ancient Near Eastern covenant, which was the context of Jesus, gives better understanding. This bypasses much speculative marriage theology that developed along sacramental lines. The idea that 'what God has joined' meant a spiritual link—perhaps for eternity (Mormonism)—which ignores divorced as if still married 'in God's sight', is unbiblical.[33]

Some have rejected remarriage to another, at least before the 'former' spouse has died. Historical theology, the broad consensus over church-time, has been that marriage is indissoluble, at least among Christians. Christian Humanists, such as Erasmus, uprooted that interpretative tradition, and unearthed a more biblical position— marriage is dissoluble but sometimes sinful, adulterous.

We have briefly looked at what are generally considered two biblical justifications for divorce, namely the Matthean and Pauline exceptions. Both are permitted; neither are demanded. Both free both parties to remarry another—or arguably to remarry each other. Following their lead, I again say that marriage is a covenant, is spoken of as permanent, and is dissoluble. The bridge built for permanence, may rightly or wrongly be demolished in certain situations. It was permanent under normal conditions, yet impermanent if fundamentally undermined. *Ipso facto*, the Sinaitic Covenant, though spoken of in permanent ways, was dissoluble.[34] Yet if dissolved, would the key term, *Israel*, become meaningless?

---

[33]   For more, see www.theologicalstudies.org.uk/article_divorce_snuth.html.

[34]   Some call it a conditional covenant because of the likes of Dt.28. Dt.28 does not speak of annulling for disobedience, but of punishing (or if good enriching) proportionately the covenant people who as a people who turn to the darkness.

Chapter 2   Jesus as Israel

Let's look at a few indicators that *Israel* was a prophetic term for Jesus messiah.[35] I have argued through the lens of marriage, that though covenant is intended for permanency, that ideal might fail. Is Ethnic-Israel's covenant, still in force? Let's look at how the term *Israel*, and the plan contained within that title, has expanded into new waters.

Since the Yeshuic Covenant speaks of *Israel* in various ways, it is important to see the range of meaning that the title carries, namely...

Stage 1	Jacob-Israel	Jacob the man
Stage 2	Ethnic-Israel	Jacob's twelve sons and descendants
Stage 3	Jesus-Israel	Born within that special identity
Stage 4	Global-Israel	The church, born by the spirit of Jesus

Servant Song—Israel

In 1892, Bernhard Duhm suggested that there were four Servant Songs in *Isaiah* (42:1-4; 49:1-6; 50:4-9[10-11]; 52:13–53:12).[36] Let's focus in for

---

[35]   MEVV policies range from reluctance to translate *christos* as other than *christ* (CEB/LEB/NCV/NKJV), to gently scratching the Zionising itch (for which the ISV—not listed—excels) to abandon the term *christ* in favour of *messiah*.

For ethnic-Jews it can be good to see a more familiar face (*messiah*) turning up more than twice in John's Gospel. But to totally dismiss the term *christ* for cultural reasons of past bitterness, can be to blinker them to the globality of the church in favour of tunnel vision, to miss the wood for the tree. Messiah went global; *Saul* became *Paul*. *Christ* is a big historical term with both good and bad baggage.

For NT believers at large it can be good to see a less familiar face (*messiah*) turning up more than twice in John's Gospel. To totally dismiss the term *messiah* for cultural reasons of past bitterness, can be to blinker them from the Jewish/Gentile life situation of the C1 world, to miss the tree for the wood. Christ came through the Jewish tunnel; Paul came from Saul. Messiah is a big historical term with both good and bad baggage.

I favour *messiah* in contexts where the ethno-Jewish feel was likely. For the Gospels I stand with the CEV/ERV/NABRE/NIV/NLT/NRSV for their functional approach, though they underplay (especially in *Hebrews*) the scope to messianise. For a balanced approach to the NT, the old HCSB perhaps best hit the mark.

[36]   Some say there's a fifth (61:1-3). Some say there aren't any.

---

a moment on his fourth. As Raphael Gasson—as an ethnic-Jew and former Spiritualist medium—put it, Isaiah 53 is "the chapter much avoided by [most ethnic] Jews" (Gasson 25). When at last confronted by it, Gasson testified that as he read through its specificity, so many even minor details ticking the box of Yeshua as messiah, he gained a sense of the Tanak being actually inspired by God.

Perhaps Duhm rightly identified Servant themes as songs, but he wrongly ignored their contexts, and while rightly dismissing the idea that Yahweh's Servant was Ethnic-Israel, wrongly dismissed the idea that Yahweh's Servant was Yeshua. Alec Motyer thought Duhm needlessly sceptical, and showed that Ethnic-Israel could fit the bill, both making sense of Yahweh's Servant being Israel (41:8; 49:3), yet with details undermining a corporate identification (Motyer 2005:26).

For when we ask if the whole, or even a righteous remnant of Ethnic-Israel, had been righteous enough to bear sin (53:11; Ex.12:5), and whether a Remnant, or some outstanding individual, has ever turned in part or whole, the nation back to Yahweh (Is.49:5-6), is it not best to look to Yeshua? These *Songs*, fully integrated within Scripture, show the Servant distinct from a spiritually shoddy nation (42:18-25) "and from the spiritually committed and expectant remnant (51:1–52:12), leaving a majestic Individual to occupy our gaze (52:13) as he died bearing the sins of others (53:4-9) and lives [again, now] administering the salvation he has won for them (53:10-2)" (Motyer 2005:27).

Is it coincidence that Jesus' messianic community would be described as in line with 49:6's prediction to be "a light for the Gentiles" (Ac.13:47), the global plan of God? Admittedly, he did not meet Ethnic-Israel's *national* expectations, but then those expectations weren't God's.

The fourth 'song' speaks of the Servant being lifted up. The Greek OT used the same word as Jesus did of himself, in such as Jhn.8:28 and 12:32,34. Incidentally, the term for 'lifted up' (*hupsos*) carries the idea of exaltation, probably a subplot in *John*. Kings are exalted.

As an aside, why join the ancient song of the Roman soldiers, lifting Jesus higher? Singing biblical terms, but with unbiblical meanings, can easily cause confusion, even blindness, but songwriters love to take us there. It is safer for songs to replace the term 'lift up,' with something like 'exalt', simply to add some verbal distance between what we mean and what Jesus meant about being lifted up onto a cross to redeem us. We cannot lift up on the cross, he who was lifted up on the cross to die once for all time, even if colourful Christian pipers offer to lead us as Hamelin's spellbound children. We should examine songs as well as prophecies, and keep only the good.

Some cite Jhn.12:32 to affirm Universalism. Universalism is an idea Origen held, that every human being ever born (and perhaps every angel ever created) will ultimately live lovingly with God. It is a position Christians can hold.[37] I'll neither damn nor defend it—John Sanders' *No Other Name* (1994) covers it well. On Jhn.12:32, the best Bible version to sail past Scylla (Parochialism), without being sucked into Charybdis (Universalism), is the NKJV: "And I, if I am lifted up from the earth, will draw all peoples to myself." It highlights the cross bypassing ethnic boundaries and being for all peoples, all ethnicities, even if some people are repelled our preaching.

In the Servant 'Songs' the term *Israel* is distinct from the historical Jacob and from the historical ethnic race that had good claim to that honour. This Servant Israel would be lifted up to redeem. There is a multi-layered approach, which includes messiah Yeshua.

The New Covenant Israel

Let's now focus on Jhn.1:51—Jesus as Jacob. The wider context in Jhn.1 is of messianic talk. John the Immerser told Jewish leaders[38] to prepare for messiah. The next day, his cousin Jesus asked to be baptised. John, knowing Jesus' outstanding dedication to Yahweh, knew Jesus didn't need to turn back to God (*repent*), which after all his national preaching and immersion were all about. Unbeknown to John, Jesus' mission was to pick up John's baton to identify with John's mission.

Once immersed, heaven approved, showing John that Jesus was messiah. But John, not seeing God's full face, pictured God's Lamb as being a national apocalyptic warrior Lamb—hence his later doubts.

---

37   Some claim 'names' out of context for this belief, indeed if some websites are to be believed, the early church was largely Universalist, and Hitler loved Jews.

38   For MEVV differentiating Jewish leaders from rank-and-file ethnic-Jews, NLT (A+); CEV (A); CEB (B+); NIV (B); ERV (C+); NCV (C); LEB/NABRE/NKJV/NRSV (D-).

One of his disciples was Andrew, a brother to fisherman Simeon. Andrew, accepting John's witness about Jesus, tried to convince Simeon. To underline the Jewishness of the setting, the Hebrew-Aramaic term in v41 was transliterated into Greek as *messias*, rather than simply using the more usual Greek term *christos*.[39]

Then Andrew and Simeon, presumably, had some table talk with Jesus, before going home. Incidentally neither of them became disciples of Yeshua at that time, though Simeon was given a prophetic mission name, *Kephas* (Rock). He would neither be always reliably steady, nor was his confession at large worth calling him Rock Man. The significance remained veiled.

But once Peter became a disciple, he along with his fellow disciples lived a year or so before knowing beyond doubt that Jesus was the messiah, in spite of the fact that Jesus was panning out as a national warrior. Once Kephas (a.k.a. *Peter*) publicly accepted that truth, he was given a foundational mission to ground the messianic community (Mt.16:18).[40] He would lead the way, even if he was fog-bound rock now and again (eg 16:23; Gal.2:11).

Some claim that his specialness was continued through leadership in Rome. Some counterclaim that he was only a *pebble* contrasted to the *rock* of confession that grounded the church—they throw in a bit of Greek. We can however dismiss the claim of Greek wordplay in Mt.16:18, for the Aramaic behind Jhn.1:42 has no masculine/feminine option, no hidden wordplay, and Greek gender is secondary. And we

---

[39] The Aramaic, *messias*, is kept only twice in the NT. It means the same as *christos*. Translations that adopt it, in ethno-Israelite contexts, can help a little. I would use it heavily in the Gospels and *Hebrews*, but neither in *Galatians* nor *Ephesians*.

[40] He also had a pivotal role, certainly among the Jerusalem church (Ac.15:7), and probably church-wide, in opening evangelism to Gentiles. Philip to the Samaritans (Ac.8) was different, in that they were held to be schismatics, not Gentiles; Cornelius was a full Gentile (Ac.10). Jesus had welcomed both Samaritans and Gentiles, showing his global plan. The so-called keys of the kingdom which were to Peter (singular *you* in Mt.16:19), were also arguably implied in the same loosing/binding mission given to all (plural *you* in 18:18), whether or not that missional aspect meant evangelism (as in Jhn.20:23) or housekeeping.

can dismiss the Roman claim, which church history didn't even allege until centuries into the Christian Era: it is at best a hypothesis. Arguably Roman popery, like English monarchy, has had saints and sinners: they make an interesting study.

Historically, Peter would be the first among equals when the church went public at Pentecost, yet would be eclipsed locally by James and didactically by Paul. What remains outstanding, foundational, was Peter's leadership in re-establishing the symbolic apostolic number to twelve, his epochal speech, and his validation of the gospel to ethno-Gentiles. The dodeka symbolism at Pentecost, grounded the community's Israel identity as founded upon the ultimate Rock as Messianic Israel. Peter was specifically prayed for to consolidate his apostolic brothers for that pivotal stage (Lk.22:31-2).

And having mentioned saints and sinners, it's good to define *saint*. Ecclesiastically, when I first wrote this book, former pope John Paul 2 was on the path to sainthood, one miracle down, another to be discovered and validated (two witnesses?): yes, he made it. That followed an idea—set up by the Church:Roman network he had led—to help its members to be inspired by outstanding examples of sainthood by sharing their epitaphs. Such can be helpful role models.

However, that idea ignores the bigger picture. Biblically, the word for holiness (*hagios*)—sometimes put as *saint*—is attached to all Christians. Type 1 holiness functions, like tent pegs, as positional: all Christians are set aside unto God by God, so all are holy, all are saints. Type 2 holiness functions as lifestyle: not all, certainly not I, actually live the totally dedicated life we ought to, even though set aside unto God by God. Holiness levels in this sense, like waves in a sea vary Christian to Christian, day to day, action to action, attitude to attitude, thought to thought. Some are saintly saints; some are unsaintly saints.[41]

---

[41]   In Rm.1:7; 8:27; 12:13; 15:25-6,31; 16:2,15, we can read *saints* (LEB/NKJV/ NRSV: D-) or *[his/holy/God's] people, holy ones*, or *Christians/believers* (ERV/ NABRE/NCV/NLT: A+). In between are the CEB (A-) and the CEV/NIV (B+). The NIV toggles between *God's people* (Rm.1:7; Col.1:4) and *the Lord's people* (Rm.12:13; Col.1:26). Yet they are not one *person*. Ananias prayed to the lord as Jesus, speaking to him about *his* holy people (*hagioi*/saints), so *the lord's people*, does work: for that matter, so would *the spirit's people*. Yet primarily

Back to text. As the early stage (Jhn.1:43) we know of only Philip being called to discipleship before they met Nathanael. Note also the mixture of Hebrew (Simeon/Nathanael) and Greek (Andrew/Philip) names, possibly hinting at globalism. Some suggest that Nathaniel's fuller name was *Nathanael son of* (bar) *Tholomaios* (Tholomew in English, hence Bar-tholomew)—Son of Ptolemy in Greco-Roman times.[42] Nathanael was sceptical: could anything good come out of Nazareth, where unkosher Gentiles rubbed should with Jews? In line with prophecy, Jesus was born in Judea's Bethlehem (but not in a manger!), became a short-term refugee in Egypt (Hos.11:1), then settled for safety in Galilee's Nazareth. So had Philip misled Nathaniel?

Well, John Calvin certainly accused Philip as misrepresenting Jesus to Nathanael, as if Philip had "foolishly called Jesus the son of Joseph and ignorantly made him a Nazarene" (Köstenberger 80)! In fact, Philip, not Calvin, was correct and justified. Lk.2:33,48 happily calls Joseph Jesus' father, for along social lines he was, and Philip would not have known deeper. Lk.1:35 gives the balance: Jesus was/is the permanent temporal mode of the eternal second person of deity, both deific and human. He is stream within of source beyond, and incarnate mode of the noncarnate son, God the son as a man, deific limitation of unlimited deity. Humanly speaking he was a Nazarene in both the sense of having grown up in, though not being born in, the town of Nazareth, and also as being a despised person, which *Nazarene* can mean. Nathanael's village of Cana looked askance at near-neighbour Nazareth, but more significantly messiah was not predicted to be born in Nazareth, a small insignificant village suburb of a large Gentile city in Galilee, Sepphoris, so deemed somewhat unkosher.

But when Nathanael met Jesus he met a prophet, a prophet who called him a true Israelite. High praise indeed, especially since *Israelite* isn't a common NT word. This story only works if Nathanael

---

we are people of *God*—Jesus highlights as the Way, not the Destination. Paul's strong policy to avoid confusing the father with his son was to keep the term *God* for the father, and the term *lord* for the son. My beef with the NIV is that in trying to balance between *God's* people and the *lord's* people as if synonyms, we might confuse the persons whom Paul kept distinct.

[42] Probably the Synoptics (ie *Matthew/Mark/Luke*) refer to him as Bartholomew, while *John* refers to him as Nathanael.

knew that Philip hadn't spoken to Yeshua about him. In line with Philip's witness and Jesus' prophethood, he identified this rabbi by the messianic terms *son of God*, and *Israel's king*. From John, Philip would have known that Jesus was son of Joseph son of David, from Nazareth, and heir to David's throne. That claim was never in dispute, even among later Judaists who disputed Jesus' wider messianic claims. However, at that time the popular messianic expectation which even John shared, was of a Davidic warrior who would defeat Rome, re-establish the monarchy and holy priesthood, and establish Jerusalem as the spiritual hub for the nations. Even the expression *God's son* was—since the Davidic kings bore this title—little more in this context than the messianic Davidide.

Let's check out *God's son* as a title. As we look back into Scripture, we can see that 2 Sam.7:14 records Yahweh's promise to David to have a Davidide, who would be Yahweh's son and build the temple. In spite of all Solomon's folly, Solomon was that son—an honorific title. Lest some think it must have meant David's 'greater son' Jesus, let it be said that 7:14 refers to this son being disciplined though never disinherited. Lest it be thought that this must merely mean that Jesus knew discipline through painful times (Heb.5:8-9), 1 Chr.28:6 named this son *Solomon*.

That David and Bathsheba's immediate son, Solomon, built the temple, is not in dispute. It goes back to what I call Alpha and Omega levels of fulfilment, initial and subsequent/deeper fulfilments (*sensus plenior*). That a subsequent and more-so son of God built, and in another sense was, the true temple, is all part of how prophecy has worked, and not all details need apply. It's good to note that the relational terms father/son, can refer to an affectionate covenant: Ethnic-Israel was Yahweh's son (Hos.11:1).[43]

---

[43]   Sadly ignoring the dynamics of covenant and friendship, some believe—and no doubt wish to believe—that the parity covenant (brother/brother) between Saul's son Jonathan and Saul's replacement David, was homosexual. Correctivism teaches that we must misread what millennia have rightly read, that to be wise we must be secular fools. 2 Sam.1:26 speaks of covenant loyalty above the normal expectations of marriage, and praises both he who attacked (ie Jonathan's father), and he who defended (ie Saul's son), David. The Hebrew *ahabah* is also used of Yahweh's love for his people (eg 2 Chr.2:11).

These terms caused C7 Muhammad—may he be blessed—needless fears that Christianity taught that God had a son through sexual union with a goddess: having just given up polytheism, he must have sighed. But 'God's son' is a valid expression for the eternal second person of deity, useful even for the unimaginable relationship beyond time, accommodating our need for pictures to improve our image of the unimaginable. *Mere Christianity*, by C S Lewis, remains a should-read book, though due (and deserving) a gender update: part 4, *Beyond Personality*, offers much insight into the trinity.

Back to Nathanael. Jesus replied that that recognition was all too simple: a too simple definition to a too simple miracle. More profoundly, he was in the pattern of Jacob-Israel, in fact of a redefined Israel, not a mere ethnic king. The Greek text has a double *amēn*, taking the Hebrew idea that immediate repetition was a superlative: "Never let it rest until the *good* is *better* and the *better* is *best*." This double *amēn* was probably a feature Jesus created, translated well as "very truly". I used to sing, "verily, verily". A verity is a truth. Only John recorded this bold expression. Very truly, Nathanael, representing sincere Israel, not deceptive Jacob, would see heaven open and angels of God ascending and descending on the 'son of man'.[44]

An open heaven

According to Köstenberger "an 'open heaven' was every Jewish apocalyptic's dream" because it meant seeing revelations, not answers to prayer (Köstenberger 85; Ac.10:11; Rv.4:1; 19:11). For Nathanael, heaven would open and remain open—the Greek of *anoigō* (open) in the perfect tense. Much speculative Jewish apocalyptic was based on the idea that some interesting characters had gone into heaven and come back with revelation.

Jesus such speculation: "no one has ever gone to heaven and returned. But the Son of Man has come down from heaven" (NLT: Jhn.3:13).[45] In

---

[44] An intentional puzzle. The CEB's 'human one'—perhaps better 'human representative' or 'representative man'—is needlessly gender neutral, IMO, no real improvement.

[45] The NLT reading is best, with the old Amplified Bible just a little behind and the Common Jewish Bible meriting a mention. Most other MEVV miss the sense, while particular demerit goes to the NKJV.

other words, don't look to noncanonical Jewish apocalyptic, look to Jesus. The revelation Nathanael would see would be from God and be in line with what Yeshua promised, namely messiah as the true Israel. Here read 'true' in the Johannine sense, such as in 1:9, where 'true' light neither contrasts true to false, nor genuine to counterfeit—though these meanings are sometimes included. In this biblical sense, it meant that before the ultimate came, came anticipations, handy hints but pale forerunners.

As with Heb.1:1-3, God's son is the ultimate (*alēthinos*) spiritual self-disclosure of God. I think that this is one of the basic keys to unlocking the whole Bible. Its significance can hardly be overplayed. The key goes under different terms. For example, Matthew preferred to speak of fulfilment, where an initial level of prophecy was subsequently fulfilled; the Writer to the Hebrews used a number of terms to contrast what we may call Alpha Level to Omega Level: *kreittōn* (better), *alēthinos* (ultimate), *typos* (paradigm), *hupodeigma* (copy), *skia* (shadow), and *parabolē* (symbolic).

What God had up and running before the Yeshuic Covenant, was neither false, permanent, nor unhelpful. It was an initial (alpha) level of what would be the ultimate (omega) level for mortal man, and what would transcend the artificial barrier of ethnicity. Jesus had called Nathanael a true Israelite, in the sense of sincerity and heritage, even though a descendant of crafty Jacob-Israel.

Then Jesus reminded Nathanael about Jacob's open heaven dream, of angels using a stairway between heaven and earth.[46] The importance of this vision was not the picture of angels, but of human need and deific response, focused at the alpha-level through Jacob. Gen.28:12-22 highlighted the Abrahamic Covenant and how it would bless Jacob and, through Jacob, all peoples. Jacob personally committed to it, beginning Israel's practice of a regular tribute tithe to Yahweh from suzerain Israel. Nathanael's vision would connect to

---

[46]   Sci-Fi fans may speak about photosomatic beings inter-phasing between one dimension and another, which might be nearer the reality. God can give visions in symbolic language, and above/below pictures, symbolising heaven/earth/hades, have long been convenient: we still speak of going up/down in the social world.

this collection of ideas. Later, Jesus would say to a Samaritan woman that he himself was indeed greater than Jacob (Jhn.4:12-4), one offering greater blessing as a greater well to quench spiritual thirst.

Pentecost and Israel

If Jesus was true Israel, who were his sons? I'll not ask who were his four wives! Analogies are approximates, partial patterns, so perhaps the analogy needn't be pressed for sons, let alone asking if eleven betrayed one and all ended up in Egypt, etc. It is, though, a question to introduce the idea that if Yeshua himself defined the Servant Songs' idea of *Israel* serving *Israel*, Jesus' circle of apostles intentionally represented the true *twelve* tribes of Israel.

In the Gospels we read how they were a little flock (Lk.12:32). An implication that they were seemingly an insignificant part of God's flock, Ethnic-Israel? After all, Ethnic-Israel had once been seemingly insignificant among the nations (Dt.7:7). Ezekiel had prophesied a Good Shepherd, Yahweh himself. And in some sense, someone else who would remind them of King David (Ezk.34:15,23-4). Ethnic-Israel had been Yahweh's vine (see Ps.80:8-19; Is.5:1-7; Jr.2:21; Ezk.15; Hos.10:1-2). The disciples were branches of God's *alēthinos* vine, Jesus (Jhn.15:5).

Incidentally, unfruitful 'branches' would be as useless to God as vine branches that are simply discarded (6). Fear not, unproductive Christians aren't consigned to hell, nor should heretics be burnt, contrary to some medieval teaching![47] The core group of twelve symbolised a new Davidide monarchy (Mt.19:28), superior to the old regime. We can see many clues to the NT church's identity, once the key opens the way.

Twelve is Big. Twenty-five times the Gospels call Jesus' inner core followers, 'The Twelve' (some later manuscripts throw in Lk.22:14, too), and Mt.10:1-2 defines them as disciples (some later manuscripts add this definition to Mt.20:17/Lk.9:1). Where the phrase has no extension it should be treated as a technical term, and preferably highlighted by at least one

---

[47]   Commenting on this being a proof text for hell's burning, Küng commented that "it is impossible to imagine a more flagrant abuse of the Gospels, and of this Gospel in particular" (Küng 257). Calvinism tends to assume that it is simply the separation of pseudo-Christians (eg Köstenberger 455).

capital—'the Twelve'.[48] But whatever the textual basis, The Twelve (*dōdeka*: Mt.26:14; Mk.4:10; Ac.6:2) was the usual form of address, the common jargon for them, and it's unlikely to have been merely incidental. For contrast, while three in particular were closer to events, they were never called The Three. No, the smallest inner circle was Twelve by design.

Indeed for John, a man who seems to have planned methodically to write into his Gospel so much symbolic significance, The Twelve would only be called such after the story of the Jewish feeding, when knowing his dormant royal inheritance, the crowd threatened to make Yeshua their king. Jhn.6:1-15 records this miraculous sign as a significant link with the Synoptics—they seldom interlink before the cross. It speaks of a new Passover: "the movement from the miracle to the discourse, from Moses to Jesus (6:32-5; see 1:17), and, above all, from bread to flesh, is almost unintelligible unless the reference in 6:4 to the Passover picks up 1:29,36, anticipates 19:36 (Ex.12:46; Nb.9:12), and governs the whole narrative" (Hoskyns 281).

What was so significant about the feeding of the oft-called 5,000? Comparing the locations and cultural words used, "from the time of [C4] Hilary of Poitiers it has been common to argue that the feeding of the [5,000] represents [God's] provision for the Jews, and...the [4,000 as] for the Gentiles" (Carson 1991:271). Not all miracles were for ethnic-Jews: the bread would go global, as the Syrophoenician woman prophesied. But initially the bread was to satisfy an ethnic-Jewish family audience, which had about 5,000 men (Mt.14:21).

Jesus multiplied a young teenage boy's budget picnic: the one would give life to the many. The twelve basketfuls remaining symbolised messianic manna still available for each of the twelve tribes of Israel in their exodus. Surely, King 'Joshua' (page 247), would lead them in battle for the Promised Land. He was surely their prophet, their king, the Moses long expected, and he would free them from Rome.

But such thinking was confused, and their hearts were hung on the wrong hook. In line with what he later said to Pilate about his

---

[48]   Best as a technical term, CEB/NABRE/NIV (A+); ERV/LEB/NKJV/NRSV (C); NCV (C-); CEV (D); NLT (D-). To suggest that Jesus only had 12 disciples/followers, underplays his impact.

kingdom, he wouldn't be their war-lord, and he escaped to the Golan Heights, lest they began a war of independence and be slaughtered. At heart level, truly "he came to what was his own, but his own people did not accept him" (NABRE: Jhn.1:11),[49] though John, himself an ethnic-Jew, quickly added that some did. Significantly, John only spoke of The Twelve here (6:67, 70-1) and in 20:24, and even after Judas had departed it wasn't The Eleven. They were drawn from Ethnic-Israel but stood separately.

Judas replaced

But for a while it was only eleven, for the Keriothite had fallen in the plot and from the plot. Jesus had died. The Twelve were down to eleven, though only for a few weeks. John used *The Twelve* in a limited way; so too Luke used *The Eleven* (Lk.24:9,33; Ac.2:14). Why, instead of simply saying *apostles* in Lk.24:9, as he did in the next line, did Luke record this expression? Was it not to say that the core group, previously The Twelve, were unprepared for the grand opening?

To get back to symbolic strength, Judas had to be replaced. Ah, replacement. Even Jesus was replaced—by the spirit (Jhn.16:7). Though the spirit was already with them at some level, he would become their paraclete and mediate Jesus' lordship: Jesus' lordship on the ground, tactical command 'in Jesus' name'. Luke's second volume picked up on this theme of replacement, a restoration of symbolic strength to Twelve, showing Matthias being added to the eleven (*endeka*) apostles (Ac.1:26) before Pentecost. Let's look at this.

While there were perhaps well over 500 believers at that time (1 Cor.15:6), either 120 in total or including 120 men, met in Jerusalem.[50] They agreed that a twelfth apostle was needed for the big day before the spirit 'came' in his new role. Matthias was appointed, and the following silence about him is no more significant than that of most of the apostles not traced in *Acts*. We need not think Peter wrong, unless one holds that the twelfth place should have gone to Paul, and

---

49   The NABRE (A+); NRSV (A); CEV/LEB (B+); NCV (B); ERV (B-); CEB/NIV/
      NKJV/NLT (D-).

50   Luke had mentioned Mary in a smaller group (?). Ac.1:15 might well be on a
      later men-only day. It speaks of *adelphoi* (brothers, possibly brothers & sisters)
      or *mathētai* (disciples), and then adds that there were 120 names (*onomata*).

---

that Pentecost could have symbolised (or didn't need to) a new kind of Israel with only eleven apostles.

It shows that they thought themselves to be in the pattern of twelve-tribed *Israel*. At that time, it made excellent sense to choose a witness who had physically walked with Jesus, whom, once they had shortlisted candidates, they either voted, or asked God to decide (Ac.1:26). Some think this rules out there having been apostles after that generation, but Paul and Barnabas had probably neither literally walked with Jesus, nor seen him before he died. Too easily we can believe that apostleship died out after The Twelve, replaced by apostolic authority only transmitted through *clergy* and canon.

Luke reflected the sense that a twelfth apostle was required before Pentecost. Some say that Paul's supporter Luke didn't believe in Matthias, but recorded his call as Peter's folly. Yet wouldn't Luke have indicated his unease over any fundamental decision relating to apostleship? And if violently disagreeing, perhaps feeling that his colleague Paul was the proper twelfth apostle, why not airbrush Matthias out of history? Luke held the pen of history.

It seems clear to me that Luke agreed Matthias' appointment as needful. The historicity must be accepted if for no other reason than that in subsequent Lucan history, Matthias made no historical waves, nor seemed relevant. For Pentecost he was however vital, a statement of intent, we might say. Since it was Peter's belief (the leading apostle of the first wave), you might wonder why we wonder about Luke's opinion anyway. The answer must surely be that while Peter deemed a twelfth apostle needed by Pentecost, Luke (a Gentile theologian and historian on Paul's team) confirmed Peter decades later, not simply theologically but with historical hindsight and acumen. That *Petrine* theology argued the case before Pentecost, seems clear from the fact that had Luke created the idea of a pre-Pentecost replacement apostle, he would have made his theological reasoning through 'Peter' clearer, and if inauthentic others would have blown the gaffe.

Whether Matthias was God's best, will still be debated. In dispensationalist circles, I once thought his appointment folly, a people-powered interim measure, similar in ways to prematurely appointing Saul to kingship instead of waiting for Yahweh to select David as Israel's first king. Later I asked why Peter, with the unanimity argued for within the sandwich of unity (Ac.1:14; 2:1), theologised the need for a twelfth apostle by Pentecost. To me the answer seems clear: it was a necessary statement of a transmutation of Israel as a community.

At Pentecost were representatives of Ethnic-Israel, even from the diaspora. To this audience, including interested Gentiles, the message of repentance, forgiveness, eschatological spirit, and water-baptism-identification,[51] was preached. In this context, forgiveness linked to repentance, with the latter being knocking on Christ's door, and the former being the father welcoming the repentant inside the messianic community, True Israel.

By the way, it was not saying that without such forgiveness, Peter's audience were all damned for eternity, but that only by it could they enter the new covenant: Ethnic-Israel was invited by Israel to enter Israel.[52] Remember, Luke was on Paul's mission team, so his verdict would probably have reflected Paul's. Bear in mind that Luke also spoke of subsequent apostles, so didn't limit history to only twelve.

12-11-12

Isaiah prophesied that Jesus would be Israel. Jesus saw himself as summarising Israel: he was its temple; the crowd rightly greeted him as King David's son; his 'coronation' (hupsos) would be to globally draw all peoples to himself (global mission), the light even to ethnic Gentiles. His followers were the true twelve-tribed Israel. Peter—and, once converted, the Pharisee Saul—saw the messianic community as twelve-tribed Israel, and their Gentile historian Luke so noted it: adding Matthias made Israel.

---

[51]   Ac.2:38 proclaimed that they needed to yield to a proper attitude towards God (repent), thus receiving his forgiveness (welcome), and then to be immersed in water to witness to their new status: water-baptism relative to (eis) forgiveness—"εις might be understood as 'with reference to'..." (Morris 1988:380.16).

[52]   This is an important distinction, for some have taught that without a conversion experience there is no ultimate forgiveness into heaven.

Chapter 3   A Tale of Three Big Texts

Many evangelicals, tapping somewhat into the ancient church, think that we can enter ultimate life without explicit welcome of God's son. This falls into the idea called inclusivism, a wider-hope. Some inclusivists think that ultimate life has three Cross-based delivery points. ① Gentiles can access it if they hear and are mentally/morally able to understand (the age of accountability, which varies individual to individual). ② Gentiles below that mental/moral age are all given it (*quasiuniversalism*: Sanders 206). ③ all genetic members of the ancient Sinaitic Covenant have it by birth right—godless Esaus apart (*covenantal nomism*: E P Sanders).

I doubt that God has different delivery schemes. Focusing on the third, can he even sort out Jews from Gentiles, since marrying in had different generational scales to become true-blooded Israelites (Dt.23:3,8)? And if there is no different salvation method between ethnic-Jews and ethnic-Gentiles, is there a different method between mental infants and mental adults? If there is any other than one method, isn't Pandora's Box open for business?

I shall later look at how ultimate salvation relates to people who die below a moral/mental age of accountability. Disagreeing with ③, this chapter will examine three NT texts to replace ethnic glasses with spiritual glasses—*Global-Israel*.

Galatians 6:16

Reviewing the obvious?

Here, I think, we find Paul having used Israel terminology for Global-Israel. If he applied the blunt, in your face term *Israel* to the church, then it's a unique text, though we should be concerned unless a general case can be made for such theology. There are no significant textual variations for this text, but interpretation is disputed by vested interests both sides.

Some say that Paul had only Ethnic-Israel in mind, partly because they say that in every other instance of 'Israel', the NT speaks of Ethnic-Israel. Who dares call Paul inconsistent? Nonetheless, the consistency argument can be deceptive. There was this time when only Tammy, Tim, and Tony, put their names into a hat. I proclaimed them first, second, and third in that order without drawing their names out. When they asked why, I argued that Tammy was first because neither Tim nor Tony was; Tim was second because neither Tammy nor Tony was, and obviously Tony had to be third, so why bother drawing out the names? With such impeccable logic, why bother with mere evidence? The 'every other instance' line works the same way: I claim victory without fighting for it; I assume the conclusion, beg the question (*petitio principi*).

But my argument fails, because without drawing the names out to individualise things, I argued from a lack of proof as to what each was not, to a proclaimed proof of what each was. That's worse than the Alpha Centaurian who argued that since all the other instances of planets in our solar system lack humanoid life (proved), so must Earth (speculation). That's dumb, but less dumb. Each biblical text should be examined in its own right, without begging the question. What did Paul mean, not what do I mean, is the question.

Once, rereading Chaucer's C14 *Canterbury Tales*, and replying to someone that I was reading a translation (to wit, Coghill's), I was advised simply to read it in the original Middle English and told that I would pick up the sense naturally. But as C S Lewis put it, such "will be so amateurish as to be nugatory, no matter how clever the reader: 'if we read an old poem with insufficient regard for change in the overtones, and even the dictionary meanings, of words since its date—if, in fact, we are content with whatever effect the words accidentally produce in our modern minds—then of course we do not read the poem the old writer intended. What we get may still be, in our opinion, a poem: but it will be our poem, not the writer's. If we call this tout court 'reading' the old poem, we are deceiving ourselves'" (Martin 2000:81). To a non-Welsh speaker, even swearing in Welsh might sound holy. Guidance helps.

Approached without guidance, 1 Pt.1:1 and Jas.1:1 might sound clear enough. But any good commentary on such will show that even a gifted amateur can overlook ingredients to sound exegesis, especially when our contextually different culture uses a different mapping system to the Bible's. Only if we have reasonably read it in its terms, not in ours, can we reasonably translate it into our terms. So now to a brief look at two 'every other instance' texts by Peter and James, before returning to Paul.

Briefly, outside of *Acts* (11:26; 26:28), *1 Peter* alone has the word 'Christian' (4:16). The question is, what group or groups would Peter have developed such oversight over. Jewish non-Christians, nonethnic-Jewish Christians, ethnic-Jewish Christians, or Christians in general? Talk about 'twelve tribes' can be about God's people, the global church. Might it sometimes mean the *True Diaspora*, the global church scattered around the Empire? As Karen Jobes suggested, as Christian *diasporans* they might also have become social *diasporans* in one of Rome's purges against Christians in Rome—that is, exiled from Rome for allegiance to Christ, double diasporans.[53] *Diaspora* could have a sociological weight (eg socially homeless for Christ), as well as metaphorical weight (eg as Heb.11:9's spiritually homeless on earth). Might *diaspora* have even been a positive term for dispersal of seed, witness (Ac.8:1)?

Might *1 Peter* imply a spiritual transformation into God's Israel (2:10), suggesting a contrast to mere non-volitional ethnicity. Its OT citations seem applicable to any Christian, and the lifestyle of at least some of his readers had been pagan (4:3). The combined Jewish/ Gentile greeting (shalom/grace) was used. Intertestamental Jewish Religion (a.k.a. Second Temple Judaism) had expected the diaspora to be ritually cleaned by God and returned to the land of blessing, but Land Theology also applies to the NT church, as Elmer Martens said. Peter's audience could well have been a multiethnic new creation audience.

Though James probably wrote predominantly to Christian ethnic-Jews (1:1), 'twelve tribes' in some contexts can mean God's people as the NT church, scattered (*diasporans*) or shunned around the Empire (Moo 1990:32-3). Similarly, while systematic theology might prefer stricter terms, in more casual writing Paul simply called the church in Corinth, *the church*, without denying that the term also applied to churches outside of Corinth.[54]

The diaspora as Jewish Christians, whom James looked after, allows a wider sense of meaning in other contexts. Some have argued that the

---

53   Jobes 61

54   Yet the definite article teaches us a bit about the ideal unity of local churches

church did not call itself Israel until the time of Justin Martyr.[55] Such ideas are disputed, but I confine my analysis to the NT writings.

Background and possibilities

Now let's approach Gal.6:16 without squeezing it into our predetermined moulds, aware that Paul could contrast a sinful-Ethnic-Israel, to a spiritual-global Israel (Rm.9:6; 1 Cor.10:18). Are its duplications (real or fancied) based on a dual audience, namely the NT church and Ethnic-Israel? The verse—its transliteration slightly simplified—is *kai hosoi tō kanoni toutō stoichēsousin eirēnē epi autous kai eleos kai epi ton Israēl tou Theou*. All will know one word; many will guess another. Unavoidably, prior commitments flavour translations. Here are two versions to contrast the grammatical poles.

- "Now may peace be on all those who live by this principle, and may mercy be on the Israel of God" (ISV).[56]

- "May God's peace and mercy be upon all who live by this principle; they are the new people of God" (NLT).[57]

Favouring the ISV, on the one hand a preposition and a conjunction (*epi* and *kai*) are used twice the same way. Therefore, two audiences? That would work, but on the other hand the semantic range of *kai* covers 'and', 'also', 'even', and 'yet' (Balfour 39). In short, in context the second *kai* may read something like '*that is*, on God's Israel'.

In the larger context of *Galatians*, "the issues focus on the question, 'Who really are the children of Abraham?' (See esp. 3:6-10,14,16,26-9; 4:21-31), [so] to conclude with a declaration that Gentile converts are rightfully 'the Israel of God' would be highly significant and telling. In this case the second *kai* should be seen as being explicative, epexegetically (that is 'namely') clarifying in a second clause the expression *epi autous* ('on those'): 'even on the Israel of God'" (Longenecker 298). The *epi* would nicely fit this context, as *per* the NLT.

Favouring the ISV, on the one hand, the word order attributes (*eirēnē/ eleos*) *if* to one audience as in 2 Jhn.3, should perhaps have been *eleos* before *eirēnē*, since mercy (*eleos*) comes before peace (*eirēnē*). That

---

55   Eg Peter Richardson's *Israel in the Apostolic Church*, 1969.

56   Unlike the MEVV, the ISV (likewise CSB) splits the concepts *peace*, and *mercy*.

57   The ISV is ethno-Zionist; the NLT is spirito-Zionist.

would work, but on the other hand the C1 Ethno-Jewish document, the *Shemoneh Ezreh*, 19, has "Grant peace...and mercy unto us and unto all Israel." Rm.5:1-11 likewise deals with peace, *before* 5:12-21 deals with mercy. The logic behind a preferred word-order must not preclude unexpected variations. The NLT is grammatically justified.

The case against the NLT and for the ISV is weak. Paul wished the so-called Circumcision Party (roughly Sinaitic Christians, later Ebionites) to cut itself off from the messianic community (Gal.5:12).[58] Theologically, the Party that called itself Circumcised, was really the Uncircumcised, contaminating the true Circumcision, akin to the unkosher yeast of the Pharisees which contaminated the holy message (Mt.16:11). Paul had said that geographical Jerusalem was more Arabian, and its Sinaitic people more like Ishmaelites (4:24-5), when compared spiritually to the Yeshuic Covenant, which was like the promised laughter of Abraham (Sarah's child Isaac), and its city God's heavenly city (True Jerusalem).

In short, there had been a true eclipse, and Sinai's old glow paled before the new messianic fire. Severance words. The best mercy for Ethnic-Israel was arguably not a continued or resurrected Sinaitic Covenant, but the entrance-door into global covenant. Paul spoke of peace and mercy as being post-conversion blessings of living within Global-Israel. God's mercy and peace are new every morning, indeed mercy in deliverance from Sinaitic Christianity, and peace from the Circumcision Party.

Paul, poacher turned gamekeeper, now had bad press among many of his ethnic people, yet yearned to return blessings for cursings. By the time he wrote *Romans* they had beaten him up several times, even left him for dead. What did he say to that? That if throwing himself into hell would save them, he'd jump immediately (Rm.9:3; 10:1). He

---

58   He yearned that preachers of false gospels, such as the Circumcision Party (later Ebionites?), would be cut off from the church for her sake and thus the world's. "The Greek word [*anathema*]...means...to be under a curse. The Greek word, in turn, reflects the Hebrew *ḥērem*, 'something dedicated,' often 'dedicated to destruction' (eg, Nb.21:3; Dt.7:26; Jos.6:17; 7:12; Zc.14:11). (All the NT occurrences have this sense: Rm.9:3; 1 Cor.12:3; 16:22...)" (Moo 2013, loc. 2291-8/16965). He left excommunication to God, not the church: temporal hell as exclusion from messiah's church, perhaps, but surely not ultimate hell.

had already had a rough ride when church planting in South Galatia, and still bore the marks (*stigmata*) of his ordeal, possibly scarred for life for standing up to what he believed was pivotal spiritual truth (Gal.6:17). Allegiance to one's ethnic people was important, yet having rubbished the central plank of physical circumcision (15), would any friendly overtures to Ethnic-Israel pacify any opposition, even had they read or been told of such friendly words? Hadn't he totally dismissed the covenant distinction, by dismissing as pointless physical circumcision (commanded by Yahweh under Sinai), and loading its true meaning onto the global covenant (Php.3:3; Col.2:11)? Indeed, by that he had denied that Ethnic-Israel was any longer God's Israel.

Yet even granting that after dismissing their covenant claim he tacked on to his ethnic people, "and mercy to the Israel of God", would he not have expanded, there and then, a bit on that new thought? Too little backtracking is worse than none at all. In fact, unlike the ISV, all my main Bible versions lump *peace* and *mercy* together. The NLT ideally puts *kai* as an explanatory 'they are'. Peace and mercy belong to the NT church, which is Global-Israel.

The middle ground is that peace *and* mercy belong to the NT church, *and* also to Ethnic-Israel.[59] Of my main versions, perhaps the CEV is worst by its implications of a works-salvation: *if...then* inclusion. A will-belong-and-will-be-blessed compared to a do-belong-and-will-be-blessed. I would otherwise rate the CEB/LEB/NKJV/NRSV worst, with probably the ERV as best.

Some, defining *Israel* and *Jews* as ethnic not spiritual terms, say that Replacement Theology (Replacementism) is both anti-*Israel* and anti-*Jewish* (so Jacob Prasch's *The Final Words of Jesus*, 1999:157). On the one hand, the idea that wherever replacement theology has flourished, ethnic-Jews and religious-Judaics have had to run for cover, is risible. But on the other hand, Replacementism allows the criterion of justice (not blind-eye favour) to judge Middle East politics.

I say that *Replacementism*, better *Supersessionism*,[60] brings out the true meaning of *Israel* and incorporates Jewish and all other

---

59   Eg the NKJV: but is it likely that these attributes, in the same way, could have been an ongoing part of antimessianic Ethnic Israel.

60   Replacement can be like for like; supersession is replacement by upgrade.

ethnicities into the true meaning previously hinted at. Its entrance is non-exclusive, treating people as people, not peoples as peoples. Nicodemus, born into God's ethnic-kingdom, was subsequently born into God's spiritual kingdom; likewise, Pharisee Paul.

Galatians is certainly exceptional. Its expression 'God's Israel', is certainly exceptional. Why for instance qualify the term 'Israel' by the genitive, *of God*? To understand it we might assume that the term was being touted by the Circumcision Party, which in effect was arguing that Gentiles needed to pick up ethnic-Jewish identify flags (physical circumcision for boys and men, kosher laws, weekly sabbath keeping). Did Gentiles have to buy into Moses in order to buy into God's Israel?

Against that attack on grace, Paul argued passionately to the contrary, and concluded by calling the NT transethnic church, *God's Israel*. That is, that's what they were, and they weren't to listen to any who said they weren't. I have shown that at least it's a possible witness to Global-Israel grammatically, and contextually fits. *Galatians'* internal teaching is strong: Christ killed the ethnic Jew/Gentile distinction (3:28); Abraham's true heirs were believers (7-29); they were like Isaac, children of the promise (4:28). Douglas J Moo affirmed this central teaching to decisively favour the idea of Christians as such being God's Israel (Moo 2013:10741-8/16965). Let's look at another big text, Rv.7:4.

Revelation 7:4

Two groups?

Does Rv.7:4,9 speak two-ways of one group, Global, Israel, or of two groups, Ethnic and Global, Israel? *Revelation* is a symbolic writing, and even its Letters speak of some ethnic-Jews falsely claiming to be true 'Jews' (2:9), allowing a non-ethnic type of Jew. Did John fit in with Jesus and Paul, or is it true that claiming genetic coding to Abraham through Sinai, ultimately defines *Israel-Jew*?

What did Yeshua say? He affirmed that his Sinai-Jewish audience were genetically children of Abraham (Jhn.8:37), yet disaffirmed the truest sense to that relationship (39-40): their inner attitude was demonic, not Abrahamic, their father the devil, not God.[61] There was an inner/outer distinction.

Paul also showed that though the genetic descendants had outer benefits handed down, there was no automatic inner benefit. Springboard diving from those blessings into the new spiritual blessing, partly depended on their spiritual attitude to the spiritual heritage they had. Indeed the real meaning, long hidden, was that being truly Israelite (or *Jewish*, a remnant idea) was an inner reality that some outwardly Jews lacked, and that some outwardly non-Jews did not lack (Rm.2:28-9). The true circumcision were those in the multiethnic congregation of messiah (Php.3:3; Col.2:11). Jeremiah, who had prophesied a new covenant, had said that Yahweh counted Ammon, Edom, Egypt, Judah, and Moab, as equally circumcised (*dedicated*)—yet by ultimate standards all were uncircumcised (Jr.9:25-6; Dt.30:6). So let us not assume that any Jew/Israelite/tribal talk in *Revelation*, must 'literally' mean Ethnic-Israel.

We have looked a little to the original apostolic team being twelve in total, significantly replenished for the day of Pentecost (*Barley Harvest Festival a.k.a. Weeks*) to represent the true twelve-tribed people of God. Twelve is a big symbolic number, and Rv.7:4 is problematic for extreme literalism. Not least is the puzzle as to why there could not be 12,001 from one tribe and 11,999 from another—unless for *symbolic* reason? According to Robert Mounce "the number is obviously symbolic. Twelve (the number of tribes) is both squared and multiplied by a thousand" (Mounce 158; likewise, Aune 460).

Saying that the total number of *Israel* is symbolic, neither demands nor denies that it may describe an uncountable messianic number from *all nations* (9), but slackens the hold of literalism. Should we stick with ethnic glasses, saying that though it was symbolic it was symbolic of "all [ethnic] Israel…[rather than functioning as] a coded name for the Church" (Daalen 83)? I shall pursue symbolism.

---

[61]   Incidentally, this helps prevent the folly that teaching that Jesus was God's son (and Christians God's children) we must imply a motherhood, perhaps Mary as God's wife. But who biblically would suggest that the devil—a father to some—has had a wife and borne human children? Paternity can mean affiliation.

Even in John's days, many ethnic-Jews had simply given up any hope of the twelve tribes reuniting, having to be satisfied with the idea that at least Israel was represented among the Jews of Judah by the dregs left by Assyria. There are strong objections to the symbolic army (144,000) being symbolic of Ethnic-Israel. In particular, the sealing was seen as not *for* ultimate life, but *from* the plagues, and those sealed were seen as servants of God (3). But *from God's wrath* upon the earth, why should ethnic-Israelites be shielded, yet Gentile-Christians be unshielded? And would Christian ethnic-Israelites be shielded on their ethnic, but not on their messianic, side? Or would only Christian ethnic-Israelites receive a protective seal, when dispensationally speaking, it was only Christian ethnic-Gentiles who, without such protection from God's anger, would survive the great ordeal to enter God's joy?

I hold v3 to refer to a sealing of all Christians throughout all history, perhaps by the Holy Spirit (Beale 1999:414). A sealing either subsequent to entering into God's family, God's 'kingdom', or else as defining their entering into it. but for poetic propose, spoken here as if subsequent. Both God and the Enemy 'know' and favour their own, particularly within a framework of conflict. I don't see God specially exempting Ethnic-Israel, not Christians (if Gentile), from his wrath.

As said, even in the C1 many ethnic-Jews believed the missing tribes were lost beyond recall. Nevertheless some, with John F Walvoord (*The Revelation of Jesus Christ*, 1989:143), hold that the 'lost' tribes of Ethnic-Israel will be revealed at the end of this age. This is based on a wider biblical look, interpreting much OT prophecy in less subtle, and more literal, ways. Dispensationalism's hermeneutical control belief, literalism, holds that a physical city will like a spacecraft either land or hover over planet earth (Rv.21:2)—I've heard that preached—and that only a literal age-end (eschatological) temple for literal Israelites from all the literal twelve tribes, explains Ezekiel's Temple Vision.

The classic dispensationalist reference book is the Scofield Bible. According to Schofield, dispensationalism's father, "prophecies may never be spiritualised, but are always literal" (Johnston & Walker 145). Yet he bowed to Heb.10:4 and Rm.3:25, unwittingly undermining this mindset. In 1917 he suggested literal temple, literal offerings, *non-literal* meaning (that is, merely memorial, not redemptive). The 1967 edition suggested a literal temple with symbolic offerings and meaning, prophecy painted with "the terms with which the Jews were familiar in Ezekiel's day" (Beale 2004:344). Yet if ditching literal sacrifices, why not go the whole hog and ditch any literal temple, exegeting both as symbolic, as metaphorical?

But demolish temple foundations, and dispensational walls crumble. Yet even to talk of *memorials* undermines the reason for sacrifice that Ezekiel gave, namely to make atonement (Ezk.45:15,17,20). Both this verb and its form, exactly match Moses' atonement context (eg Lv.6:30; 8:15; 16:6,11,24,30,32-4; Nb.5:8; 15:28; 29:5). Doesn't dispensationalism implode under the burden of literalism, even allowing for metaphor where literalism seems too much?

Unlike the Scofield 1967, I suggest that images of change were painted using the then familiar paint for a new kind of deific dwelling, prophesied in images of sacrifice within a stone temple within a literal nation (1 Pt.2:5). Darby's dispensationalism had real problems in keeping a strict ethnic/spiritual ('law'/'grace') divide, even in splitting Abraham from Moses.

What of the prophesied new covenant (Jr.31:31)? Being so obviously related to the spiritual covenant, Jesus and Paul spoke of a messianic community/church *fulfilment*. And Heb.8:8-9 and 10:16 made the Jeremianic link—patently ignored by Darby, dispensationalism's grandfather—patently obvious.[62] Progressive Dispensationalism seeks to keep dispensational epochs, yet welcomes limited OT fulfilment by the church. Darbyism needs correction or replacement.

Isn't Sinai valid?

Lost tribes

Many speak of the 'Ten Tribes' (1 Kg.11:31-5) that they hope will be reunited with the Jews. A technical aside cometh. I prefer to speak of the Northern Kingdom, or Lost Tribes, because it's at least as accurate

---

[62]   This prophecy spoke in terms of reuniting North & South Israel. "The new covenant [would] express the prophetic conviction that there [could] be, and that there has been, only one unified people of God" (Dumbrell 145). Paul could speak of Christ's cross overcoming religious apartheid to reunite the global breach between Jew and Gentile—symbolised by divided Israel—creating a unified humanity (Eph.2:11-22).

and perhaps clearer. Simeon is a problem. Let me explain. Simple mathematics says that 12 minus 10 equals 2. Yet was not Judah left with Benjamin and Simeon, a *three*-tribed kingdom, in which case should we not rather talk of the missing Nine Tribes?[63] How should we account for the apparent equation that 3 plus 10 equals 12? One approach takes out Simeon, leaving Judah as a two-tribed kingdom: 2 plus 10 equals 12. The reason for exclusion is that Simeon had towns but no fixed land within Judah, was not blessed by Moses because of its rebellious reputation (Dt.33), and had appreciably reduced in size during the exodus. This size reduction is calculated as being by a third down to 200 (and Dan slightly more so), *per* Colin Humphreys, or by about two-thirds down to about 22,000 (reduced far, far more than any other tribe), *per* traditional translation. Whatever the numbers, it's suggested that Simeon migrated to the north to regain status, with some filtering back.[64] This would square the mathematics. Perhaps under Jeroboam's orders the northern alliance ceded land to Simeon for friendship. This would make sense.

Another approach is the minimalist, which assumes original literary mistakes, since it assumes literary composition way after the events, doubting the veracity of the 'events'. Minimalism—the belief that only the minimum of biblical 'facts' are right—rejoices in, or suffers from, a presumption to disbelieve. Thus, it can argue that Moses' Blessings were created centuries after an alleged exodus, when

---

[63] Representation of a fourth tribe, Levi, can be left out of any count as scattered spiritual salt rather than secular meat: it had become the sanctuary tribe.

[64] Did Simeon and Levi disgrace Jacob-Israel by unjust homicidal frenzy (Gen.34:30), with Phinehas-Levi redeeming itself when Zimri-Simeon led an anti-Yahweh rebellion (Nb.25:11,14)? This is less likely if Humphrey's calculations are correct, but highly arguable on tradition translation of the pivotal Hebrew term *eleph*. Does 2 Chr.15:9 imply that Simeon had migrated *en masse*, only to have some for religious reasons permanently return south along with representatives of Ephraim-Israel, in line with 11:16? 34:6 might well imply a purge from the North Kingdom's south (West Manasseh/ Ephraim), through its midlands (Simeon) and into its far north (Naphtali). That 1 Chr..4:39-43 speaks of Simeon south in the South Kingdom might fit with the prophecy-curse of Gen.49:5-7 to divide both Levi and Simeon.

Simeon (or the idea, *Simeon*) wasn't in anybody's mind. If minimalism were true this would make sense.

Sure, some say that what claims to be the original record of twelve tribes was written back (concocted) into Israel's history to 'create' a common paternity (Jacob). But "there is no factual basis of any kind for denying the premonarchic reality of early Israel's tribal structure as a federation of officially related tribes with a claimed common ancestor of that name. Quite to the contrary" (Kitchen 219). Rather than take Simeon to swallow minimalism, take a good dose of Kitchen to cure from minimalism. Sure, some argue that such as Simeon, missing from Dt.33, shows that the group (they often suggest in Josiah's reign, a 'Deuteronomist') that coined the name *Simeon* for the fictitious history, then forgot to mention him when *redacting* (ie weeding out and merging in their changes). But we can reply that extant (as we have it) Hebrew text also lacks some referencing to Reuben (6), Levites (8), and Issachar (18). Possible data corruption? Sometimes the Greek text carries otherwise lost information, but couldn't an earlier Hebrew text have lost a Simeon reference? Alternatively, as suggested, Simeon might have been unmentioned as a deliberate snub by Moses—but was that tribe exceptionally worse than any other?

An alternative approach allows for symbolic language. Thus, the number 12 coordinates the whole garment, and mathematics be blowed. What Jeroboam got was nine 'secular' tribes plus a representative amount of Levitical 'salt' thrown into the count, making ten, in order to legitimise the temple-dedicated tribe (Levi) operating both sides of the new political border. Rehoboam's kingdom would have two tribes (Benjamin and Simeon), which including Judah made three: Levi was excluded from this count. Mathematic inexactitude, symbolic speech? I leave it with you. It's to avoid these intricacies that it's simpler to speak of the Northern Kingdom, or Lost Tribes unnumbered.

Blurred distinctions?

It's true that there had been some intermingling of the tribes. But generally, tribal ties remained strong under the basic settlement structure of the tribes—each got their tribal turf and plots of land for tribal families. Intertribal marriage was more an option along tribal boundaries, but even so, women would take on the tribal identity of their husbands. To keep tribal cohesion, if women became tribal land inheritors, marriage was prohibited outside their tribe (Nb.36:7-9: vv 7 and 9 sandwich this strong principle). My guess is that if intertribally married, either they would be debarred from inheriting if, say, the male heir then died without succession, or that compulsory land redemption—a 'cash' buyout—would come into play. Tribal cohesion was to remain theologically significant, although the district divisions of Solomon's administration would have weakened the connection to tribal land. And the big shake ups of the North Kingdom being exiled by Assyria (completed 722 BC), and the South Kingdom about 125 years later, would have erased family records of exact land plots, breaking down ties with the past glory. Indeed, the actual tribal network, based on a network covenant, was undermined by Assyria. Babylonia allowed repatriation of Southerners who wished to return (*Ezra/ Nehemiah*), though as *Esther* shows, some preferred self-exile in Persia, perhaps feeling that returning to a contaminated land was too painful. Can we keep our cake yet eat it; we keep indistinction with distinction?

Eating *Revelation's* cake with distinctions

Revelation has its own arrangement of the distinct twelve tribes, but there was no set pattern to compare to. The initial order (Gen.35:23-5) was in line with Jacob's 4 wives, Leah {Reuben, Simeon, Levi, Judah, Issachar, Zebulun}, Rachael {Joseph, Benjamin}, Zilpah {Gad, Asher}, and Bilhah {Dan, Naphtali}. Soon Levi dropped out and Joseph was split into Manasseh and Ephraim tribes. About a hundred years ago G B Gray pointed out that "in about twenty lists in the Old Testament there are eighteen different orders" (Morris 1995:113), so presumably no benchmark was ever intended. In a mini chart I did of seven listings (shortened below), only one grouped the tribes according to their maternal lines, and five began with Reuben and Simeon, of which three ended with Naphtali. Some say that for symbolic reasons, John departed from the benchmark order, but I ask, what benchmark order? As little order appears elsewhere in Scripture, we may safely put symbolism on the back burner, except perhaps Judah heading the list. After all, John's only other mention of Judah is about "the Lion from the tribe of Judah" (Rv.5:5; Gen.49:9)—a military icon: Nb.2:3 and 10:14 also listed Judah first on a military basis. Judah's lead position is likewise in one or two

Jewish extrabiblical lists (eg C1 LAB [*Liber Antiquitatum Biblicarum*, a.k.a. *Pseudo-Philo*] 25:4).

Sample variations of Jacob's tribes[65]

Genesis 46	1	2	3	4	5	6		9	10	7	8	11	12
1 Chronicles 2	1	2	3	4	5	6		11	7	8	12	9	10
Ezekiel 48	11	10	12	7A	7B	1		4	8	2	5	6	9
Revelation 7	4	1	9	10	12	7A or 11		2	3	5	6	7	8

Did a copyist drop Dan?

One or two other peculiarities in *Revelation* are also worth mentioning, such as the apparent omission of Dan. It is just possible that the only copy of John's *Revelation* to be smuggled out of Patmos misspelt (or botched) John's *Dan* as *Man*. An easy error. In Greek, which was written only with CAPITALSWITHOUTSPACING, it's not too difficult in a rush to confuse a Greek D/Δ with a Greek M. In quick copy mode, our imaginary copyist might have felt that John had contracted *Manasseh* to *Man*, an abbreviation expanded in later copies. *Revelation* was a dangerous document in dangerous times, and its autograph (kept with John?) might soon have been destroyed after the sole copy escaped into the Christian domain.

Had John written *Dan*, and no copyist error come into play, no puzzle generating speculative solutions would have been imagined. We simply don't know if anything like this happened, and the suggestion can be neither falsified nor verified—reasoning must be *a priori*. Certainly, any change *after* a first copy would probably have left traces in the manuscriptal witness, what scholars call the tenacity of the text once it takes off. But if, as I believe, God inspired the autographs to be without error (giving full scope to different genres not structured for literal truth), once in the public domain must we hold that he also made sure that each and every letter remained in some manuscript or another throughout the millennia? On the other hand,

---

[65] Key: [1 = Reuben]; [2 = Simeon]; [3 = Levi]; [4 = Judah]; [5 = Issachar]; [6 = Zebulun]; [7 = Joseph]; [7A = Manasseh]; [7B = Ephraim]; [8 = Benjamin]; [9 = Gad]; [10 = Asher]; [11 = Dan]; [12 = Naphtali]. Using Gen.35:23-6's sequence.

if John deliberately dropped Dan, was it because Christians should have a down on Dan?

Did John drop Dan?

Some assume that John blacklisted Dan, and go back at least to the days of Irenaeus. Irenaeus was a good C2 bishop with a name for peace, who was convinced that Antichrist would be a Danite (Haer. 5.30.2). He found various OT texts that gave Dan a bad name. Let's look at these, beginning with Jr.8:16. An attack would be from the northern *land* of Dan, not the long-exiled *people* of Dan—so why blame the people for the land? Babylon would attack from the north—so what? Yahweh even called Babylonia his army against his people (Jl.2:1,11), so it had his blessing. And sure, Dan had refused to help Israel fight against the Canaanites and Sisera (Jg.5:17)—but so had Reuben (15-6). I agree that without apparent opposition, Jeroboam set up one of his golden calf-idols at Dan—but then he also set up one at Bethel in Ephraim (1 Kg.12:29), so why single out Dan?

I agree that Amos used the town of Dan in the far north as a geographic point of idolatry—but then he also used the town of Beersheba in the far south as a geographic point. Indeed, like a sandwich the couplet could express the whole people in-between (eg Jg.20:1; 2 Sam.3:10; 17:11; 1 Kg.4:25). And Gen.49:17 seems negative, but was Dan biting an invader's horse any worse than Gad attacking an invader's heel (19)? And before we jump at any hiss from the Snake of v17, let us see how the exalted Snake of Nb.21 was redemptive at that time, and a prophetic pattern for the greater uplift of Jhn.3:14. The Snake motif cannot be determinative. All the tribes had demerits. Singling out Dan for special censure is, I think, unwarranted.

Dan is in all the full OT tribal lists, except perhaps the extended family trees of 1 Chr.2–7. (It is in 2:2, as is Zebulun, and in some versions Dan is in 7:12). But "it would seem that with the founding of the monarchy the Danite clans in the south were assimilated into the kingdoms of Judah and Israel and lost their distinctiveness," while those in the north "apparently intermingled with their neighbors, especially the tribe of Naphtali and even the people of Tyre" (Roth and Wigoder 1258). Ethnic-Israel had an expectation that messiah would be born to a Danite mother and Davidic father (Gen. Rab. 97.9). As to claims of rabbinic negativity, "the tradition is not found in any [ethnic] Jewish sources and cannot therefore be confidently thought to be pre-Christian" (Aune 463). According to George Ladd, the argument of Irenaeus "founders on the fact that Dan was included in the salvation of the eschatological people in Ezk.48" (Ladd 115).

If John dropped Dan it was possibly because, if ethnic-Jews asked whether 1 Chr. 2–7 did or did not include Dan, John thought the question irrelevant, since it missed the reunion that Yahweh had prophesied, and in fact John ruled in what ch.7 had ruled out, Zebulun. In other words, it's not a case of thinking out of the box, so much as thinking within a different box (paradigm). Was he saying that getting back to Ethnic-Israel wasn't God's agenda? If so, Dan would have become significant by exclusion, even as true significance is through shelving our ethnic identity, our true kingdom being beyond this world. We can only guess whether, and if so why, John dropped Dan, but the Bible doesn't float the idea of a Danite antichrist. To briefly mention some other points, it seems that within the criterion of twelveness, John could play around with the tribes of Levi, and Ephraim and Manasseh (or their father-tribe, Joseph). Arguably he wished to reinstate Levi, and get in the two tribes of Ephraim and Manasseh, though replacing the name *Ephraim* (which had stood for North Israel: Ezk.37:16) by the rejected *Joseph*.

Ethnic reunification or spiritual unity?

The idea that the Samaritans were thought to be northern tribes is a non-starter. The general hostility against the Samaritans from Jews, who were yearning for a sense of twelve-tribed unity, would have been incomprehensible. There had been a sense of unwelcome familiarity on the part of the Samaritans, who even had their religious link to Abraham and their take on the OT (Samaritan Pentateuch), Jhn.4: they were snubbed. Samaritans could believe a Good Samaritan story but not a Good Jew story—until Jesus came. He was that Good Jew at Sychar's Well, and the woman was that battered Samaritan. And it's highly unlikely that Ac.26:6-7 should be taken as anything more than meaning all Ethnic-Israel within the Roman Empire. If the Lost Tribes existed as coherent tribes well beyond kith and kin, naturally Paul wouldn't have known their hope and obedience levels, nor need we hold that he reckoned that the 'Lost Tribes' had reunited with Judah—his fellow Jews didn't.

From C1 ethnic-Jewish historian Josephus, it seems clear that some believed that the Northern Tribes still existed well beyond the Jewish diaspora scattered within the Roman Empire (Aune 461). As said, there was a touch of the North within Judah, such as Asher (Lk.2:36). Still, after the major disunity done politically by Solomon and geographically by Assyria, reunification remained a yearning hope. Sometimes sin divides permanently, and Ethnic-Israel showed by its dying hopes that reunification prophecies had not been literally fulfilled. It certainly has not been literally fulfilled between then and now. Nor is there any thought of it becoming so after messiah's return. If it is to be literal, it must happen between now and his return, as dispensationalists predict. Yet did John speak of the 144,000 as the fulfilment of such prophecies, and separate from the NT church? Will literal reunification fulfil this text?

The possibly impossible

OK, with God everything is possible, but can God turn stones into people (Mt.3:9)? Neither the Baptist nor his audience took that literally, and what Matthew recorded might well have been prophetic announcement that the stones Jews walked over—representing Gentiles treated as spiritual dirt—could by God be given covenant status even as ethnic-Jews could be cut off like firewood (see 8:11-2). After all, Abraham had had many children who hadn't become covenant holders (Gen.25:1-2). Some 'impossibilities' are mere figures of speech. Could God trace the ancestry of every mortal human being, then call out exactly 12 000 [men?] from those he judged represented each ancient line of the North and South kingdoms?

There are different kinds of impossible. To attribute the in-itself impossible to God is folly. Mt.19:26 has its obvious context in the fact that spiritual salvation (25) is *humanly* impossible but not *deificly* impossible: it is not a philosophic assertion that God can violate the Law of Non-Contradiction. Can he create a rock too big for him to lift, thereby disproving the claim that he is all powerful? Create a contradiction? Know that he knows nothing? No. Biblically he can do all things that are intrinsically (that is, within their nature) possible: God cannot be Satan, only himself; God cannot create a being greater than himself and more eternal, etc. Is there a people that can trace back three millennia of ethnically pure paternity (the biblical inheritance test of who was an Israelite) or even the current ethnic-Jewish idea of maternity fixing ethnicity? I have my doubts.

The lack of concrete knowledge about the fate of the large majority inheritors of the North Kingdom (Ephraim) is, I think, clearly indicated by the minority and then contemporary report, recorded by Beale. Indeed "one strain of Jewish tradition held that the ten tribes would never be restored (b. Sanhedrin 110b; 'Abot de Rabbi Nathan 31b)" (Beale 1999:419). What would that strand make of today's dispensationalist claims that two millennia on, scattering on scattering, it will literally happen? The divide was perhaps between those who believed themselves realists and those who believed themselves biblicists.

However, I suggest that their dollop of biblicism on this was based on faulty hermeneutics, insisting on a fulfilment that God had never planned. End of the day, they expected a national messiah, not a global one. In short, two positions contend. Either God can do it because he promised to do it, or God can't do it and never promised to do it. It's just as important to not hold God to what he has *not* promised, as it is to hold God to what he *has* promised. Sure, he may surprise us with a revivification, though I do not see the biblical promise to do so. What then does the 144,000 symbolise?

<u>The church militant</u>

The 144,000 symbolise Yahweh's imagination-defying human army: "this is explicit in the fact that 7:4-8 is a census of the tribes of Israel. In the Old Testament a census was always a reckoning of the military strength of the nation" (Bauckham 77). Let it be immediately added: "we use God's mighty weapons, not worldly weapons, to knock down the strongholds of human reasoning and to destroy false arguments" (NLT: 2 Cor.10:4): too much Gun and Gospel has been used to civilise the world, that is, to give it both our culture and Christ. In John's poetical style, apocalyptic, the contrast was between two kingdoms, the unfallen and the fallen, and the point was that God's people were like an army that, defeatable, was not ultimately defeatable (see Mic.7:8).

Spiritually it had a cohesive structure, the number of Israel multiplied by the number of Israel, multiplied by a millennium. *Revelation's* Letters had spoken of overcoming, conquering. Then there was a contrast between hear and see (Rv.5:5-6). Rv.7 seems to follow this pattern. John *heard* of the 144,000, then *saw* the Great Company. He was, in Ethnic-Israel garb, presented with themes of eschatological battle, led by the Davidic king. God was affirming the earlier revelation, the Tanak, and tracing salvation history into its Yeshuic phase. In 5:5-6, the Lion led; in 5:9, are the innumerable of the Slaughtered Lamb, the Passover Lamb? Gen.13:16, 15:5, and 32:12, spoke of innumerable descendants, and the only counted lists in the OT are of her army. The phrase used by *Numbers*—*ek tēs phu'ēs* (Nb.1:21,3, etc) was basically utilised by John's *ek tēs phulēs*. There is thus a military link: that of *Numbers* was thus, and Rv.14:4 seems to likewise look to the men-only army, which practiced cultus celibacy in times of war.

Hence there is reference to wartime cultus purity for the men in it (Dt.20; 23:9-10; 1 Sam.21:5; 2 Sam.11:9-13; 1QM 7:3-6). That is, spiritual purity symbolised by cultus purity, perhaps also a link to OT idolatry as spiritual fornication (see Daalen 126): see 1 Jhn.5:21. In short, this indicates neither misogyny, male Christian chauvinism, nor lifelong celibacy, as wrongly asserted by some,[66] but is indicative in the NT of moral purity, whatever one's age and gender, and symbolic of supreme commitment to God (holiness). Jewish expectation was of an eschatological Ethnic-Israel army brought together at the end of the age to defeat the Gentile foes.

In *Revelation,* it was of all peoples under the Lion of Judah, to oppose a kosmic worldview.[67] Just as 5:5-6 depicts Jesus Christ as the Messiah who has won a victory, but done so by sacrificial death, not by military might, so 7:4-14 depicts his followers as the people of the Messiah who share in his victory, but do so similarly, by sacrificial death rather than by military violence. This interpretation is confirmed by 14:1-5, in which the 144,000 reappear.... In 14:1 the Lamb and his army stand to oppose [their enemies] on Mount Zion, the place of the messianic king's triumph

---

[66] For example, a documentary on serial killer Ed Gein, whose dominant mother apparently raised him on a twisted form of *Revelation* that asserted that most women were sexually immoral. Crazy ideas can lead to crazy people and can also *come from* crazy people twisting the good.

[67] I use *kosmic*, from the Gk. κοσμος, for its main and negative idea of global hostility towards God, and *cosmic* in neutral or positive settings.

over the hostile nations" (Bauckham 78). The symbolic count shows Global-Israel's structure (the NT church painted in Israel paint), and its full count being beyond human computation.

Israel has had transethnic meaning and fulfilment. Stephen Smalley added that whatever might be military overtones or undertones here, "the 144,000...like the saints elsewhere in *Revelation*, are worshippers more than soldiers" (Smalley 186), highlighting the global church, not simply some section or aspect of it. We may also reflect on messiah's death as having been a military success against man's enemy, and the church as fighting against sin and the powers behind it. It is also perhaps well to note that Ethnic-Israel as Yahweh's Army was, apart from initial conquest of Canaan—where the larger local and morally repugnant population numbered perhaps about 50,000 and could fight the invaders or leave in peace—was never authorised to fight to extend its domain: no jihad or holy war. In theory it banded together only to defend its domain.

Romans 11:25-6

Some might still be unhappy with my takedown of literalism, and seeming exclusion of the ethno-Jewish people. They might think me too quick to symbolise away literal statements. And after all, has God revoked what Paul said God wouldn't revoke (Rm.11:29)? Yes, even if *Revelation* has sidelined Israelite ethnicity, *Romans* hasn't, right?

In fact, I think that while those of that ethnic race were precious to Paul and are to God—and they are not totally excluded—they were precious as individuals. So, ethnic-Gentile Christians should never totally exclude them, as some in Rome were possibly pondering. Paul had to write them back into salvation history, while explaining their general exclusion from the gospel, without any special road to true life beyond death.

In *That Hideous Strength*, C S Lewis pictured opposites in Mark and Jane: Mark feared exclusion; Jane feared inclusion. In *Romans*, Paul pictured opposites among his ethnic people, who unlike Mark and Jane will not all turn to messiah. Like Mark, many fear exclusion from ethnic-society and tradition; like Jane, many fear inclusion into messiah. And like Bree in *The Horse and His Boy* (C S Lewis), no ethnic-Jew will necessarily be special in messiah's community, "but as long as

[they] know [they're] nobody very special, [like other peoples they can be]...very decent...on the whole—taking one thing with another" (ch.10).

I think that Rm.11:29 affirms the idea that Ethnic-Israel had served its time in God's mission, would not be ultimately worse off for their obedience, and theoretically had a great theological springboard to dive into global salvation. Obviously, their national mentality hadn't tracked God's directional change. So, had God made a mistake in his selection of them? That's where Rm.11:29 answers 'no'.

Ametamelētos can simply have the contrast to something you give, wish you hadn't, and take back. Was its context about continuing specialness, or simply about affirming God's wisdom in the un-regretted former specialness? If the latter, Paul simply said that God did not in the least *regret* having called and gifted Ethnic-Israel (2 Cor.7:10). It was the ethnic road to the messianic road, God's plan.

Arguably Bible versions (eg NLT) that assert extended life in the previous charismata (Rm.11:29; 9:4-5), go beyond Paul's meaning. The NJB puts Paul well: "there is no change of mind on God's part about the gifts he has made or of his choice", even if he has subsequently precluded any ongoing role. The NCV is similar, though worded more as a general principle about the *now* rather than about the *then*.

Several Bible versions use the term or meaning, *irrevocable*—not called back. The previous wave of English versions, up to and including the Revised Version, preferred the term *repentance*. There is a difference between 'I have not changed my mind (*repented*) about having given' and 'I have not taken back what I gave.' God never regretted having used King Cyrus as a messiah but doesn't continue to use him (Is.45:1ff.)!

God extended his gifts and calling, even throughout Ethnic-Israel's extended disloyalty: even Judas had had gifts and calling. But Lk.20:10-7 concludes that new tenants would work the vineyard, the final verse ('the cornerstone')—echoed in Ac.4:11, Eph.2:20, and 1 Pt.2:4-7 —as symbolising Jesus. I reckon that the old chapter was only closed ("job done": Jhn.19:30) when the new chapter began. Paul's heritage was the adoption to ethnic-sonship; his had been the deific glory, the covenants, the torah, the temple worship and the promises. His was the patriarchs, and from his people was traced the human ancestry of the messiah, deific forever praised. As far as the gospel was concerned, he had been an enemy for the benefit of the Gentiles; but as far as election was concerned, he had been loved (privileged) on account of the patriarchs (see Rm.9:4-5; 11:28—personalised).

Yet Paul, an ethnic-Jew and Pharisee, counted these historic gifts and calling as loss compared to knowing messiah. Seemingly the glorified messiah put no value on them (Php.3:2-8): "We are the circumcision. We are the ones who serve by God's spirit and who boast in Christ Jesus. We don't put our confidence in rituals performed on the body..." (CEB: v3).[68] If we—Christians whether ethnically Jew or Gentile—are the circumcision (linked to call & gifting), then old Israel/Judah are not. Nor had they ever been, though physical circumcision and the physical temple had been prophetic signs of new covenant fulfilment.

And contrary to what Julian the Apostate claimed to subjugate Christianity, Mt.5:17-20 does not extend Sinai's covenant-specific stipulations into our age. Jesus validated Moses against unauthorised reductions, and affirmed that contrary to hostile rumour, he wasn't out to destroy Sinai—his was no hostile takeover bid and as the king of the inbreaking kingdom of heaven he commended loyal Sinaitics and they would be held in honour. Yet as messiah he was authorised, indeed commissioned, to bring Sinai to its intended end (to fulfil: plērōma) turning its dream into reality. Otherwise, Yeshua would have failed Moses. The difference is like in relay races, you aren't there to destroy your team member behind you, but you are there to take the baton from them, their part superseded.

So on the one hand, as God's plan Sinai couldn't ever be destroyed, and "until heaven and earth pass away" expressed its durability—not longevity—under Yahweh's sovereignty.[69] As with any covenant, the suzerain could annul it for gross violation (eg messianic rejection: Jhn.1:12),

---

[68]   The Greek sarx, 91x in Paul's writings, carries a range of meaning. In Php.3:3, 'flesh' is ambiguous, nor should we compare human effort to covenant nomism (ie covenant as losable, not gainable).

[69]   Lv.26:44 graciously says that for grossest disloyalty (stage 5) temporary separation rather than annulment would be the punishment (implications for the marriage/separation/divorce theme here). However, promising permanency precluded not the justified replacement of the grossly violated Sinai once it reached its prophesied terminus ad quem, blatantly too rejecting messiah.

yet the ideal time would have been when what it prophesied, the new lap, superseded it. At the cross the dream ended and the reality began: myth became fact in Christ.

In fact, the right to annul had long existed, and only global grace kept Sinai going until the new age arrived, preserving the ethnic husk of old age for the spiritual wheat of new age. The story of the two stone tablets told both of right, and of grace from the very start of that relationship (Ex.34:1). Once we see this, we can see that Jhn.19:30's key word, *tetelestai*, carried the good death of Sinai in messiah's death, he whose blood represented the new covenant.

So, Ethnic-Israel ran for God until Jesus took over for the final lap, or should we say until the then next big event. Let's not forget that Matthew's Gospel highlighted the theme of *fulfilment* by Christ.[70] We could at this stage look at other 'literal' promises that fare no better under a good hermeneutical lens. But let's look at the 'missing tribes'—the ethnic-Jews were never more than incomplete Israel.

But let us get back to Rm.11—what was good for the Roman church is good for us. Indeed, its theme of hardening is useful to soteriology (salvation teaching). It may be added that if this text is deemed so pivotal by some, might that indicate that their idea of it is unlikely elsewhere? After all, if it crystallises a big biblical theme, why does that big theme have so few alleged clear texts and teaching blocks, remaining at most a hidden undercurrent, elusive?

The eschatological plan

With a double negative, Paul spoke of a *mystērion* he did *not* wish his audience *not* to know. Why did he consider it in his context? It's not the thread we need to examine first, so much as the thread within the weave. In the OT, *mystērion* indicated confidential speech, some eschatological secret. The Synoptics used it, so did Paul (Mk.4:11—the hardening theme shared with Rm.11), and so did *Revelation*, carrying its OT basis. It became a fad in speculative critical circles (those devaluing the idea that Scripture was alone God's particular revelation) to claim *mystērion* as a link word to the world of pagan *Mystery* Religions, from whence they

---

70   *Matthew's* Fulfilment Quotations are 1:22-3; 2:5-6; 2:15; 2:17-8; 2:23; 4:14-6; 8:17; 12:17-21; 21:4-5; 27:9-10.

said it came (see John Drane's *Introducing the New Testament*, 1986:258). Paul's other use in Rm.16:25, was about Gentiles coming to faith.

What was the historical backdrop to *Romans*? Around AD 49, Emperor Claudius had banned ethnic-Jews from Rome. After he died in AD 54, many returned to Rome's church, but some ethnic-Gentile Christians wondered how they should fit back in. Being as Jewish as Jesus, should they be given the best jobs? Some of them seemed to have thought that they should be privileged.

Paul helped level the playing field. Yes, both sides had historical advantages and disadvantages, yet all came within newness and oneness in messiah. For leadership, none were automatically ruled out, or in. Into that situation Paul wanted all to think a really useful thought, a *mystērion*. Paul "did not state that what he was imparting was a new revelation, or that it had been revealed only to himself; and it can be maintained not unreasonably that the contents of this mystery are to be discerned in the OT seen in the light of the gospel events" (Cranfield 574). In short, what had been the concealed OT plan?

Although the Greek terms vary between *sklērunō* (multiple *sclerosis* is about tissue *hardening*) in Rm.9:18—similarly *pōroō/pōrōsis* in 11:7,25—most Bible versions follow the C16 Geneva pattern, rather than the C16 Bishops Bible, and render as *hardening/obstinacy/resistance/stubbornness*, rather than *blindness*. Yet at the end of the day the two pictures amount to the same thing, and there's none so blind as they who are stone deaf from a hard heart.

Should we approach hardening as evil, so that if God's responsible, he's evil? Has he deniability? Or should we approach it from God's goodness, so that if he's responsible, hardening is good? I follow the latter, that the doctrine of hardening, spiritual blinding, is from God, therefore is ethical since God is Ethics, God is godly. But the doctrine of hardening can conflict with our faulty expectations.

<u>Hard Cheese or Good News</u>?

"...'Everyone who calls on the name of Lord[71] will be saved.' But how can they call on him to save them unless they believe in him? And how can

---

[71]   I have removed the article, for kurios could function as God's name, Yahweh. I wish to underline that although "will be saved" fits NT citations, Jl.2:32's context spoke of people who already saved into Sinai's covenant, would be

they believe in him if they have never heard about him? And how can they hear about him unless someone tells them?" (NLT: Rm.10:13-4).

Are all Chinese who died before the cross, and all Australian aboriginals in the century after, ultimately doomed because they never heard missionaries? One ancient pagan, C3 Porphyry, believed that Christianity was ridiculous, because he believed that it taught that ultimate salvation only came after the cross, and then only to those who heard of it and accepted it.[72] If I believed it taught what he believed it taught, I reckon I'd join his camp, even as C S Lewis reckoned that siding with some vicars meant joining atheism.

Well before Neal Punt, Porphyry of Tyre asked, What's Good about the Good News?[73] Did the Christian god damn all generations before the cross? Even limited exceptions through Abraham's line and its limited interface with Gentiles, couldn't justify that, could it? Why accept a parochial religion whose limited atonement merited scorn and defamed God?[74]

The Christian reply should begin with God not being a god, parochial or otherwise. We are not polytheists, so why should we speak like them? A parochial god cannot be God—not even a triune god can! *Contra* Porphyry, Augustine said that the unevangelised deserved damnation, and that God's goodness was shown by the fact that he was prepared to save even some: even the charitable limit their

---

spared death from the invaders led by Yahweh against his evil people. So, a NT context does not demand a meaning of salvation after death, but could speak of being saved into the messianic community from the rest of their people as the remnant. And a pastoral application from *Joel* might be that "Christianity.. is asked whether it will bring shame or honour to the name of Jesus as it listens to *Joel*. In many of its members it is ripe for God to lead its enemies against it in order to cast it into perdition (2:1-11)" (Wolff, 1977:70).

[72] There is a similar issue with the idea that messiah ethnic-Jewry is ultimately damned except for its last generation who will all be saved. Some moderate this idea by asserting that those generations have a different kind of salvation a different way by virtue of their different ethnicity.

[73] Compare Neal Punt's *What's Good About the Good News?* (1988), an Inclusivist book of F F Bruce's position: www.ukapologetics.net/evinc.htm.

[74] Evangelist John Wesley agreed: a limited atonement to rule out a salvation offer, is such that "makes your blood run cold" (Sanders 72).

charities. After a 'starmageddon' storm a boy was mocked for returning handfuls of the surviving multiple thousands of starfish that had been beached back to the sea. But it made a difference to those he saved. So let God limit salvation any way he's chosen, for even saving one from sin's storm shows more grace than humanity has deserved, said Augustine. Yes, but it does show finite grace, and *contra* Porphyry, Augustine was arguing that God was infinite.

I admire Augustine better on 1 Pt.4:6. *Contra* post-mortem evangelism—as some said 1 Pt.4:6 taught—he refused "to entertain the thought that the gospel was once preached, or is even to this hour being preached, in hell...as if a Church had been established there as well as on earth" (Sanders 55).

Porphyrian argument still deafens some to Christianity. Arguably neither post-mortem evangelism, nor Augustine's be-thankful-for-limited-mercies approach, best shows biblical teaching on ultimate salvation. It is a bigger issue I shall look at later, as I explore ultimate life as having always been available to all peoples.

Is Christianity parochial, and how parochial is global? Sci-fi such as *Star Trek*, have featured planets finding out that their gods are aliens merely a scientific/psychic level or so above themselves, cosmically neither creators nor saviours. Sounds a bit Mormonist to me. I don't recall a single episode, whether in the Original, Second, DS9, or Voyagers, that considered that God, as revealed best by Christianity, might embrace the universe, though *Star Trek 5* (*Final Frontier*) affirms that God cannot be parochial. Is it any surprise that Star Treks laid almost no weight on concepts such as chastity and marriage?[75]

As it stands, there is no problem with God pervading the whole universe, nor do we need think, theologically speaking, that humanity is the highest specie in the universe. Angels aside, are there morally self-aware creatures beyond Earth? Larry Norman reckoned that "if there's life on other planets, then I'm sure that [Christ] must know, And he's been there once already, and has died to save their souls." That begs some big questions. If such life exists, has it needed

---

[75] By sexual indiscipline T'Pol (Enterprise) let down Vulcans and viewers, and ST Discovery's 'fun' use of the F-word is best undiscovered—I beamed out.

redemption (is humanity the one sheep that went astray)? If fallen, would redemption have to come *via* incarnation and death in their contexts?

Actually, for any possible races in our universe capable of fall/ redemption, Jerusalem's cross, parochial in time and space, might have universal significance. Jerusalem's cross blessed neighbouring Cana, and separated by sea, Canberra under the Southern Cross. So why not bless Kepler-22b around the Northern Cross, and extragalatic worlds where no man has gone before?

And as for time, the C1 cross has in fact had retrospective global significance throughout all of human history. Parochial? Nonsense, even *UY Scuti* is parochial. But if there are spiritual aliens, who is my neighbour? "Our loyalty is due not to our species but to God. Those who are...his children are our real brothers and sisters even if they have shells or tusks. It is the spiritual, not biological, kinship that counts" (Lewis 1975:93). We do not have a big god; bigness coheres in God.

I have already touched on the idea of the Scandal of Particularism, the Exclusion of the Many, and wish to look later at the Wider Hope idea of ultimate salvation, inclusivism/inexclusivism. At this point I merely say that my evangelicalism has enlarged from a narrower base, though enlargement does not prove validity—the glutton's belly was once narrower and healthier.

But parochialism can be smallminded indeed, and overly hard. I used to be big on the phrase 'born-again'. Everyone not in that circle had a dead/dormant spirit (at least to God), which God could at best, by the gospel smoulder into flame, jumpstart, breathe into life. Conflicting ideas from Calvinism and Arminianism vied within my head to make best sense of the data. How could the totally dead/depraved accept life or even desire it? Surely some spiritual life, albeit fallen, at least *sought* its source, *was* prepared to hear the true Voice? Indeed, King David within Sinai had been 'dead' to God (Eph.2:5), and Christians should reckon themselves dead to sin (Rm.6:11): David was relatively alive to God, and we are relatively dead to sin.

I also assumed that if the waters were stirred, one's spiritual walk from Bethesda could only begin from intellectually welcoming Christ. Regarding Ethnic-Israel, I held that before the cross all or some (plus a few non-Israelites) were saved legally—let off by God the judge—even if not internally changed, and that after the cross God would only (apart from those 'born-again' few) include the entire final ethno-Jewish generation for some level of salvation, extending at least into a millennial reign. Ethnic-Jews had been hardened—as before the cross the whole Gentile world had been—and indeed had called down God's wrath upon their heads (Mt.27:25). Yet we Christians were beholden to them, and along with God should especially love them as a people and probably evangelise them to bless them. But hardness was negative, hardening tending as a punishment to harden them from the evangel and probably into hell beyond. Yet why should a C20 ethnic-Jew be punished for ancient sins?

<u>Hard news</u>?

Having rethought deific salvation, nowadays I approach deific hardening as more of a barrier to current meaning and opportunity, than as a barrier to ultimate life. At best it's a spiritual haze, or veil, through which God is largely hidden and unknown (2 Cor.3:14,17-8). If this is biblically true, then it could mean that ultimate life has always been accessible to every human being across the world, and in this age always shall be, even to those who die as Judaics—if evangelism is an eddy, then ultimate life is its undercurrent. It would also imply that in God's central plan, Ethnic-Israel was the almost-only player, and that since the cross, Gentiles have become the almost-only players, with ultimate life common to players and spectators alike.

I do not believe that God hardens to ultimately damn, yet I believe that some whom he hardens are ultimately self-damned and thus self-hardened. Let's look at an example of God hardening the self-hardened for a good purpose. It is written that Yahweh would harden Pharaoh's heart (Ex.4:21), that Pharaoh began the hardening (8:15), and that Yahweh reinforced that hardening (10:1). Yahweh knew his man, who as expected (known) reacted to intervention by hardness; Yahweh intervened more: I don't assume that Pharaoh is ultimately damned.

By calling Judas of Kerioth the son of perdition, John was commenting that Judas was by his very nature fit to act as a child of Satan. You might not hold out much hope for Pharaoh or for Judas, but surely we may for preconversion Jews who simply weren't able to swallow Jesus' heavy teachings in Galilee (Jhn.6:66). Maybe their hardness even ended with the resurrection (Ac.2:37). Is it wrong for

God to hasten and confirm us along our chosen road, even to protect us from a premature birth of faith?

Egypt itself was not the big bogeyman against God's people, though it had some anti-Yahweh leaders. The very miraculous signs evoked by the hardness of Pharaoh would predispose Egyptians with eyes to see and ears to hear, towards a covenant relationship (Ex.14:18). Hinting at globalism, Yahweh said that he would eventually save and adopt Egypt (Is.19:19ff.), slavemaster and slave. "Isaiah foresaw the conversion of the Gentiles under the image of that of Israel's most ancient oppressor and seducer (see Is.30:2-5)" (Carson 1997:645). Ethnic terms can have a meaning by extension—*Egypt* representing the world, *Israel* representing Yeshua's messianic community.

In attitude like Pharaoh to Moses' words, Jesus' self-hardened people were hardened by Jesus' words, lest messianic light dawned too soon before the works of the night were over (Mk.4:11-2).[76] The journey, safe to begin in the morning, should not be started in the dangers of the night. A study of this theme will show that its source, Is.6:9-10, carried within itself two truths. That a hardening would sometimes simply follow God's speech, and would sometimes be his intention.

The Gospels convey both these aspects. *Mark* lines up with the Hebrew text, while *Matthew* with the Greek, as two sides of a coin. Indeed "Is.6:9-10 is central for the early Christian understanding of why Israel as a whole did not accept Jesus" (Keener 380), and was even quoted in Jhn.12:40. Although the Galileans had danced in jubilation around messiah, the Jerusalemites were hardened enough on their morning of infamy, to cry out with their leaders, "Crucify, crucify".

What a day it was. Beginning in God's schedule for that eventful year, as required on Nisan 14, the Passover lambs had been slaughtered, and as twilight began Nisan 15, messiah had eaten the Passover Meal at the start of Passover Week.[77] There is a good case for Quinto-decimanism. Having proclaimed the new covenant to his apostles

---

[76]   Alone from his people at large, Jesus spoke of "their hardness of heart and unpardonable sin (see 2:6-7,16,18,24; 3:2,5,22,30) resulting in a further hardening of the heart" (Stein 5572-5/29605).

[77]   For clarity here, ERV/NLT (A+); NCV (A); CEB/NIV/NRSV (B); LEB/NKJV (C+); CEV (D+); NABRE (D-). None are flawless.

that evening, he was led out early next morning to become the true Passover lamb, thus setting a new Passover Day. Hardening had opened up the Good News.

That day he died, not for an ethnic people nor for an ethic covenant, but for the global population and a global covenant; for the true exodus from Satan's Egypt and into God's Canaan. Incidentally both *John* and the Synoptics (*Matthew/Mark/Luke*) record the same historical execution date, Nisan 15. The Keriothite had already decided to betray Jesus, but Jesus' encouragement was the hardening he needed to complete the task without further delay—and it was night (Jhn.13:30).

<u>Hardening why</u>?

Even before the glorious sight when the new dawn comes, we can from history at least hazard some guesses as to why Ethnic-Israel has now been hardened. It is significant that *Acts*—which shows some ethnic-Jews softened—ended on this note of Isaianic hardening *and* Saul-Paul having turned to the Gentiles. Yet by 'all' (Ac.28:30) we may assume that individuals of Ethnic-Israel, as well as Gentiles, were welcomed to hear and to be taught. So why was the majority of Ethnic-Israel hardened, as history shows?

If hardening neither excluded Gentiles before the cross from ultimate life, nor excludes ethnic-Jews from ultimate life after the cross, what gains and losses were in the hardenings? There are always personal losses by walking in spiritual haze, even as there are gains by walking in spiritual light. Before the cross, messianism prepared for the cosmic stage. It was the experimental group (Ethnic-Israel/Judah) to the control group (Gentiles).

Sinai showed what could and could not be done by external rules and regulations (ethnic covenant)—a nearerness to God but not quite there. So even the best education, Sinai, can't deliver ultimate redemption to students—even Moses failed. The hardening of the Gentiles (control group) showed the insidious spiritual mess without deific teaching. With deific teaching (experimental group) Sinaites were a lesser mess.

The universe has looked on. As *Denomination Blues* (*That's All*) put it in 1977, "...you can go to your college / you can go to your school / But if you ain't got Jesus / you'se an educated fool / And that's all / I'll tell you that's all." Well, pagans went to primary, but the Israelites went to secondary, but even they weren't prepared for college level, and many sank back into or below primary level. It seemed that any new covenant level had to be hardwired within its students, with a new student-teacher relationship. Besides a global demonstration with perhaps universal observation, the special group also played a central part in preparing for God's son to interact directly at just the right time. This is why the Gentiles were hardened just for the right time, as salvation history unfolded.

Ethnic-Israel's turn to be hardened came. With a new covenant dimension, the explicit offer of redemption went global. Then, for the greater good, the ethnic race that had birthed messiah, was detached from Yahweh's central plan, his focus, even as the chaff that birthed the wheat becomes detached and useless.

Obviously, the hardening of Ethnic-Israel did not apply for all its people. Paul the Christian was happy with his ethnic-Jewish roots, and stilled called himself a Pharisee, having cut himself off from Sinai—true circumcision. But an attachment to Sinai—the what-had-been—was a barrier to the what-had-come, a false circumcision. Paul wished that those who tried to squeeze Gentile Christians into Sinai (Gal.5:12), should go the whole hog and get themselves ideologically castrated (more cutting than circumcision).

Douglas Moo noted that Dt.23:1 used the same verb to exclude such from entering Yahweh's congregation (Moo 2013:9063-4/16965). Now Christianity is Yahweh's congregation. Probably this Circumcision Party was trying to smooth Christianity over for racial harmony, but their idea of doctoring out God was as misguided then as it is today in Marxist politics. Man is in the dock, not God. They were spiritually blind, still part of the hardening that seeks to subsume.

Is Paul's suggestion of cutting-off from messiah's church, still relevant? Whether or not ethnically Jews, some teach some kind of spiritual superiority of ethnic-Jewish Christians, Judaism-creep. Is there an ingrained spirit of racial superiority in Ethnic-Israel, a Sinai factor? Has the wider NT church needed deific protection against Ethnic-Israel's inclination to ethno-centralise spirituality? Charybdis can suck down even big ships, as Chrysostom feared. Paul told the story of how the disobedience of those previously blessed, opened up blessing to those previously disobedient, who in turn enable God to bless the former party—Rm.11:30-1:[78]

30	Ethnic Gentiles	at one time	were disobedient	now	have received mercy	[by ethnic-Jewish] disobedience
31	Ethnic-Jews	now have	become disobedient	now	they receive mercy	[by God's] mercy to Ethnic Gentiles

There was a definite benefit for the previously excluded side, but the switch in fortunes did not preclude either side from evangelism, nor automatically include each and every ethnic Gentile/Israelite/Jew. Paul was among those ethnic-Jews who had come into the global mercy of God. But he avoided ethnocentricity like the plague.

One Christian and ethnic-Jew, Stan Telchin, was a more recent witness to the fact that an anachronism towards Moses, or towards the rabbis, can still arise within Christian ethno-Jewish 'churches'. In the West there was a big swing to Jesus *ha mashiach* among ethnic-Jews in the late 1960s, a big youth rebellion against racial traditions. Integration difficulties sadly led to both creeping disassociation and Judaising tendencies, increasing separation from fellowship with mainline churches. Hebrew buzz words—Hebrew often to these Jews being an unknown language—crept in along with the name change to 'messianic Judaism'. Telchin strongly repudiated such trends. He argued that messiah came to make "a single new humanity" (CJB: Eph.2:15), with racial and Sinaitic tags being totally irrelevant (see Telchin's *Messianic Judaism is not Christianity!*, 2004:150). Aaron is out, Melchizedek is in.

Once upon a time, ethnic-Gentiles could only access ultimate life and, by and large, were excluded from entering God's central salvation plan. The blessing then was that Ethnic-Israel could access covenant life and was corporately included in developing God's central salvation plan. That era is long gone. Sadly, ingrained nationalism/peoplehood-pride precludes messianic Judaism from the multinational and multiethnic stage of God's design—just like

---

[78]   See Morris 1988:424, following Cranfield.

someone committed to living in the past can burden those looking towards the future. Similarly Dr. Rich Robinson, also an ethnic-Jew, lamented his people's ethnolatry ("veneration by a people of themselves and their traditions"), that under a We-Are-One slogan, Yom Kippur nowadays tends to be more about them forgiving God, than about him forgiving them.[79]

Unhardening when?

If we put the cart before the horse, we might expect hardening to end with the final ethno-Jewish generation. However, if we see that Paul himself had been hardened, yet turned to messiah, then we have surely put the horse before the cart and can take a biblical ride.

Although Judaism only began a little after Paul's death,[80] we can see that he followed a very different path once he moved from hardening to enlightenment. Indeed it was at his missional home base that disciples were first called Christians (Ac.11:26): Simeon encouraged Christians to rejoice that they bore that identifying name (1 Pt.4:16). The NT Letters, probably all by ethnic-Jews, reflect that ethnic majority living in this hardened phase, refusing to accept that the Sinaitic regulations (about the kosher, the sabbath, physical circumcision, holy days, et al) were over.

[79]   https://jewsforjesus.org/publications/issues/issues-v04-n04/the-yom-kippur-dilemma. His biblical quotes from the NIV, unsurprisingly, downgrade the scandal of God's name even from LORD to Lord, and there is polytheistic talk, yet he nicely presents a trilemma—should ethnic-Jews hold to an incohesive Judaism that lacks Sinai, hold to a Western pluralism that treats religions as merely subjective, or hold to Christianity as fulfilling the deific speech through messiah?

[80]   For simplicity over accuracy, many biblical scholars refer to even early Sinaitic Religion as Judaism and some even call Moses a Jew. The term Jew comes from the tribal name, Judah, to which King David belonged, but calling Moses a Jew is a bit like calling Rabbie Burns an Englishman—and Abraham an Israelite. Judaism began in AD 70, when several stands of Intertestamental Jewish Religion, itself the modified representative of Sinaitic Religion, Yahwism, was restructured basically along Pharisaism lines. One can be an Arab and a Judaist, or an ethnic-Jew and a Muslim, and 'are you a Christian or a Jew?' is a category error. Belief need not coincide with blood.

Some still—even some Christians unaware it's futile—wish the stone temple to be rebuilt. A Wailing Wall is venerated as a visual reminder of the glory departed, which they hope will return. But Paul's blindness was removed—he had been unhardened (2 Cor.3:16).

<u>Unhardening for whom?</u>

According to *Romans*, for an unspecified time Ethnic-Israel would (as Paul had been) in some degree be hardened, premier players now relegated, but 'all Israel' would be (as Paul had become) saved. But are we really talking of Ethnic-Israel here, for "it is impermissible to argue that 'Israel' cannot change its referent within the space of two verses, so that 'Israel' in v25 must mean the same as 'Israel' in v26: Paul actually began the whole section (Rm.9:6) with just a programmatic distinction of two 'Israels', and throughout the letter (eg 2:25-9) as well as elsewhere (eg Php.3:2-11) he has systematically transferred the privileges and attributes of 'Israel' to the messiah and his people" (Wright 1991:250).

Is Wright right here? I don't think his is the best of options, and while wordplay is obvious in Rm.9:6, it is not in 11:25-6. And if 11:26 is about the NT church, talk about *mystērion* would be an anticlimax if the simple point was that all the NT church would be saved. Yet to take *Israel* as ethnic in 11:26 does not mean that *pas* must be taken quantitatively as 'all'. Might it have been used in its rabbinic sense? The C2 rabbinic Mishnah says that "all Israelites have a share in the world to come" (Sanh.10:1), and immediately lists classes and individuals within the ethnic people—such as heretics who believed that the Bible was primarily engineered by man, not by God—as excluded, limiting 'all Israel' to mean the righteous of Israel.

I am happy to say that at the end of the day, all the righteous of Ethnic-Israel shall, in line with God redeeming the nations, be saved in the same way of all righteous Gentiles being saved.[81] That surely requires the same pathway of hearing the gospel properly preached. If Gentile Christians were thinking that God had abandoned the ethno-Jewish people because they had five years earlier caused riots

---

[81] The righteous/just are those of a certain spirit before conversion, which while not making them righteous in God's eyes or granting them Christ's righteousness of eternal life, nevertheless indicates a pro-God disposition which God sees.

in Rome, and hadn't turned *en masse* to Jesus, Paul was saying that that was because God had indeed hardened the majority while he shaped the Gentiles into his ways, but all those truly seeking him would be *saved*—a tricky word.

Indeed, if Paul's *pas* (*all?*) in Rm.11:26 had meant every individual Jew, then presumably likewise with v25's *plērōma* (*fullness*) Paul was "thinking of the Gentiles in the same inclusive terms" (George Buttrick 9.575). John Knox maintained that such universalism was un-Pauline (Buttrick 9.577) and that the 'all' of 26 and 32 was the 'all' of classification (all of a certain type), not of individuals, and alluded to the fact that not all who are descended from Israel in blood are in spirit Israel (9:6: Buttrick 9.575). I can go with that.

Alongside the strange idea that after most ethno-Jewish generations get a Go-Directly-to-Hell card, a final generation will all get a Go-Directly-to-Heaven card, is the strange idea that Paul was grieved enough to potentially offer to be damned if only his people wouldn't be. How would his damnation have pleased God or helped anybody?

Actually, I think he was talking about the immediate life of the now relationship of Christian insight (Jhn.17:3). That is, that he would have gone blind, given up his Christian relationship with God—compared to which Sinai's best was but unkosher dung (Php.3:8)—if by such sacrifice the rest of his people would have become Christians (Rm.9:1ff.). But whatever his meaning, his attitude undermines a naive claim sometimes made that Christians only believe in order to gain benefits. C S Lewis had been a Christian for about a year before he had any belief in heaven; converted to deism, Antony Flew rejected both atheism and postmortal life.[82]

In short, the *all*, the fullness, may refer to God's will—to reveal himself in messiah—upgrading all those of Ethnic-Israel he can

---

[82]   Attributed to Antony Flew, as recorded by *The Sunday Times* (London:2004), "I don't want a future life. I want to be dead when I'm dead and that's an end to it. I don't want an unending life. I don't want anything without end", seems consonant with the idea that an afterlife is a mere survival, especially—and he thought the most likely religious option the Christian one—had he the idea of endlessly praising God before a celestial throne. Flew 2, maintains disinclination in an afterlife. Had what he thought he wanted clouded his judgement? I guess he's gotten what he wanted, but not what he wished.

within his chosen pathway, even as was the case *apropos* Gentiles, and an issue separate from ultimate life. Saul of Tarsus had showed less tolerance than had his mentor Gamaliel 1 of Simon of Hillel, yet in God's plan only Saul became a Christian. Yet will they not both—the unhardened and the hardened in *Acts*—end up in heaven?

The deliverer has come

Some of the futurist assumption assumes that Paul predicted the deliverer to come *from heaven*, perhaps meaning from the heavenly Zion. But the deliverer *had* come from Zion. When *Zion* refers in the NT to the heavenly Jerusalem, the text makes that special sense clear (see Heb.12:22): "if arguments are given [in support of the second coming], they are few and not very strong" (Hvalvik 38.92). It is better perhaps to work within a framework of something already begun in Paul's lifetime, what C H Dodd called *realised eschatology*. Clearly Paul was quoting *Isaiah*.

But was what was future *to Isaiah*, future *to Paul*? One may quote what was to be, as if it is still to be, even though it has happened. For instance, in Rm.9:33, "I am placing a stone", which had been future to Isaiah, had happened before Paul quoted it. Was not this a stone that had been placed the Deliverer? The Deliverer had come.[83]

Paul spoke of the stone laid *in* Zion (*en Siōn*:[84] Rm.9:33) and the deliverer *from* Zion/Jerusalem (*ek Siōn*: 11:26). Interestingly, he used neither the Masoretic Text's "come to Zion", nor the Septuagint's "come for the

---

[83]   Keith & Kristyn Getty's *Oh, How Good It Is* (2012), rightly says that "the redeemer has come".

[84]   Some older versions translated *siōn* as Sion, thus confusing it with *seōn/siy'on* (Dt.4:48), the latter sometimes put as *Sirion* (see Dt.3:9). Sion/Sirion is fine for only that one text. For all other texts, if following the Greek *Sion* would sound right, but if following the Hebrew (*tziyon*) *Zion* sounds better. I have seen a weak argument for more translations to use *Sion* rather than *Zion* (Steve Santini): he loved the idea that Mt. Sion was a holy place (Elijah's ascension). I have seen a somewhat better argument that *Zion* must be preferred because Mt. Sion had been a place of sexual orgy between fallen angels and human women, a place of false gods, and would be a place in Dan where the antichrist will reign (so Barbara Aho). I am not happy to speculate about the mountain's holy or unholy past, nor about its future; I am happier to read *Zion* rather than *Sion* in English.

sake of (heneken) Israel". Probably, as Craig Evans suggested, he melded ideas from Nb.24:17—"'a star from (*ek*) Jacob...a man from (*ek*) Israel,' into Is.59:20-1 + 27:9. In short, Paul placed himself in the tradition of the prophets. But his continuity with this prophetic tradition was in one important sense different: whereas the prophets of old longed for fulfilment of God's promises, Paul the 'sent' prophet proclaimed Scripture's fulfilment in Christ. Thus, Paul joined the prophets who have been sent out into the world, bearing the good news foretold in Is.52:7 and 61:1" (Soderlund and Wright 128).

From Zion might, for Paul, have signified Jesus' kingship and/or his Jewishness (see Rm.9:5), or his resurrection at Jerusalem, and an emphasis on temple theology. That is, the deliverer had already come from Zion (33). 15:8 speaks of God's promises confirmed and outworked by messiah's decisive and ongoing commitment to Ethnic-Israel—that is, Hans Conzelmann's inaugurated eschatology, which unites the aspects of *Realised Eschatology* (C H Dodd) and *Future Eschatology* (Albert Schweitzer),[85] with *Ongoing Eschatology*.

Paul addressed both 'sides' of Rome's church, into which ethnic-Jews were returning. His immediate concern was reintegration, rather than future eschatology. Gentile Christians puzzled over why, having been his people, the great majority of them didn't walk with him when he came through his son (Rm.1:3-4). John made the point from a loyalty perspective, immediately adding that a minority did (Jhn.1 11). Paul made the point from a theological perspective of sovereign hardening, within the context that some, as he himself, walked with messiah after an initial hardening: in the mystery of God neither all in nor all out. That the majority of ethnic-Jews were deaf to the gospel was true—too deaf to work with God, even if not fully deaf to God. That a Caiaphas, a Gamaliel, or a Pilate, would be ultimately damned for lacking positivity towards messiah, is not clear to me, but seemingly they were never saved into messiah's church. The deliverer had come from Zion, delivering all who welcomed him.

---

[85]   Schweitzer's form however was of an anticipated eschatology that failed to materialise even though Jesus died for it, so that Jesus was consistently wrong on that.

It is easier to be exhaustive rather than conclusive, but I do not wish to exhaust. Being content to be suggestive, I shall but briefly sketch some related ideas from this section of *Romans*. In line perhaps with Is.11:10, Paul's emphasis was on the Olive Tree root (*rhiza*—origins) rather than on the tree. As with hardening, I suggest that function, rather than ultimate life, was the underlying issue. That in effect, the cry of newness, *tetelestai* (Jhn.19:30), ended the chapter on Sinai; that all Sinai's readers were no longer following the plot; that this may be pictured as a branch cut off from its tree, the tree itself alive by its root—we may say the root idea, the core plan.

A friend follows my car down the road by. I take a left or right fork in the road, but my friend continues straight on. My friend has left me by not changing direction; I have left my friend by changing direction. Paul was a microcosm, an ethno-Jewish example of one who in solidarity with Sinai, had been cut off from the root because their faith did not move with the root change. They held to the husk.

Similarly, any ethnic-Gentiles who were reckoning that the Claudian expulsion Edict had been a godsend to purge the NT church from Jewish 'losers', misunderstood God. Paul warned them that ethnic-cockiness mislead them. God could disintegrate the proud children of Romulus, even as he could integrate any humble children of Judah, if they were open to hear.[86] Ethnic-Gentiles too could be cut off from their new spiritual land, as geographical land symbolised (Lv.20:22; Dt.28:63). Paul, an ethnic-Jew, had been cut off from God's plan, hardened, but through faith was soon grafted into its new phase.

Indeed it was in principle easier, more natural, for ethnic-Jews, since they already had spiritual history that anticipated such newness (eg Jr.31:31; Ezk.36:26). They had but to humble themselves into seeing that people is people, that God is impartial (Ac.10:34; Rm.2:11), and that God had, so to speak, gone global. The church at Rome had to see that the hardening had been to help the global reconciliation with God to begin aright, so they were to welcome Christian ethnic-Jews, who as fellow Christians were likewise part of the new creation of Global-Israel through Christ's resurrection, his global gift for all peoples.

---

[86]   An argument here for diseased Christians to be removed from the Vine (Jhn.15: life Level 3): restoration is not ruled out.

Chapter 4   Has the Evangel Changed?

You may wonder whether true OT Yahwists were the same in relation to God, as are true NT Yahwists, Christians, or whether there has there been a fundamental upgrade instead of a mere update. Terms such as *regeneration, born anew*, and *indwelt*, spring up. Martin Luther taught that OT believers weren't indwelt by the spirit. John Calvin disagreed: the perseverance of saints in both Testaments required God's spirit to live within (indwell), even if the regeneration is deeper for Christians.

Feeling blocked by Jhn.7:37-9, George Jeffreys argued that regeneration predated the cross and was by the 'Spirit of Christ', not the Holy Spirit who only came after the cross: true miracles were never from the unregenerate.[87] Luther held that Christians alone were indwelt and regenerate, but Yahwists had simply interacted with the spirit. More recently, B B Warfield (*contra* Walvoord) held that the spirit indwelt OT believers, and that they were regenerate, not simply as *per* Walvoord, influenced by the spirit. I side more with Luther and Walvoord. Has the good news upgraded?

OT Indwelling?

Indwelling is not a metaphysic, nor some symbiont a surgeon could discover, but is a metaphor for residing fellowship. Working with this basic metaphor, indwelling—as a virtuous guest sharing your table in your caravan—let's look at the idea that the Holy Spirit wasn't *within* OT believers, who were nevertheless born from above, regenerate (James Hamilton: *Themelios* 2004:30.1.12-22).

Hamilton argued that the OT text doesn't explicitly say that God's spirit was *within* any individual person, yet does explicitly say that he was *among* Yahweh's people, and was even *upon* some he chose to do certain top jobs. Yet that for the general population, God's spirit had a special residency (*loci*) within Jerusalem's temple. The temple was deemed a special place to visit to be blessed, and was the centre for removing the sin that contaminated fellowship with Yahweh.

---

[87]   I suggest that the prophet Balaam (like Caiaphas?) was unregenerate yet worked the miracle of prophecy. "The distinction Jeffreys drew..is not one that has recommended itself to other Pentecostals or biblical scholars" (Kay 226).

That was close, but could it ever be closer? Well, some prophecies predicted an indwelling stage, meaningless if the people were already indwelt, but meaningful if the weren't. Some who believe that he indwelt folk before the cross, point to Nb.27:18. But its contextual meaning is probably that Joshua was "a man in whom [was] the spirit of leadership" (NIV), ie the right kind of man to lead.

Other texts might be looked at, but even if some texts allowed for indwelling, they would have to be taken as exceptions to the rule, proving the rule that at most, indwelling was uncommon within God's ancient people, a stark contrast to the rule that all NT believers are indwelt. Some who believe that the OT lacks clear statement about indwelling, simply don't believe that Christians could remain loyal without deific indwelling, *ipso facto* loyal OT believers had to have been kept by God's indwelling.

Similarly, to bolster trinitarianism, some say that OT believers knew God's son, [88] even if the OT lacks trinitarian texts. Is gaining credence for one speculation, gaining credence for the other *ipso facto*? Should we use backdoor theology to argue that what is explicit in the NT was implicit, explicitly implicit, in the OT? But why would trinitarianism have been so well hidden under Sinai?

Anyway, back to indwelling. To argue for pre-crucifixion indwelling at the individual level, we could argue that focusing on solidarity required communal, rather than individual, terms, and that the communal indwelling was never meant to deny individual indwelling. If the latter co-existed with communal indwelling, it was certainly a well-kept secret!

---

[88]   This includes speculations about whether the three men (*ishim/andres*) of Gen.18:2 included God's son (eg Augustine) and two angels (19:1), and Jhn.8:56. The first is better understood (as with Jacob) as a principal angel as Yahweh's agent speaking with his voice. The second speaks of messiah's *day*, not of seeing messiah, and could be prophetical insight expressed at the birth of Isaac, the guarantee of greater fulfilment through the covenant line (Carson 1991:356-7). I think the second is too thin a straw to support exclusivism's claim that Christ was seeable *before* the cross so 'proving' that ultimate life could come to apparently countless masses at least among Ethnic Israel who saw him *before* the cross.

Yet even here, there seems to me that those who at times raised individualism's flag, such as Ezekiel, could prophesy indwelling to be a new feature then-future (eg Ezk.36:26). I wouldn't simply assume that the minimum needed to remain loyal is indwelling, and I fear it is an argument of desperation lacking textual support. How many on the battle field, or in a marriage (is there a difference, some ask!), remain loyal simply because loyalty is part of the common *Imago Dei*?

Loyalty can exist, both us-to-God, and us-to-each-other, because we are Imago Dei. Scriptures like Hg.2:5, show that Yahweh's spirit was *among* his people, rather than *within* certain individuals. The OT does not make a case for its believers being indwelt by Yahweh's spirit. It makes a case for him not indwelling them. It makes a case for a future new stage of common individual indwelling. Indwelling is basic for NT believers, and a distinction between Global-Israel and Ethnic-Israel. Individual indwelling is unique to the new covenant.

OT Regeneration?

A few words from *John*: "...some people did accept [the Logos]. They believed in him, and he gave them the right to become children of God" (ERV: Jhn.1:12); "the spirit had not yet been given, because Jesus had not yet been raised to glory" (NCV: 7:39). If we hold that the Holy Spirit was never *within* OT believers, is it still possible that they were born-from-above, regenerated, by Yahweh's spirit? Are there not two stages, potentially simultaneous, that he births into life those whom he will indwell? If so, some say that 7:39 meant future indwelling (reception), partly because they assume that 1:12 was about previous spiritual birth by the Holy Spirit.

I agree that Jhn.7:39 was about a future dimension, but so was 1.12.[89] You see, we should think historically. John was speaking about spiritually sensitive Jews *before* the cross, who before the *new covenant* couldn't be *new covenant* children of God, but were in line to become so after Jesus had died and begun the new covenant reality of God's messianic family and kingdom. They had been given, so to speak, a 'reservation ticket' all ready to hand in once the cross opened the gate.

---

[89]   The term *genesthai* is a clear future term—*to become*.

All that is history. They welcomed the one who would die but hadn't. Now, we welcome the one who has died. Now, to say that receiving Jesus entitles people *to [in the future] become* children of God, wrongly implies a second stage of welcome (and/or submission), or that believers only become family members after death. Now, this side of the cross, whoever welcomes Jesus instantly enters God's messianic family, and reservation tickets are neither issued nor needed. So, 1:12 was not about a previous new birth and therefore isn't a basis for asserting a pattern of new birth followed by indwelling.[90]

Does Jhn.14:17b—"he lives with you now and later will be in you" (NLT)—show that the spirit was *with* Jesus' disciples and would later be individually *within* each? Did 'with you' mean stage 1 new birth, regeneration, in preparation for a later stage indwelling? Perhaps, but it's unclear on a couple of points. For my part, I think it's far more likely that Jesus contrasted a there and then-ness (the Sinaitic covenant he himself was living within) with a future new birth/indwelling. True, the Greek could mean *in* the community of believers, rather than *in* each believer, but isn't the new covenant message about him eventually being *in* each believer? It's a radically new operating system, not a major upgrade. Grading: NIV/NLT (A+); ERV/LEB/NCV/NKJV/NRSV (A-); NABRE (C); CEB/CEV (D-).

So, I do not take the jump from the spirit being with them, to with-ness meaning new birth/regeneration. But did not Jesus represent *a group* who were already born anew: "we tell you what we know and have seen" (NLT: Jhn.3:11)? If so, were some born anew before the cross?

Before tackling that, let's look at the English term *born anew*, for to some it's unfamiliar. It is different from *born again* but is more biblical, and goes back to William Tyndale, but got lost in Bible translation. Sadly, the KJV followed the *born again* of the Geneva, Bishops, and Douay Rheims.[91] None of my main Bible versions get the

---

[90] An annoying nearby grave has "Behold the Lamb of God, which *taketh* away the sin of the world". True the Baptist's side of the cross; untrue our side of the cross: we behold him who *has* taken it away: "it is finished" made the difference. All who welcome him immediately become children of God.

[91] Best, Tyndale/Coverdale/Matthew read as if Jesus twice said *born anew*, and Nicodemus jestingly said *born again*: ABA sequence. The Great Bible, understanding how the Greek could mean *from above*, read as if Jesus twice

flow perfect, but here's my conclusion. Jesus said that the only way to see God's kingdom is to be 'born anew' (CEB: 3); Nicodemus asked how can anyone be "born again...born a second time?" (NCV: 4); Jesus replied: "I said to you, 'you must be born from above'" (CEV: 7). Whether or not in friendly jest, Nicodemus had taken have a word the wrong way, asking if Jesus preached reincarnation. Back in the 70s, I had some work colleagues ask me if I meant reincarnation, when I spoke to them about being *born again*. Perhaps to help others avoid Nicodemus' folly, John recorded the dialogue in such detail.

Technically, Jesus' initial *gennēthē anōthen* (3) allowed either *born again* or *born anew/from above*. Theologically Nicodemus' *born again* was a good-natured academic saying "you can't really be meaning *that* idea?" to which Jesus had replied, *of course not!* It's a qualitative thing (a new type), not a quantitative thing (a second of the same). And no, I haven't switched from being a born again Christian to being a born from above Christian, since to be born from above is to be a Christian, and to be a Christian is to be born from above—the only kind of Christian is a Christian Christian, and we should not need any addon.

Yes, some falsely call themselves Christian, and for some it has been a fashion to dress as if a Christian.[92] Moreover, some true Christians decay in wisdom and knowledge, fading from God's revelation and into sub-Christianity. But Christians shouldn't treat *born again* as a holy cow; anti-Christians shouldn't treat *born again* as a hated cow: to me *born again* is an affectionate but gelastic old cow.

---

said *born from above*, and Nicodemus foolishly said *born again*: CBC sequence. Wycliffe/Geneva/Bishops/Douay/KJV read as if Jesus twice said *born again*, and Nicodemus implied it (BB'B sequence: Wycliffe/Geneva/KJV) or said it (BBB sequence: Bishops/Douay). None showed the ABC sequence of *anew/again?/from above* (ie spiritual).

92   "In [Jane] Austen's era fashionable people went to church in such elegant attire, mainly to be seen by fashionable people. However, 'serious' religion— religion that affected people's hearts and actions—was ridiculed as 'enthusiasm'. Among the upper classes, fashionable manners allowed for Wickham's gambling in Pride and Prejudice, Maria Rushworth's adultery in Mansfield Park (socially acceptable as long as it was 'discreet'), and Sir Walter Elliot's extravagance in Persuasion." (Cox 13)

So, the correct term sorted, I hope, were some born anew *before* the cross? To say yes is to face a number of objections, not least by Nicodemus, an OT believer seeking a deeper life with God and needing new birth, and Yeshua, who was God's messianic kingdom (*autobasileia*, C3 Origen) so had never needed new birth to see God's messianic kingdom, so wasn't one within a born anew camp.

Let's go on. The eminent rabbi had invited sensational and controversial Rabbi Yeshua, to explain his framework. It was, 'you' (plural, applicable to all) must be *gennēthē anōthen*. Nicodemus was genuinely surprised, and Jesus was surprised that he was surprised. Shouldn't any leading OT scholar (10)[93] twig that he was talking about an OT prediction? OT prediction was basic to entering God's messianic kingdom, and Ethnic Israel needed to see that the long messianic gestation was coming to birth. The OT prediction of newness bespoke something begun *after* and *by* the cross.

New Birth: a picture of New Kingdom identity

Of course, Nicodemus was already a kingdom member, since Ethnic-Israel was already God's kingdom—he had been born into it and could see it. What messiah spoke of was a prophetic theme about a *new form* of kingdom—some deeper, truer, messianic, definition that needed a new dynamic, a new righteousness, to enter, and therefore new eyes to see. Nicodemus lived in the alpha level, but the omega level was coming.

Yeshua began to explain the access to the redefined kingdom. He spoke of birth by water. He hardly meant the meaningless platitude that for a human being to be birthed by God's spirit, they must first have been birthed by a mother! Nor was he talking about water-baptism. After all, Nicodemus could hardly have been surprising slow on the uptake, about something that was still only a twinkle in the master's eye.

The closest to that idea would have been the Baptist's challenge for ethnic-Jews to get right with God, since God's kingdom was near. John's converts had simply been immersed in water *with reference to* (*eis*) their inward returning (*metanoia*) to the covenant (Mt.3:11). They

---

93   'The teacher' means one with national repute, not the only one.

had rededicated themselves to the Sinaitic Covenant, possibly expecting a messianic victory over Rome. But water-baptism was about cleaning/commitment, not about birth. Moreover, John's baptism was never a Christian practice, and Christ soon dropped it. It refloated Sinai in order to launch messiah—prepare ye the way.

In contrast, the new birth was something messianic. Messiah would do away with Sinai, even as chaff, having done its task, gives way to wheat. He would invite the Righteous Remnant into the next step (Ac.19:4-5). The inner weakness of the Sinaitic Covenant was clear in the OT, and its prophets yearned for inner change (Jr.31). It was hoped that God's spirit would transform the heart, cleansing like water (Ezk.36:25-6): thus 'water/spirit' would be two sides of a spiritual coin, of spiritual currency, speaking of a new spiritual dimension or layer based on a predicted phase in God's global plan, and dawning in Nicodemus' lifetime.[94]

This new dimension—which surely Nicodemus yearned for—would transform converts into being individually messianic children of God. Even for ethnic kingdom members, *gennēthē anōthen* meant entering a new realm of knowing God, a profound transformation from above by his spirit. Predictive prophecy of personal heart transformation like cleansing water, was soon fulfilled.

So if neither he nor his disciples were born anew, why did the Jesus say that "we speak of what we know, and we testify to what we have seen..." (NIV: Jhn.3:11)? Perhaps to say that though he, Yeshua, was indeed a brother rabbi, he was also the prophet of prophets and represented them. Paraphrasing: Nicodemus, you are slow to comprehend the OT witness, but we prophets have seen that a newness of kingdom is coming and witness to the fact.

This reading would make sense, without implying that the new birth had begun. Or less likely, maybe the 'we' alluded to the discipleship

---

94   The OT combined the images of water and spirit to speak of renewal or cleansing, and spoke of the spirit poured out (eg Nb.19:17-9; Ps.51:9-10; Is.32:15). Water and spirit together could "forcibly..signify cleansing from impurity...[and] the transformation of heart.... reminiscent of the 'new heart' expressions that revolve around the promise of the new covenant" (Carson 1991:195).

team he led: he and his team were doing the rounds as witnesses that a new day of spiritual birth is dawning. He certainly wasn't saying that he himself was spiritually reborn—he was born uniquely unique, the only one who had come from heaven ontologically (13—see note 45). 'We speak' probably included such as Ezekiel and Jeremiah (11), even though OT prophets had not fully understood their own message (1 Pt.1:10-2). No prophet had returned from heaven to witness to mortal man; Jesus (God's son from heaven) was uniquely placed.[95]

This last bit could have hinted to Nicodemus of Israel's messianic representative, having perhaps returned from God with visions to establish the Ancient of Days' kingdom (Dan.7:13-4). Could that explain why Nicodemus' voice fades from the text? Did Nicodemus, like Mary, fall silent to ponder such things in his heart, becoming convinced enough—even after Jesus' apparent defeat—to side with the minority (Jhn.19:39)?

In fact, through death Jesus defeated death. Jesus would save his people (3:14; Nb.21:4-9), as when surprisingly the snake had been raised as salvation's flag, and all who had saluted it were healed. In the fuller context of *John*, the word 'exalted' (*hupsos*) combined in Jesus the ideas of heavenly dignity and literal lifting up onto a cross. God's glory was shown in Jesus' death. Is.52:13 (in the Greek LXX) has this same word, as well as have Jhn.8:28 and 12:32,34. But as said earlier, it is better to avoid singing of us lifting Jesus up, lest we confuse what we're to do (evangelism and praise), with what's been done for us (the atonement). We cannot lift up, in *that* sense, he who was lifted up once for all time.

---

[95]   Jesus did not assume that heaven was vertically above the earth. The Flat Earth idea was not the only idea in town. Rather, he spoke in metaphor, even as we speak of 'the moral high ground' without meaning spatially higher above sea level than the moral low ground.

For how Jhn.3:13 should be put, see the NLT. Variations of an ending, for example NKJV's 'who is in heaven', suggesting that Jesus was in heaven even as he spoke, may well reflect later editorial comment added when *John* was copied, reflecting the idea that Jesus who had spoken to Nicodemus had since ascended back to heaven, his home. Alternatively (and far less likely) Jesus had said something about existing as deity in heaven and co-existing as a man in time and space.

Of course, if this spiritual birth/ regeneration[96] wasn't available before the cross, did it mean that the OT believers would never see God's kingdom? Don Carson's *The Gagging of God* is a good remedy to post-modernism, which admittedly has had some positives, not least in dethroning modernism, but no human monarchy is perfect. Though extreme subjectivism is a sad legacy, there can indeed be gaps between speech and hearing, especially between cultures different in time and place. Each word can indeed have a range of meaning, and though there is absolute truth, the net pickup of truth can vary from person to person. While it's true that we should be canny of post-modernism, it's true that we should also be canny about contexts and cultural glasses. We won't always fully understand another's words, and their beliefs and ours can vary, since human intellect and perception are imperfect.

Talk of God's kingdom has had layers of meaning. Though God's Sinai kingdom had existed over long centuries, *John* announced that God's expected kingdom was dawning. You can keep a cake and eat a cake if you have two cakes. Like Nicodemus, they were in and saw Yahweh's kingdom *as an ethnic kingdom*, and like Nicodemus they couldn't see or enter Yahweh's kingdom *as a messianic kingdom* unless they were born anew (See Salvation History's Two Levels of Immediate Life, below). That chance they neither yet had, nor needed for ultimate life. Yet with new birth would come new identity, good news.

---

[96]   A Latinised form of *palingenesias—regeneration*—was used twice in the KJV (Mt.19:28—birth of a new age; Tts.3:5—birth of new lives). Nowadays it tends to be kept only for Tts.3:5 in order to keep a theological term for conversion: adequate, even if not ideal. Paul's point was that in mortal life we need another experience (*palin* is *again* is below his meaning) of birth (*genesis*)—birth by the spirit. Biblically *palingenesias* does not mean regeneration as a body repairs itself, so is about birth into holiness, not ongoing holiness.

The levels of kingdom

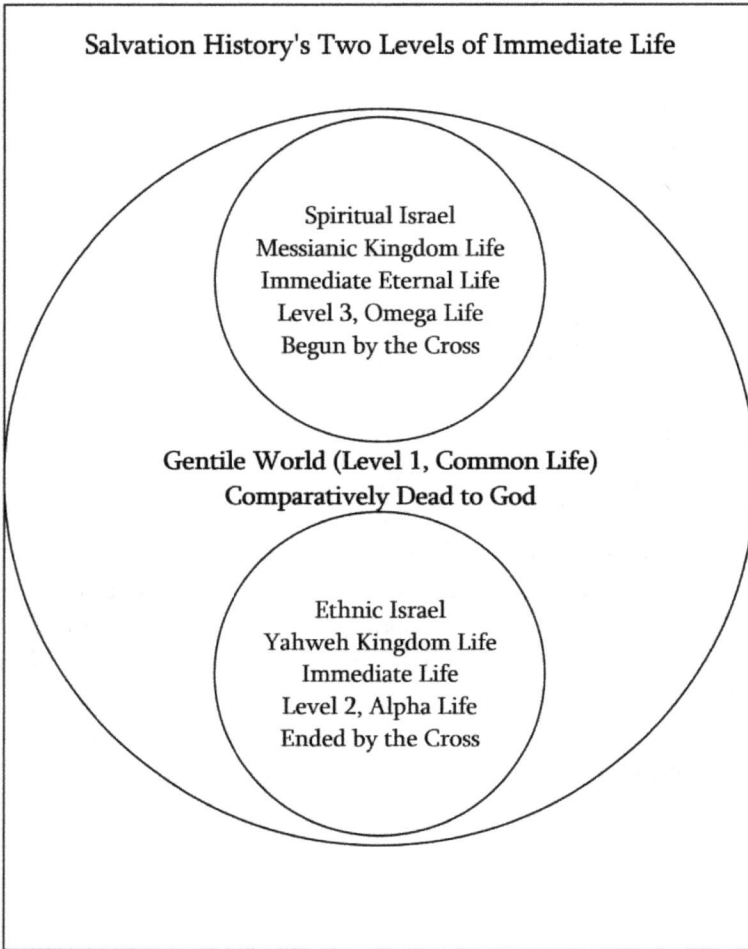

Salvation History's Two Levels of Immediate Life

Spiritual Israel
Messianic Kingdom Life
Immediate Eternal Life
Level 3, Omega Life
Begun by the Cross

Gentile World (Level 1, Common Life)
Comparatively Dead to God

Ethnic Israel
Yahweh Kingdom Life
Immediate Life
Level 2, Alpha Life
Ended by the Cross

Yahweh's throne was in heaven; his kingdom reigned over all (1 Chr.29:11). His reign was wider than Sinai, but Ethnic Israel was closer to its epicentre. Sinai as a focus of Yahweh's kingdom, tended to be a background yet foundational theme. Sinai was a holy kingdom (Ex.19:6), soon realising that it fell below holiness and holiness loyalty.

A core change happened when Ethnic-Israel *en masse* sought new management, seeking to have a human monarchy like its neighbours (1 Sam.8:7). There had come a glitch in Yahweh's representation structure. Was Samuel a misguided nepotist? Why didn't he appoint better people for the job, since his sons were rightly unpopular? Yet the real problem was with Ethnic-Israel, inwardly yielding to the temptation to be more like its neighbours, less like its king (20).[97] Thereafter, human monarchy became the norm, while Yahweh's direct kingship tended to be exfiltrated. The ethnic ideal had been the United Kingdom of Israel (1 Chr.28:5), but the Southern Kingdom had taken over this honour and witness (2 Chr.13:8).

Ideally, Yahweh would have established a human monarchy for his people, one unlike the other nations, and according to his own timetable. Some say that there are conflicting strands in *Samuel*, labelling them as A (promonarchy) or B (antimonarchy). However, they're not from different sources, and merely reflect mixed feelings to people power—Yahweh had planned change, but not for so soon. Saul was the best man available at the wrong time.

Even under Yahweh's reign, the same sin that demanded a copycat kingdom, was part of the underlying reason why his ideal kingdom level could never be established without a new type of covenant. A covenant at heart level was his bigger plan, the end towards which Ethnic-Israel was a means. A type of covenant that came with Jesus, which gave the spiritual insight that allowed folk to see and to enter it (2 Cor.3:13-6). A covenant in which we and the spirit would be family.

Putting all this together, we can see that Jesus didn't say that to have *ultimate* life, Nicodemus had still to be spiritually born, but rather that the new birth—long anticipated by those who had ultimate life as individuals and not as Israelites—meant globally an in-depth insight hitherto unknown for the here and now.

---

[97] Even David would in solidarity with his people place his confidence in human resources, possibly planning to extend his kingdom. This sin of attitude was brought to the light by action in God's, and Satan's, will (Gen.50:20; 2 Sam.24:1; 1 Chr.21:1), and they were punished to teach them. Incidentally, Yahweh taking human life is no more immoral than taking students out of a school when their course is over. Remaining students may sadly miss them, but death ends mortality, not life, and opens the door to the beyond. Salvationists rightly speak of their people being 'promoted to glory.' But students expelling fellow students (by accident, war, mercy killing, or murder) is a serious matter, as is wilfully detaining those packed up and ready to go.

New birth is seeing God's heart at the messianic kingdom level. This applied also to those ethnic-Jews (Jhn.1:11-2) who already believed that God had sent Jesus, and if holding onto faith would become God's new-kingdom children—a covenant individualisation—just as soon as there was the new kingdom to see and to enter. Ethnic-Israel had a there and then taster of the future, when Jesus came (eg 4:23; 5:25; 16:32)—a pre-dawning of this new kingdom/new covenant level, glimmers of light from God's plan. Before the cross, the veil over God's face was pulled back just a little. An embryonic New Israel community was doing the rounds, still tied to the umbilical cord of their rabbi and hidden within Ethnic-Israel.

It is ill-judged to base ideas of God's spirit *indwelling* the OT believers, on the presumption of spiritual birth before the cross. Even the Twelve lacked this insight, this spiritual birth. OT believers, such as Nicodemus, saw and lived in God's kingdom in its earlier ethnic stage, as had Aaron, David, Isaiah. To see the next kingdom stage, the global stage that Jesus was beginning to preview, would require folk to be born anew. We speak of a penny dropping. To be born anew is, by the spirit's grace, seeing the dropped penny and picking it up. It is Jesus glorified. The disciples were born anew, not as a batch, but individually—beginning with Mary—as each picked up that dropped penny, personalised it, and bought into God's Yeshuic kingdom.

The breath of Christ

Finally on this point, let's look at when Jesus *breathed* that special time (Jhn.20:22), because some say that this was them being indwelt/regenerated by the spirit, what some call a Johannine Pentecost. Those within this camp who believe that *John* was historical, then assume that this was before Pentecost. Almost all Bible versions add a preposition—mostly *on*, but occasionally *exhaled/into/upon/inspired*. Any added preposition adds interpretation, for the word structure itself does not indicate *in* (insufflation), *out* (exsufflation), nor *on them*, nor *into them*. No preposition should be added, and Rotherham's 'breathed strongly' was right, for in fact it was not an impartation of the spirit, whether to indwell or to energise.

As Theodore of Mopsuestia long ago taught, it was to symbolise the round-the-corner event of Pentecost (Carson 1991:653).[98] Nor need we linger with the question of whether Jesus had ascended by that time—thus allowing the spirit to be given (16:7; 20:17)—since Jesus had been glorified by the cross, his exaltation an ascension. Whether he inhaled, as if to say that they would receive the spirit like breathing in, or whether he exhaled as if to say that he would impart the spirit like the breath of life, we are not told. Neither was the main point; both perhaps are secondary points within synergism.

It was a prophetic expectation to prime them for what Pentecost would bring. And that wasn't new birth—that day individually dawned by welcoming the resurrected lord. No, Pentecost brought the Grand Opening ceremony of the new age. That day, when The Twelve were in place, they would begin a new global interactivity with the spirit. It was not the birthday of the church, but it was perhaps their graduation day, their premier. A sea change has been expressed by new-level terms, such as indwelling and spiritual birth (*regeneration*), terms not necessarily explained by ontological reality (as if the spirit comes inside our bodies), so much as by a significant increase in revelation and cooperation with the spirit within Global-Israel.

---

[98] See also the major Johannine commentaries by Witherington (1995) and Köstenberger (2004).

Chapter 5   <u>NT Regeneration and Indwelling</u>

As said in the previous chapter, some reckon that the OT believers were regenerated, born anew, before the cross. However, the cross both allowed ultimate life and redefined immediate life levels.

Prophetic sight spoke way back in the Garden: a woman's son would crush the serpent's head; by taking the venom would overcome the evil sting. Abraham rejoiced to see Jesus' *day* (Jhn.8:56 (see note 88 above); Gen.12:3). For Yahweh's temple plan would focus down to one man, Yeshua, then be multiplied into mobile temples, wherever Yeshua's disciples would go and worship. Jeremiah prophesied that the covenant would be within, rather than without, God's people (Jr.31).

On the border of salvation history, Simeon was content to die having seen Yahweh's global redemptive plan dawn (Lk.2:29-32). Excited by messianic rumours, Nicodemus yearned to know more of the plan, but still had to await the cross before he could see the kingdom that messiah would open by the cross (Jhn.3). At work since creation, the spirit's mission of new birth—that is global revelation—could only begin after the cross (7:39). By the cross, people began to really see and to enter God's messianic kingdom.

With-ness has now been superseded *within-ness*, an extra dimension in human relationships with God and insight into his plans. It is an added value of relational enrichment, along with the deeper aspects of community, and God moved into the common individual level. In a sense, it's like a baby finally getting to see the light of day (Jhn.3:3)— we can drowse in the sun. The father is our visible destination, his son is the way, and the spirit is our individual navigator. Each Christian has direct throne entrance, temple worship, and prophetic insight, since community assets have internalised in Christ.

Though profoundly personal and individual, its community aspect remains vital, and we "should not stay away from the church meetings, as some are doing" (NCV: Heb.10:25). At least while reasonable age, firmity, and mission, allow. And to play our parts. As Roman Catholic theologian Hans Küng said, it "is important that the positive significance of the priesthood of all believers be realized.... [Every Christian is able to have] direct access to God, [make] spiritual sacrifices...in a spirit of love and self-giving...preach the word and administer [water-]baptism, the Lord's Supper, and [proclaim] the forgiveness of sins [having come into] the mediating work of the one and only mediator" (Küng 372,381). Küng said that Protestants who preached that every Christian is a priest, were right, but wrong if on that they did not practice what they preached. On this he addressed what some call, Body Ministry (Eph.4:16). Nevertheless, our primary identity is now in Christ, not in community, a spin-off.

I hold that while ultimate life extends beyond the messianic church, by linking to its core revelation, only messianic believers are true priests, temples, royalty, etc. But believer-priesthood is in practice somewhat disempowered, especially within networks that have hierarchical network terms such as *bishop*—even if only adopted for political clout—and top-down control over local church autonomy.

I like the term *indwelling*, yet I think it functions best as a contrast to the previous top level of neighbourliness, which was *with* but not *within* (Jhn.14:17). It's a good way to express the betterness, the deeperness, which the Writer to the Hebrews put in so many different ways. Technically, it's a pictorial way to indicate a much fuller joy, insight, and activity with God, than that foreshadowed in the Tanak.

A companion picture of closeness and intimacy is of us in deity—obviously not our spirits within a somatic body. Some picture a sponge in water; water in the sponge—mutual residency. Indeed, some picture the trinity a bit like this—interpenetration, perichoresis, like a ball of three intertwined colours of thread, indivisible yet one. Along the lines that water-immersion is a drama Rm.6:11 tells us to consider ourselves as being "dead to sin but alive to God in Christ Jesus' (NIV). That is, that where it most matters, Christians through identity with Christ should live in the light of transference from the lordship of sin to the lordship of God the father. And with that comes a sense of being family members by redemption, brought in by his son.

- In the father: 1 Ths.1:1; 1 Jhn.3:24
- The father in: Jhn.14:23; 1 Jhn.3:24
- In the son: Jhn.6:56; Gal.2:20
- The son in: Jhn.6:56; Gal.4:19
- In the spirit: Rm.8:9; Rm.14:17
- The spirit in: Jhn.7:38-9; 1 Cor.6:19

The Spirit on Believers

While comparing terms, it might be good to refer briefly to an OT emphasis that carries through into the NT. Namely that for special assignments, some had God's spirit come on/upon them in the sense of enabling and overseeing them. The missional theme, whether the mission was for a permanent priestly post or a one-off prophecy, has a reference different to regeneration and concomitant indwelling. This is nicely charted in Petts 125, which shows that whatever the expressions *Baptised in/with the spirit* and *Receiving the [gift of the] spirit* might mean in other contexts, that in the context of Luke's pentecostal accounts of Caesarea, Ephesus, Jerusalem, and Samaria, they are synonyms for the spirit coming 'on' (Gk. *epi* + genitive).

There is a missional and relational dimension, potentially of immediate subsequence (at/after), available to all Christians. It is good to realise that besides the individualisation theme of all Christians being indwelt, they are all able to engage in special mission with God's spirit. Indeed if it is correct that Rm.15:18-9 suggests "that the gospel is not 'fully proclaimed' unless it is attested by signs from heaven" (Petts 97), then with a low charismatic skills base the gospel can still be preached under a pentecostal level, but not as fully as from a high charismatic level. The gem is undersold when not all its facets sparkle, though few pentecostal Christians will operate as fully as apostles (2 Cor.12:12). That's a fact of life, Christian life.

Still, the good news remains that all Christians have the spirit of mission, so all can take part whether at higher (*epi*) or lower levels, and we all have the option to make the good better and the better best. Is there not at least some correlation between the new creation and *Genesis*, where "God's wind swept over the waters" at creation (CEB: Gen.1:2) and God's word was spoken? *John* begins with a *Genesis* tie-in (Gen.1:1; Jhn.1:1), and features the Five Paraclete/Spirit Sayings. Surely the Christian life is fuller when we have both teaching and the spirit's fullness. Whoever is in the new closeness can have God's spirit on them, talk the talk, and walk the walk.

How Did it Work?

Speaking for many others, C S Lewis had been put off Christianity by the idea "that Christians must believe...one particular theory as to what the point of [Christ's] dying was. According to that theory God wanted to punish [or perhaps had to punish] people for having deserted and joined the Great Rebel. but Christ volunteered to be punished instead, and so God let us off. Now I admit that even this theory does not seem to me quite so immoral and so silly as it used to; but that is not the point I want to make. What I came to see later on was that neither this theory nor any other is Christianity. The central Christian belief is that Christ's death has somehow put us right with God and given us a fresh start. Theories as to how it did this are another matter. A good many different theories have been held as to how it works; what all Christians are agreed on is that it does work.... Christians would not all agree as to how important these theories are.... But I think they all will agree that the thing itself is infinitely more important than any explanations that theologians have produced....We can accept what Christ has done without knowing how it works" (Lewis 2002:53-5 passim).

I'd rather speak of pictures, than theories, and say that biblically and otherwise we have many pictures hinting how it works. Theology is a landscape, not a picture. "I speak after the manner of men because of the infirmity of your flesh" (KJV: Rm.6:19a), or as the CEV puts it, "(I'm speaking with ordinary metaphors because of your limitations)". Picture an iceberg imperfectly—and can we perfectly picture one? Then see that from a ship we see only a side of its tip. Then see that the side we see is only its 2D face, not its 3D core. Then see that that tiny sight fails to check out the molecules and its atomic parts. How deeply can our mortal finite minds grasp God's fullness, and even his salvation plan? Revelation helps our limited minds in limited ways.

Recently a Christian told me that they weren't hot on PSA. Er, what's PSA? I asked. Once he expanded that to Penal Substitution Atonement, I knew he referred to that idea that Lewis had thought immoral, silly, and offensive to God and man. I agree—it would be folly for a Christian victim to voluntarily die in order to let their rapist go free, therefore PSA is foolish, isn't it? Or is it only foolish if it isn't part of a package deal? What if he (or she) knew that the rapist would become a Christian, would come to enjoy the wonderful life they had enjoyed? Wouldn't that be the greater love Jesus spoke of, and what Paul would die for to have life for his people (Rm.9:3)? It's a mistake to isolate any one picture (model), and to thrash it into absurdity (anyone can debunk any picture), such as the guilty going free to cause mayhem—immoral silliness indeed.

So, PSA or not PSA? Sinai sure had PSA, but why, if it wasn't prophetic symbolism? "Many passages of Scripture...speak of Christ dying for sin, bearing our sin, or dying as a propitiation" (Grudem 581).[99] And this picture goes back to *Leviticus*, where animal sacrifice (besides usually providing meat) was symbolically vicarious and prophetic of a perfect sacrifice not then available. The innocent lamb/ram would die, symbolising both what sinners deserved and God's love gave, in order to invite godly response—when I survey the wondrous cross.

Yet surely the killing-for-forgiveness was not itself metaphysical, as if by me killing a lamb I kill my sins (Johann Tetzel)—it isn't mechanical transaction so much as request. Forgiveness comes by grace, not over a shop counter. Sinai forgave by inner grace, not by outer ritual. And even as Sinai's sacrifices weren't perfect (prophetic symbols merely keeping folk within covenant), nor was its picture, but both had some value.

Theology is a landscape of many pictures. Another picture is the lord as a redeemer-slave (total commitment, altruism, and success): "...the son of man did not come for people to serve him. He came to serve others and to give his life to save many people" (ERV: Mk.10:45). The idea of buying back or winning back the bought/captured, is well respected, and Origen never needed to ask whether Satan got a ransom who tricked him, though like Mordecai and Haman, that can be fun to preach.

And *Christus Victor* (Gustav Aulén) returned to an earlier picture of the supreme soldier dying to defeat the enemy on the battlefield of death: Remembrance Day symbolises the price of freedom, the lives of many willing and unwilling victims of death. Edmond L Budry's *Thine be the Glory* (1884), loudly lauds the "risen, victorious one", who "endless... victory" over death has won, so now "his church with gladness, hymns of triumph sing". Paul asked, "Death, where is your victory?" (1 Cor.15:55).

In principle, we can even understand the anger (*orgē*) of God. Isn't it right to get really mad when we see a mugging, a wanton robbery,

---

[99]   To die to impress my beloved would be folly; to die to save her would be noble. I think Abelard did well to highlight Golgotha as demonstrating the extent of God's love—perhaps redressing its under emphasis in his days—but underplayed its metaphysical/objective necessity, its transactional value.

and if we don't feel angry, and perhaps wish to correct it, aren't we part of the problem? At our best we at best a dim reflection (*Imago*) of God (*Dei*). So let justice be done, and if possible, mercy combined. C H Dodd noted how God's anger is often remedial, but severance-anger can also show his inability to redeem the irredeemable, those merged with sin beyond redemption: those ultimately damned have defeated God and lost their souls. We honour one who used the whip to save.

The metaphysics of Christ's death is beyond us. For that matter even universal physics are. PSA is, for my money, a fragment of the tapestry, an image that helps us understand, but incomplete as an isolated thread. If you pull out all imperfect threads of the tapestry, you will have no more cloth. Woven together the threads will make sense. PSA's concept of justice is valid, even though it is invalid to shackle that to a Marcionite caricature of an angry god itching to shoot us, with his kindly son jumping between us and bullet.[100]

One church network rejected Townend & Getty's *In Christ Alone* (2001), specifically because it disallowed the line, [the wrath of God was satisfied]. On principles of Christian lyrics, I grade their song as a B+ (marked down for some archaism and arrogance), and would make several alterations, such as replacing its *Christ-alone* bit (*Solus Christus*)[101] to either [in Christ the lord] or [in God's own son]. But I nevertheless defend its picture of God's anger against sin, and of anger being satisfied by the sinless one's death in our place. That's because the transaction went beyond the courtroom into metaphysical reality—a satisfaction of outcome: death transformed us into Christ's likeness.

But apart from going free from the courtroom, we have other pictures of the atonement's result, such as birth (or adoption) into God's family, though it would be folly to say that family membership is the same for us as for the trinity—there was a time when we were not. These pictures all carry the implicit prefix, "It's as if in some way/s...".

---

[100]   That caricature also tends to overlook that the father, son, & spirit are equally angry at sin, so the son's own anger led him to become sin's victim.

[101]   To me the Holy Spirit is an unintended casualty of this Reformation battle cry, which also offends the Athanasian Creed.

Chapter 6   Good News and World Religions

Christianity

We move on with the idea already mooted, that ultimate life, as distinct from regeneration and indwelling, was available worldwide since the dawn of man. But has immediate life with God, been? Have you heard that the word 'religion' is a dirty word, a man-made word, perhaps a satanic word? When in the '70s I enjoyed *How to Be a Christian Without Being Religious* (Fritz Ridenour), religion sure sounded dirty to me, but when I read that James commended good *religion* as pleasing to God, I washed out my ears.

James used a Greek word, of course, *thrēskeia* (Jas.1:26-7), but "the word religion captures well the meaning of the Greek *thrēskeia*.... The word is not specifically Christian and [was] used widely in Greek religion to denote the reverencing of a deity (or deities)" (Moo 1990:86). Religion that pleases God is "caring for orphans or widows who need help, and keeping yourself free from the world's evil influence" (NCV: 27). In other words, inner holiness with helpful community ethics: heavenly minded and earthly good.

Quite a bit of Middle Ages Christian monasticism had on the one hand used insularity to keep itself free from the world's evil influence, and on the other hand missionised outwards in community service and preaching, helping orphans, widows, and other needy people, sharing its light. Like James it might well have had this text from *Jeremiah* in mind: "'[King Josiah] helped those who were poor and needy, so everything went well for him. That is what it means to know [me]' says Yahweh. 'But you only look for and think about what you can get dishonestly. You are even willing to kill innocent people to get it. You feel free to hurt people and to steal from them'" (NCV: Jr.22:16-7). Our goodness did not make us (as Ridenour said), but it can reveal us. Josiah had known Yahweh; his son Jehoiakim hadn't.

C S Lewis likened the three aspects of morality to a ship within a convoy headed for a destination. Morality keeps itself shipshape (inner life), coordinates with its convoy (social care), and together is sailing for the only good harbour (God), when the *alēthinos* heaven and earth shall be ours to enjoy. James' definition of good religion covers these three aspects too.

Peter and John, members of the Jewish community, had to inform their social leaders that to be true to themselves they had to put God above civil obedience, and that true social care required that resolve. Religion can extend even to a mindset that opposes formal religions. Lewis called the spirit of the age, religion: "we who defend Christianity find ourselves constantly opposed not by the irreligion of our hearers but by their real religion. Speak about beauty, truth, and goodness, or about God who is simply the indwelling principle of these three, speak about a great spiritual force pervading all things, a common mind of which we are all parts, a pool of generalised spirituality to which we can all flow, and you will certainly find interest. But the temperature drops as soon as you mention that God has purposes and performs particular actions, does one thing and not another, who is concrete, choosing, commanding, prohibiting, with a determinate character. People become embarrassed or angry. Such a conception seems to them primitive, crude, and even irreverent. The popular 'religion' excludes miracles..." (Lewis 1960:85–adjusted).

Lewis addressed his generation, but ours too is less embarrassed by vague *spirituality*, than by definite *religion*, and shies away from truth. True spirituality is within the harness of religion, yet shines forth into human darkness. Even within postmodernism's truth decay, there are still glimpses of God's image, points of contact. Those who oppose Christianity *for the sake of man*, have from God a sense of man's well-being, though foolishly thinking Christianity, possibly even theism, the problem rather than the solution.

Christians feel the hostility of what Scripture called 'the world', the *kosmos*, sin's mindset opposing Christianity. Taking this use of *kosmos*, and aware that disloyalty to Sinai had been analogous to disloyalty to one's marriage covenant (see Rm.7:4), James castigated Christians disloyal to the Yeshuic Covenant: "You adulterous people, don't you know that friendship with the world means [hostility] against God? Therefore, anyone who chooses to be a friend of the world becomes an enemy of God" (NIV: Jas.4:4).

Aligning with society can mean disaligning from God. It is seductive to treat our society's religion as familiar, world religions as unfamiliar, and mistrust world religions but not secular religion. And many Christians throw Judaism into a trusted religion status, simply because it has younger-sibling status. Some even deem it, or some earlier form of Sinai, as a mother from whom Christianity should learn from and live with as an obedient daughter, rather than Judaism being a wayward sister or half-sister born in AD 70.

We could look at examples of how other religions have persecuted Christians as Christians. Grievously some still do. We could compare examples of Christians persecuting other religionists as other religionists, and construct a list of justifiable and non-justifiable reasons, and accept that true Christians truly have persecuted some unjustly because of their different religions. Along the way we could pick up that many nominal religionists have arguably sinned more than true religionists, and we could belie the humanist secular myth that theism has been a major invoker of wars.[102] We could grade the proneness of each of the major formal theisms along with ambivalent Buddhism, towards unjust persecutions. People is people, and we are prone to persecute those who live behind different fences to us.

We can see from its core documents, that Christianity itself is not a proactive persecutor of other-faith believers, does not seek extension by spatial conquest. It allows people as people, to defend themselves, and yet it is often unfairly and dangerously maligned by Christo-phobic media as malignant. The Christian flag should be held high with humility. High, because it's God given; humbly, because fallible man, to whom it is given, has sinfully raised it in tyranny and bloodshed. It is wantonly blood stained, yet sheds much light into this dark world.

We might conclude that when it comes to the theisms, the big problem is the human itch to turn religion into one's culture and to be xenophobes. This leads to perceiving dissenters as cultural enemies, even dangerous traitors warranting victimisation, possibly in a mindset of being cruel to be kind. Ideally people as people should

---

[102] "According to the Encyclopedia of Wars (Phillips and Axelrod, Facts on File, Dec. 2004) of the 1,763 major conflicts in recorded history, only 123 of them were classified as having been fought over religious differences. That's just under 7% ...and the number of people killed in these conflicts amounts to only 2%". And of the 7% theistically motivated, about 70% have been Islamic, a religion begun in the C7, according to www.movieguide.org/reviews/Religulous.html, which blames atheism and Islam as the real religious militants.

not be squeezed into religions by their families and/or cultures, and should use their hearts and minds to decide whether to align with deity, and if to, how to. Belief should be conviction belief.

One overreaction to inter-theistic disagreement, has been secularism's spin that all are basically the same, for Equality's ideology is to explicitly accept none as truer than others, and thus implicitly imply none to be true—even to the dumbing down of the concept, truth. The poison of subjectivism. Equality affirms its own position as the highest god—while muting the term *God*—and thus opposes God.

Equality's claim that all theisms are equally true, rides on the idea of their similarities—often accepted as positive (benign) but sometimes asserted as negative (malignant). As intended, Equality undermines theisms by squeezing them into one anthropic mould. But "distinctiveness is not less important than similarity; a mouse and an elephant can each be described as a four-footed mammal with a nose, ears, and a tail. We wrong the integrity of Muhammad, Buddha, and Christ, when we reduce them to three holy men who said very much the same" (Ives 48).

They do differ, and assessing their unique selling points makes sense. "When I was an atheist I had to try to persuade myself that most of the human race had always been wrong about the question that mattered to them most; when I became a Christian I was able to take a more liberal view. But, of course, being a Christian does mean thinking that where Christianity differs from the other religions, Christianity is right and they are wrong. As in arithmetic—there is only one right answer to a sum, and all other answers are wrong: but some of the wrong answers are much nearer being right than others" (Lewis 2002:35).

Do they offer salvation? John Wesley held that God doesn't penalise Gentiles for not having access to human evangelism and for therefore not accepting Christ. He held that it was nevertheless biblical to hope that if they live up to the common spiritual light that they have, they will be separate from those around them, having "another spirit; being taught by God, by his inward voice, all the essentials of true religion" (Sanders 250). His position was more of true salvation in spite of local religions. Might they be positive?

With Wesley and Lewis I stand against secular religion that says aloud—lest it offend and since it likes to think that all truth except its is relative—that all formal religions are of equal validly, and mutters under its breath that they are all equally invalid. For God has joined with humanity through a permanent temporal mode, giving us Jesus whose death remains the only key that could and did unlock globally accessible ultimate life throughout human history.

Ultimate salvation comes only by Christ, who created the ultimate religion. But we will now consider whether other world religions carry, even encourage, the salvation message, even if they carry mixed messages. Christian converts can appreciate their preconversion religion: "the white man's religion[103] [is] in many respects...better than the religion of my fathers. However, I have always prayed, and I believe that the Almighty has always protected me" (Barrett 1906:1704-5/2001).

Hinduism

Some suggest that when Europe was shaping the development of Hinduism (the Aryan period around 1500 BC), Indian worship was similar to that of Abraham's background, with a sense of a Most High who was worshipped in simplicity under various descriptions, descriptions which by c.1,000 BC had become names of individual gods.[104] Today there is "a highly politicized antisecular 'syndicated Hinduism' based on the artificial census-derived notion of a 'Hindu majority'" (Smith 435). That is, Hinduism has been reshaped to look like a unified, syndicated religion to which so many millions subscribe, useful for political bloc voting.

In reality, believing Hindus range from pantheistic to polytheistic—some Hindus believe that there are hundreds of millions of gods; some believe that God is all. It is a family of variations around core ideas of reincarnation (transmigration: life flowing through many existences) based on karma (merit/demerit). Figures are elastic, even as Hinduism is polythetic (family variations). Whether or not their parents treated Hinduism as the best way of interpreting life and meaning, and whether or not they really believed it or simply worked their lives

---

[103]   Not that it began among whites!

[104]   Eg Chapman 143.

around it as around a social convention, the assumption is that anyone born to Hindu parents is a Hindu.

Sadly, like Union strike-breakers (a.k.a. *scabs*), those who break ranks are deemed to be traitors to their community. To some Hindu adherents, this deserves forced reversion or death. Atheistic Communistic communities have imprisoned and tortured many Christians because they were Christians: Hindus and Muslims can share the same itch to crucify—death to traitors.[105] This is based on the perception that solidarity in community requires faith-loyalty as an essential gel to keep community body and soul together.

Christianity has suffered from the idea that one's theism should be as one's community (eg Luther's *cuius regio, eius religio*: "whatever your government is, your religion should be").[106] Likewise some Christian networks have had electoral rolls, listing all within a geographical area as Christians. Likewise, many 'Hindus' will have as little regard for deity as many nominal Christians will have. We should not judge a person's spiritual beliefs by the colour of their skin (white, brown, red, whatever), birthplace, parents, or whatever: God looks at the heart and some hearts look at him. But those factors can affect influence on us as identity, and beyond doubt many millions are basically within some form of Hinduism as an identity marker. Is that bad?

Hinduism has a spiritual richness from its diversity, but in this sketch we must generalise and leave much out. Formally, it tolerantly holds that "all religions are equal, but [that] Hinduism is a bit more equal than the rest" (Alexander 178). There can be strong desires to get back to the Godhead, the idea of a universal identity, a spiritual ocean from which all droplets seek to leave the traumas of individualism and return. Within this idea, three main aspects of an ultimate Oneness

---

[105]   In practice most Atheistic Communists, Christians, Hindus, and Muslims, as individuals allow others freedom of religion.

[106]   A policy that meant that any local prince could choose their side and his subjects should then fall in line, offering them safety from him and him safety from dissenting princes. It didn't do much for individual conscience within each princedom, and begs the question as to whether on the Day of Pentecost Peter should have targeted Pontius Pilate, instead of bothering with Jerusalem's public.

(Brahman) are personified into gods. Hindus name these as three (*trimurti*): Brahma, Shiva, and Vishnu.

Perhaps the most personable concept is Vishnu as a kindly preserver, deemed to have become human nine times, and with another time to come (ten avatars—descents). Two big heroes, Rama (Rama-Chandra) and Krishna, are said to be his seventh and eighth avatars. Krishna, the hero of the *Bhagavad Gita*, is considered very personal and a god in his own right.

Heroes can make great movies, but what of the inner mentality of Hinduism? Hinduism is traditionally *fatalistic*. It assumes that we cannot stop good and evil happening because of fate, that good and evil leave their mark, and that we will suffer or rejoice in a future reincarnation, according to our fated life in this one. This, it is held, is the law of *karma*, but need not be perpetual.

Perhaps motivated by a defence mechanism, this idea of perpetual recycling (samsara) was gradually modified about the C7 BC, by that of an exit door, *moksha*, whether defined as a way into joy or simply a way out of sorrow (Alexander 189). So eventually one would be released. But what to? It says that we are composed of *atman* (soul), which some say is part of Brahman as streams are part of a lake, and that salvation, *moksha*, is to do with reunion—back to Godhead. Hinduism deems this as a state of peace beyond this life—*moksha*, "liberation from space and time" (Anderson 58). Some say that *moksha* is liberation from reincarnations to the real self, blessed freedom from everything that is individual to us.

Some Hindus hold that this current life—an idea fed back from Hinduism's child, Buddhism—is illusion (maya), that individual selfhood does not really exist at this level, this current subreality. The Vedas' position of *we individuals and Brahman*, has shifted to monism's *you are me and we are Brahman* (Alexander 183). The Sanskrit expression *tat tvam asi* (that you [singular] are), from the *Chandogya Upanishad*, is a central belief expressing reality: *you really are*.

But this is taken to deny any real existence outside of one reality: the atman of man and of the universe are one: 'atman = Brahman'. Is *moksha* when the illusion called *you* no longer exists? "It is not correct to say that the dewdrop slips into the Shining Sea; it is nearer to the truth to speak of the Shining Sea invading the dewdrop. There is no sense of loss but of infinite expansion when, 'foregoing self, the Universe grows I'" (Christmas Humphreys: Chapman 145): sponges plunged into the bath might be a fair illustration, or a lava lamp. However, "a condition in which I shall cease to think, to feel as an individual or, indeed to be an individual, is a condition in which I shall cease to be at all" (C E M Joad: Chapman 145). Ethically, the idea of people being illusions questions whether it is really sin to kill an illusion.

Hinduism says that there are three main ways for people to be *liberated* from personal identity. *Moksha* was added to the original ideas of *pleasure, power,* and *principle,* perhaps as a cry from the human heart that the cycle of rebirth (*samsara*) must have a way out to join with the creator. These three ways are *jnana marga* (meditation), *karma marga* (religious rites), and *bhakti marga* (devotion to a deity). We might disagree with the theory of reincarnation, and associated ideas such as payback/reward according to right/wrong moral choices made in a previous incarnation, but is there not something right in the desire to seek beyond the world? Is there not a strand of real love towards some strand of deity?

In the Bhagavad Gita, "Krishna...teaches a path that combines...karma marga...jnana marga...and bhakti marga. Devotion is the culmination, for even after one has mastered well duty and wisdom, one 'attains the highest devotion to me,' says Krishna to his disciple Arjuna, because 'I love you well' (18.54,64)" (Smith 831). Indeed, salvation through love/ devotion is the most popular path. In a sense it is a plunging into the deific through desire for it, and thus becoming one with it. This picks up on the idea of the impersonal reality manifesting itself through personal forms, and thus allowing a personal response.

"The Bhagavad Gita speaks of Arjuna seeing in Krishna countless visions of wonder, as Krishna asserts that 'only by [devotion] can you see me and know me and come to me'...salvation is...a gift from God" (Alexander 192). Such devotion involves ritualism and worship through idols that represent some aspects of God. Some believe that lover and beloved continue united as two, rather than the worshipper losing their individual status. Does Hinduism sense the Image of God (Gen.1:27) and its desire to love God? Has it some faint glow?

Islam

The oneness of God

For a realistic pulse on Islam and Muslims, readers can do worse than looking into www.opendoors.org, and Ed Husain's *The Islamist*.[107] As said, my aim isn't to uncover the darker side of any adherents, but to highlight any glimmers of light. Muslims must hold that Muhammad was Allah's supreme prophet, the prophet, but must Christians hold the exact opposite? Is it just possible that God, *Allah* in Arabic, spoke to Muhammad indirectly through local Christians and Judaists, and directly? If deific revelation, did Muhammad over-zealously frame it into supreme terms, in order to best win over his people from the follies of polytheism? That is, did he over-extend any prophetic brief, to help to overthrow polytheism?[108] It is possible to paint him as a prophet inspired by Christian and Judaic witness, who spoke sincerely yet too totalitarianly, unintentionally doing us a disfavour.

About two millennia earlier, the Egyptian pharaoh, Akhenaten (a.k.a. Amenhotep 4), father of Pharaoh Tutankhamen, had attempted a somewhat similar yet unsuccessful coup over polytheism. His was perhaps a genuine attempt to express a profound revelation of monotheism, exalting the sun god (Aten) to chief position, then removing all other deities as accretions. A surviving hymn goes... "Your dawning is beautiful in the horizon of heaven / O living Aten, Beginning of Life / When you rise in the eastern horizon of heaven / you

---

[107] Husain's journey was from moderate Islam (*jnana?*), to militant Islam (*karma?*), to devotional Islam (*bhakti?*). The percentage given at the presentation of militant Islam was, I suspect, wildly downgraded, though I accept that militant Islam, often undercover and including Hizb ut-Tahrir, is the small minority. "...the Hizb's leadership issued a condemnation of what had happened, saying it was a non-violent party. This myth was swallowed by investigators who never really understood the seriousness of the Hizb's form of violence. Even today, a primary reason for Western failure in the War on Terror is this same cause: an innate inability to understand the Islamic psyche" (*The Islamist*, 2007:153). For his part Husain's fascinating book ironically showed his inability to understand the Christian psyche (and doctrines), but at least I think he tried.

[108] Polytheism is wrong, but pragmatically even Sinai used some of its language as it slowly prepared the way for philosophic monotheism.

fill every land with your beauty / for you are beautiful, great, glittering, high over the earth / your rays, they encompass the lands / even all you have made / You are Ra, and you have carried them all away captive / You bind them by your love / Though you are from afar, your rays are on earth / Though you are on high, your footprints are the day." A hymn can be a love song; a zealot can be a lover.

Even before Jesus, many Gentiles had preferred Ethnic-Israel's monotheism to their own polytheism, some becoming either proselytises or God-fearers. Even before Muhammad, Mecca had martyrs to monotheism. However, he was a powerful enforcer who had grasped the basic revelation, and claimed prophethood through miracles, victories, and supernatural writing. Some deny his claim.

For instance, a sympathetic Syrian Christian, Chawkat Moucarry, argued that Muhammad's credentials to prophethood fail on a few counts. One, even if Islamic miracles were proved, miracles can be counterfeited. Two, initial military success no more proves one's religion, than the military dominance of ancient superpowers proved their religions (eg Egypt, Rome). Three, granting at least a high degree of internal coherence to the Qur'an,[109] its external coherence to the Bible (which it claims alignment to) is at best very limited.

Moucarry allowed for some overlap between the Bible and the Qur'an, and in line with Muslim scholars,[110] effectively argued that the biblical text has not been corrupted, that it makes internal and external sense, and that it boils down to *either* the Bible *or* the Qur'an. The Bible does not affirm the Qur'an, but if the Qur'an affirms the Bible, then for all its merit the Qur'an is at best a secondary witness to the primary. Likewise, any papal claim of equal (or higher) weight with the Bible it affirms, or primary school student's claim to equality with the professor they affirm, is possibly specious and at best secondary, one-way traffic. Mutual affirmation of parity is missing.

Yet even if the Qur'an does not supersede the Bible, nor Muhammad supersede Jesus, at the level of subservient witnesses can they not truly bless? Christianity affirms *ash-hadu an-la ilaha illa-llah* (I bear

---

109   See www.answering-islam.org/Quran/Contra

110   Such as Baqillani (c50-1013), Avicenna (980-1037), Ghazali (1058-1111), Fakhr-ul-Din al-Razi (114c-1209), and Muhammad ʿAbduh (1849-1905).

---

witness that there is no god but God), but not *wa ash-hadu anna muhammadan rasulu-llah* (and I bear witness that Muhammad is the Messenger of God). Moucarry sided with C14 Islamist Ibn Taymiyya, to say that to accept Muhammad to have been a prophet requires accepting him to be the global prophet and the Qur'an as God's word supreme (Moucarry 265). But surely this conclusion is insecure if prophets can be fallible.

Could not a prophet hear partially from God, then offer their best guess? The prophet John didn't know that the Lamb had to die to redeem. And interestingly Agabus, a NT prophet mentioned twice in Scripture (Ac.11:28; 21:10-1), wasn't quoted the first time, and the second time was quoted but his words were non-directional and personal prophecy to Paul: Paul rightly ignored their accurate warning. God doesn't always call us to avoid danger. Agabus had great insights into God and how we should live, but had he chosen to write a church guidebook, the church would have been right to discount it as no doubt useful in parts, as many Christian writings have been, but ultimately not canonical text for all. Thus can prophets be.

Christians may rejoice in the hope that Muhammad loved Allah—even though they grieve both that he never made the jump from Sinaitic *monopersonal* monotheism to Golgothic *tripersonal* monotheism, and that he created Islam's consequent one-way door relationship with Christianity. He rightly rejected the idea of tritheism, but I wish that trinitarianism had been clear to him. He now sees; may he be blessed. Judaism and Islam both affirm the oneness of God; Christianity supersedes their insight—God is the one eternal uncreated *society*. Thus God's societal sense of morality, is our sense of morality howbeit infected by sin—humanity is Imago Dei.

Submission to God

The terms *Islam* and *Muslim*, speak of submission to Allah. Whatever methods are associated to this, in itself it is a good theme, and we may wonder how many Christians are strongly submitted to Jesus as lord under God (Php.2:11). Too often affluence and ease water down full obedience. Aleksandr Solzhenitsyn noted that these comforts make us vulnerable.

Through regular communal rituals, Islam has sought to keep Muslims mindful of God throughout the days and years. The residual result of such reinforcement is—as with any theist left to their own devices—only apparent if one is on their own. Put another way, there could be a big dropout between communal Muslims and individual Muslims. Beyond all pretences God sees what each of us really follows. It's said that we only have what we can keep under pressure. Let's add that we only are what we are without pressure.

The rise of Islam makes fascinating reading, and at first "the idea that opponents were given the option of 'Islam or the sword' is false, except in the case of pagan Arab tribes" (Alexander 316). Sadly, Islam carries the idea that any under its lordship who would depart are traitors at heart, and much force and fear is used to prevent desertion and to keep community cohesion: the perceived needs of the many outweigh the needs of the few, or the one. In short, its entrance door invites all—speak but the words—but its only official exit door is death. Like marriage, it's literally till death do us part,[111] so is difficult to leave alive due to its concerns for social cohesion.

What is its promise to its people? As regards a final state, "for the unbeliever we have prepared fetters and chains, and a blazing fire. But the righteous shall drink of a cup tempered at the Camphor Fountain, a gushing spring at which the servants of Allah will refresh themselves: they who keep their vows and dread the far-spread terrors of judgment-day; who for love of Allah give sustenance to the poor man, the orphan, and the captive, saying, 'we feed you for Allah's sake only; we seek of you neither recompense nor thanks: for we fear from him a day of anguish and of woe.' Allah will deliver them from the evil of that day and make their countenance shine with joy. He will reward them for their steadfastness with robes of silk and the delights of Paradise. Reclining there upon soft couches, they shall feel neither the scorching heat nor

---

[111]   "While Muslim terrorists take [the Quran's verses of violence] literally, and understand that Islam is incomplete without [lesser?] Jihad, moderates offer little to contradict them—outside of personal opinion. Indeed, what do they have? Speaking of peace and love may win over the ignorant, but when every twelfth verse of Islam's holiest book either speaks to Allah's hatred for non-Muslims or calls for their death, forced conversion, or subjugation, it's little wonder that sympathy for terrorism runs as deeply as it does in the broader community—even if most Muslims prefer not to interpret their personal viewpoint of Islam in this way"
(www.thereligionofpeace.com/pages/quran/violence.aspx).

the biting cold. Trees will spread their shade around them, and fruits will hang in clusters over them...They shall be arrayed in fine green silk and rich brocade, and adorned with bracelets of silver. Their lord will give them a pure beverage to drink. Thus you will be rewarded; your endeavours are gratifying to Allah" (Qur'an 76:4-23). The idea of love for (or at least fear of) God, is worth noting, and the encouragement to help the needy, although it might be felt that if he weren't watching, the poor man might have missed out. But where is loving as God loves?

Love for God

It is right to deem the eternal as most important, yet Islam rejects the doorway of the cross. It claims that since prophets only proclaim, the death of the prophet Jesus ('Isa) would have been pointless, and that either Allah rescued him and let the mob crucify another, or that Jesus fainted on the cross and later revived. The idea of 'Isa doing jihad against Satan that required his death and resurrection, is not accepted. For Islam, salvation is one of individual merit, combined with Allah's mercy and Muhammad's intercessions: God can't be forced. Its five-pillar way to salvation are the *Shahada* (affirmation of monotheism and Muhammad as God's prophet), *Salat* (communal prayer five times a day), *Sawm* (fasting during the daylight hours of the month of Ramadan), *Hajj* (a pilgrimage to Mecca, the holy city), and *Zakat* (giving at least 2½ per cent to the needy). Allah can't be tricked. Islam says that Allah watches how folk live, and at death they are interrogated by two angels (Munkar and Nakir), "who will examine a person's faith and weigh out the good and bad of one's life" (Smith 527).

Submission is one thing, loving God is another. Mainline Islam considers man as worshipper and servant, not family, and that Allah does not wish fellowship with creatures (they are at best created to serve). Paradise is not in terms of fellowship with Allah. The *Hadith* (various collections of what Muhammad might have said and done)[112] says: "O my servants,

---

[112]   Islam has varying hermeneutic keys. For example, some take the Qur'an's verses of violence to override the verses of peace, because the violence texts come after the peace texts; some speak of equal weight and balance. Some take the Hadith to be as canonical as the Qur'an; some separate authentic Hadeeth from later, non-authentic ones, and stress that even the authentic need careful interpretation.

you can neither do me any harm nor can you do me any good" (Sahih Muslim Book 32, Hadith number 6246), and the Qur'an says, "I created the jinn [spirits] and mankind only that they might worship me. I seek no livelihood from them, nor do I ask that they should feed me" (Qur'an 51:56-7; see Ps.50:12-5).[113]

Muslim mystics (sufis) take a warmer approach. They seek to meditate themselves into such fellowship, believing that Allah has a heart to fellowship with man. Should it be intrinsically impossible to reach the Beloved, and has he not given us the option to love him? Sufis exist within both sides of Islam's main succession division, that is, the Sunnis and the Shi'a, though Sunnis are more welcoming. About 90% of Muslims are Sunni, and 10% are Shi'a. Sunnis emphasise community before philosophy, and Shiites emphasise philosophy before community. Their division was based on the question of whether Muslim leadership should be dynastic or non-dynastic. On both sides of that question, a yearning for God exists.

The Bible presents fallen man as still in God's likeness/image (eg Gen.5:2; 9:6), even if that is but a preliminary likeness compared to Jesus as God's *alēthinos* image (2 Cor.4:4), in whose likeness we ought to be (Rm.8:29).[114] Does the Adamic *Imago* account for the search for God, which the Qur'an misses and Sufis follow? Followers of *Sufism* seek God by seeking to wean themselves off worldliness. Some claim to have broken through to Allah. Anderson suggested that much mysticism is seeing God's likeness within, and that some is satanic delusion, yet some is from God (see Anderson 22). Not all agree the methods and results of the Sufis, but is their yearning for deific fellowship mistaken? Are they not a case of Muslims affirming Islam's teachings of submission and accountability, but seeking to touch Allah though he slay them?

---

[113]   Christianity agrees creation cannot harm, benefit, or feed God, but prefers the notion that creation was to share beauty and joy, an act based on the sheer creativity and love of God. On fellowship terms, it notes that God is the eternal society and has made humanity in his likeness.

[114]   Historically, it pans out as all mankind in the *Imago Dei* (God's image) in rough, Christians alone as in the *Imago Christi* (reforming), and ultimately the new humanity in the Imago Dei (fulfilled) as Christ alone will have been.

From a Christian perspective, even if Sufis are closer to God than other Muslims, the message of Level 3 salvation is still for them, as it was for Cornelius, who even spoke with an angel (Ac.10:36-43). The message of salvation extends far beyond the question of living with God after we die. Anderson claimed that he had "never met a Muslim convert who regards...God [as they] previously sought to worship, as a wholly false god; instead, they are filled with wonder and gratitude that they have now been brought to know...God as he really is, [through] Jesus Christ our Lord" (Anderson 110).[115] Likewise Phil Parshall's *The Cross and the Crescent: Understanding the Muslim Heart and Mind*, 2003:27. Islam contains good teachings and a yearning for deific fellowship. Is it a stepping stone to Christ or a rock that crushes? Let the reader reflect.

Buddhism

Let's be briefer with Buddhism. In disquiet towards the passivism of ancient Hinduism towards social sufferings, Buddhism was born, founded around the reflections of Siddhartha Gautama (probably born between 624 and 448 BC). He felt that Hinduism lacked neighbourly care. He probably gave up an affluent lifestyle—perhaps wine, women, and song—to seek for the meaning of life for himself and for others: a seeking heart, a servant heart?

Buddhism carries the chief idea of enlightenment. Indeed, its founder is called The Buddha (The Enlightened One). After decades of affluence,

---

[115]   This could be based on later philosophical reflection of the question not necessarily asked by all converts from Islam. For instance, Mosab Hassan Yousef, contrasted (in polytheistic terms) "the god of the Qur'an" as inspiring terrorism by converting the moderates (Yousef 12), to "a god who would help me save others" (248). Since he also spoke of "the one true god" (258), his polytheistic language (surprisingly common between those who agree that there is only one god, God) probably means *concepts* of God, not contrasting *gods*. That he never went overboard to compare the Islamic and the Christian concepts of God, suggests to me that he was not following J N D Anderson's point of common ground. We can *contrast* between an apple and an orange, yet *compare* them as fruit. Yousef might have argued that the contrast is between poisonous and beneficial fruit, though he also praised his father ("the beautiful [yet blind] side of Islam", 105), a religious founder member of Hamas, as similar in some good ways to Jesus, so implying some commonality.

followed by almost a decade of asceticism, his rethink led him to reject either theism, or at least the traditional priestly theism of his day. Some say he was an *atheist*, the same term used by many ancient Romans against Christians, because Christians rejected the idea of many gods. Was he merely rejecting a too easy attempt to buy into heaven *via* priests instead of by heart?

Gautama's schema (the Four Noble Truths) was that man's suffering (*dukkha*) was caused by intense desire (*tanha*)—for example gold, glory, and girls—arising out of the will to live and to possess. Therefore, he reasoned, the way out of suffering was the way out of our strong desire to live and to own. It does not mean to be without them, but it does mean to be without a craving for them: avoiding self-denial and self-indulgence was the Middle Path. It resulted in a passionless peace called *Nirvana*. "Godliness with contentment is great gain" (1 Tm.6:6). Any who achieved *Nirvana*, became an enlightened one (a buddha), having achieved Nirvana through working themself out of the cycle of reincarnation. (Zen-Buddhism, began about C6 AD, aims at concentrated meditation and feeling in order to attain enlightenment—*satori*—here and now.)

That 'way out' (exodus) is often called the Eightfold Path. These eight ingredients for proper living may be categorised as three strands: morality (no killing/stealing/lying/abusive sex/intoxicants), meditation (eg breath control and dismissing mental interruptions), and wisdom (maturing in spiritual insight). To improve their next incarnation, common folk should simply be good. Those on the next level up, monks and nuns, should renounce family ties and material goods, and live a simple, contemplative life. This could vary from living alone in a forest to living in a monastery and each morning begging food from the locals, an act to benefit the monk/nun with food, and the giver with good works leading towards better reincarnations.

Of the main divisions, Theravada and Mahayana, the former demands a more severe life towards buddhahood without aid from temples and deity, while the latter has arguably a bigger vision of deity and of helping others. Mahayanans give greater weight than Theravadins do to compassion, though they somewhat offset this by reckoning human reality to be less real than Theravadins suggest. Both divisions are effectively on a spiritual quest, unhappy with the merely secular life. This beyondness is a central tenet of Christianity, and sometimes put in terms of christlikeness. Some Buddhists believe that nothing that is uniquely 'us' ultimately exists, while others hold that individual consciousness ultimately exists, though dependent on a higher reality—the higher affirms the lower.

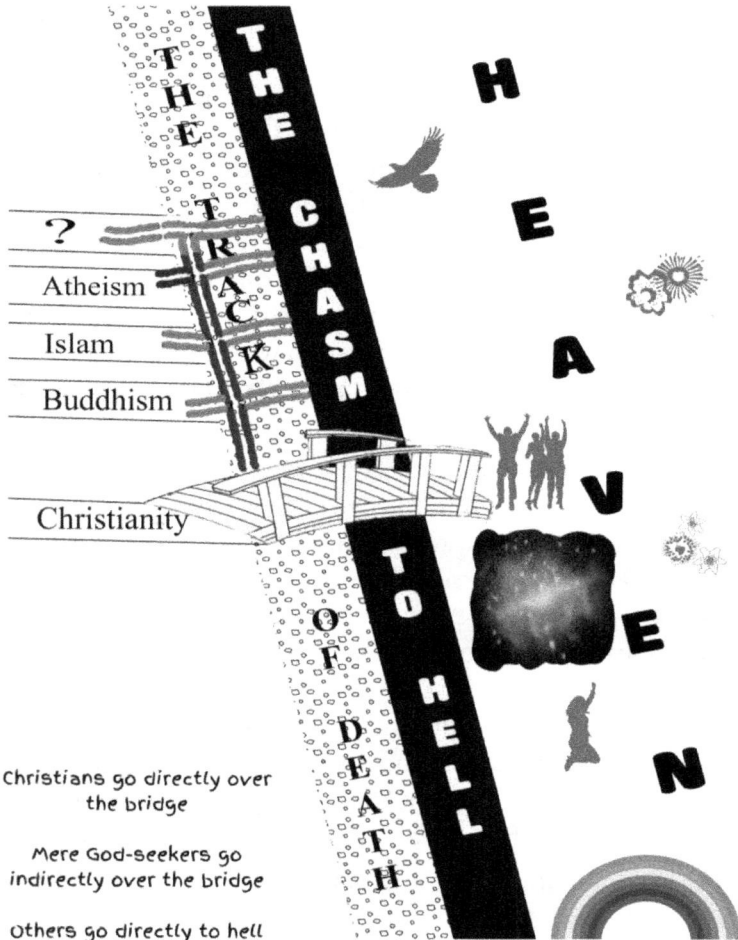

?

Atheism

Islam

Buddhism

Christianity

Christians go directly over the bridge

Mere God-seekers go indirectly over the bridge

Others go directly to hell

To summarise a bit of this, I'd say that God delivered Ethnic-Israel from oppressive slavery into a religious community that, if loyal, would grow in a relational knowledge of him, enjoying border security and abundance within. This is the kind of life he wishes for all, but he has now gone even into the very heart. Whereas members of Ethnic-Israel could at best know him as a neighbour, the gospel allows us to know him as a resident. He has internalised himself, in a sense incarnated himself, in all who have welcomed the vision of the cross. Whereas Ethnic-Israel had tokens of himself among them—a temple, a monarch, prophets, etc—these elements are within each Yeshuic believer.

Indeed the temple once invited believers to seek forgiveness, but he who delivered us from slavery to sin has made the once and for all payment—cancelling the debt of sin—a once and for all act that has broken our inherent link to its power. The blood on Sinai's temple altar is dry. Today's temple is of joyful praise and gratitude as we, the temples, move through life. In short, the Good News once offered to so few, has now a new dynamic level and is offered to all, and those entering this level of kingdom do so in a much deeper way. They are also given a mission and God's help to do it. The spirit has now been unleashed in new covenant dimension.

Other world religions either pick up or transmit eternal light, but are not roads to God: the true evangel came with Christ and is limited to Christ, the Way, the Exodus. But are there not at least signs that some adherents within these religions yearn for God, and that the religions are shaped by that desire—redemption Level 1? Must God ignore all who seek by faulty roads? Might he not at least touch base with them at heart level? Have they searched for one who didn't search for them? Might some of their teachings not have developed through earlier likeminded people yearning to touch God, however much conflicting and confusing teachings might have developed alongside? Jesus spoke of lookalike weeds, planted by the enemy to tempt the lord's servants to damage the wheat (Mt.13:27-8). But are world religions not fields of wheat and weeds, tares and truth? But let's move to an area that evangelism can't touch—prebirth and infancy.

Chapter 7   Death in Prebirth and Infancy

General Infancy Damnation?

Don Carson was not happy with John Sanders presuppositional case for inclusivism, and rightly so, for it lacked the distinction between immediate life and ultimate life. Yet Carson saw the target of inclusivism, not the target of inexclusivism.[116] I think that through the prism of latter idea we can the better consider the ultimate fate of even the unborn. My short analysis of Carson's attack on inclusivism:

- On Tts.2:11, I agree with Carson that Paul didn't mean global throughout history and peoples. I disagree with Carson/Sanders that it was about ultimate salvation. (Carson 1996:288)
- On Jhn.14:6/Ac.4:12, I agree with Carson that we do need to know the saviour to know salvation. I disagree with Carson/Sanders that it was about ultimate salvation. (304)
- On Rm.10:9-10, I agree with Carson that the positive that all who do thus will gain, prefers the negative that all that don't *will* lose. I disagree with Carson/Sanders that salvation here is ultimate/ontological, instead of immediate/epistemological. (312-3)
- I somewhat agree with Carson that inclusivists underplay the object of faith. I disagree with Carson that they necessarily do so. They can hold that while immediate salvation totally demands faith in Jesus as its object, ultimate salvation totally demands faith in God as its object. (296)

Sanders ended with a note on this theme: "the thorny issue of the salvation and damnation of...infants who die [lacks] consensus. Serious theological reflection is yet needed on this topic" (305). It raises deep hamartiological, soteriological, and ethical, questions. Any tiny hand that rises to answer, after so many giants have spoken, must be timorous—mine quakes. Intellectually I am far below an Augustine, an Aquinas, a John Calvin, a John Wesley. A quirky man with a quirky

---

[116]   I coin this term to better define issues. As an inclusivist Sanders nevertheless could contrast a broader salvation to a more limited one. Having noted that the evangelical subculture tends to unhelpfully limit 'save/salvation' to "eternal life beyond the grave", he went on to say that Cornelius "was 'saved' in [this] sense before Peter arrived and...received salvation in its fullness when he heard about Jesus" (Sanders 66): a *sensus plenior* position.

suggestion of a different way, which may be a cul-de-sac. I offer my folly. If demolishing it, may you become wiser in construction; if discounting my cul-de-sac, may you focus better on the highway. But if my way is at least a snickelway to the main road, I am content. Let me first review four heavyweight options on the table.

In the early centuries within a persecuting world, this issue probably had different replies, depending on which church a person attended. Churches didn't really have the luxury of conferencing together, and letters from those with high credibility—like peripatetic and/or secretarial leaders—functioned to share and shape thinking. The Bible has the data, but how should we interpret it? Local churches would listen/read and discuss.

An early idea developed of global infancy damnation. It had a number of ideas mixed in, such as the ultimate damnation of all outside the church, forgiveness of sins as essential for ultimate salvation, and forgiveness only coming through Christian baptism (sacramentalism).[117] It was an enemy to the general idea of globally accessible ultimate salvation, such as Justin Martyr and Irenaeus taught, but was a friend to sacramentalism that deemed water-baptism as salvifically essential. The idea formed that all who die in infancy are damned (whether just from heaven or to hell) except those water-baptised as infants. The East prefers immersion for all, but the Roman West reduced this to sprinkling—gentler on infants, and what's good enough for infants must be good enough for adult converts.

This theory of damnation began from a core idea voiced in the C3 by Origen and Cyprian of Carthage, put in Latin as *extra ecclesiam nulla salus*—that outside the church there was no salvation.[118] Somewhat similarly Augustine wrote that "no one has God for a father, who does not have the church, that is the one visible catholic church, for a mother" (Berkhof 231). Perhaps its most primitive meaning was simply that those who broke away from the church lost their salvation, if they ever had had it—traitors, rebels. The doctrine would later be used by

---

[117]   A similar idea has been that the church and only the church spiritually marries people—a rite carrying grace.

[118]   Its roots in fact go back at least to Ignatius of Antioch (Philadelphians 3:2), Irenaeus & some others. If they meant immediate life I'd agree with them.

Roman Catholics to deny that Protestants had Christ, and by Protestants to deny that Roman Catholics had Christ.[119]

I fear putting too much weight (or too little) on the church. As regards the so-called visible what-you-see church, there is some truth in the idea that there are many sheep without, and many wolves within. It is the lord of the church who is our ark of salvation in the deep waters of this life. Almost inevitably *extra ecclesiam nulla salus* led to the idea that if infants cannot enter the mystic church, they couldn't enter heaven. *Extra ecclesiam* combined with another early core idea of entry into the church being the rite of baptism—a potent mix.[120]

If heaven is only through the church, and church is only through water-baptism, then of course unbaptised infants must ultimately miss out heaven. But as Hans Küng argued, *extra ecclesiam* is too misleading to keep, yet since it's become an old guest its best graciously sidelined into disuse in favour of the positive formula, "salvation inside the church" (Küng 317)—*salus intra ecclesiam*. I agree. But what about water-baptism?

At this point, it's enough to say that many traditionally think that water-baptism for infants and physically/mentally infirm people, generally procures rather than postdates conversion. This is coupled with the idea that its waters wash the baptised's sins away, at least from God's records: washing can certainly picture conversion. In earlier days, since biblically water-baptism is indeed a one-off event, water-baptism was thought to be best left until one's death bed, so that all their sins were washed away.

---

[119]   Perhaps the idea of limiting the word *Church* to denominations sprang from this doctrine, resulting in many conflicting *Churches*. There is only one catholic Church, messiah's family subsequent to his cross, expressed through many local churches and denominations. Brand names such as *The Church of the Nazarene* have secular justification, lack biblical justification, and advocate heresy by their very branding, muddled ecclesiology that requires repentance and repudiation. Ecumenicism has some biblical justification—all in Christ are in one church.

[120]   Theologically there is a profound difference between saying that by a rite a child has been welcomed into *the* church, and welcomed into a particular local church. A canine welcomed into a church has not been made a Christian.

Mulling over it, Augustine eventually sided with the newer idea, that never knowing when death will knock at our door, it's best to get water-baptism's benefit from birth. And since the Gospels show that deific healing didn't always come through the individuals' faith, let parental faith save their infants spiritually. The idea of proxy-faith even extended (as it does in Mormonism) to water-baptism/sprinkling—as essential for ultimate life—being performed by others on the behalf of some who had died in infancy or outside the faith.[121]

The idea of baptising babies is often called *baptismal-regeneration*. Reflecting on the fate of those who missed out, "Augustine has the distinction of being the first theologian to teach positively the damnation of all unbaptized infants", though to lesser suffering than had they committed sins (Sanders 291-2). After all, if we are born, indeed conceived, with a sinful, fallen, infection, would it be fair to let us contaminate heaven, even if we had died too young to show the symptoms? Do not the blemished form hell's leper colony? Also, if we somehow colluded 'in Adam' aeons before being born, so sinned damnably before conception, then God rightly condemns people who die in infancy for their lack of repentance, unless another repents for them invoking the grace of water-baptism.

Pelagius raised his hands in horror: No, God wouldn't consign anyone to hell without them having had a chance to repent. He was widely rejected as having rejected water-baptism as essential for salvation. Many hold a midway alternative known as Limbo, a popular unofficial modifier of Augustinianism. Both Augustine and Pelagius[122] (with some support from Ambrose) made logical conclusions—granting certain premises.

Those who hold that mortal individuals must repent of Adam's sin, and/or that all born to Adam have been infected with an inextirpable

---

[121]   1 Cor.15:29 is unclear, the more reason never to base a doctrine—especially a major one—on one text. There were early teachers (eg Chrysostom) who suggested that it was shorthand for non-proxy baptism. Did it refer in some sense to our preconversion spiritual deadness (Col.2:13) symbolised by water-baptism as dying to that deadness and rising to life? See Garland 16416-35/28028.

[122]   A man perhaps unjustly condemned, whose real position might remain unknown.

sin bias which bans them from heaven, and can only be washed away through a water-baptism sacrament, will have some sympathy for Augustine's stern position.

Yet the control beliefs in Roman Catholicism, that each damned person is self-damned by rejecting grace, and that all have sufficient grace to choose their ultimate destiny, made way for Hincmar of Rheims, about 400 years later, to throw into the equation, all who *would have wished*[123] to have been water-baptised. So, any pagan infant who died but who would have wished water-baptism, would be accounted by God as water-baptised though not physically so. In Catholicism, a modified Augustinianism is dominant, but without espousing any, Rome sensibly allows a range of conflicting ideas.

You may choose to throw out sacramentalism and throw in Calvinism. Calvin probably held—and in this regard infant water-'baptism' being incidental[124]—that some who died in infancy were among God's elect, therefore heaven-bound and sovereignly regenerated out of sinful nature, and others sovereignly reprobate (justly damned in sin). Yahweh gives and Yahweh takes, praise him.

Some elect for a modified Calvinism, buying into Zwingli's sweeter assurance that all children who are born to the elect and die in or before infancy, will have been elected (Synod of Dort, 1.17). If they are, is it simply because they have had at least one Christian parent?[125] Is this

---

[123] I think he meant what I call, faith-welcome. We may call this a predilection towards God. I have come to this idea independently of Hincmar.

[124] He was a pedobaptist, convinced that physical circumcision had been a rite of welcome into Sinai (Ruth was never circumcised!), and that rather than being a pattern of faith circumcision it had been a pattern of Yeshuic welcome into the church, planting a seed of faith to flower into Christian life. He believed that entering Sinai was entering the church—regeneration—rather than seeing that regeneration and the church post-dated the cross (Calvin 4.16.4). He disliked credobaptists, holding the idea that the prophesied 'seed' of Abraham included all children of Ethnic Israel and Christians—continuation but with different entrance ceremonies.

[125] Dort, IMO, mishandled its three proof texts here, *viz* Gen.17:7; Ac.2:39; 1 Cor.7:14. Gen. was about earthly, not heavenly, life; Ac. simply spoke of a continuing offer (not guarantee) of heavenly life; 1 Cor. declared both children

spiritual nepotism? Is everyone born to elect parents, elected if they die in infancy, but perhaps not elected if they live even seconds into rebellious years? Calvinism generally takes the next position.

Infancy Universalism at Death?

Universalism is the attractive idea that all sinful rational-spiritual creatures will become saints. Brian Doerksen's *Come, Now Is the Time to Worship* (1998), sells this idea.[126] Perhaps most Christians hold a limited form for infants, as Zwingli was tempted to do. For well over a thousand years, most church parents knew that by accepting water-baptism, they and their family were ultimately safe in the boat, though all others, sadly, would either drown or be marooned: fiducial faith in the church.

That was clear, until Gottfried Leibniz (1646–1716) rocked the boat: that 'OK for us' idea undermined God's goodness, he said. Let God damn only the unrepentant who have sinned, yet infants can't sin so shouldn't be damned. This wasn't a new deal—remember Pelagius? But Leibniz' packaging sold it to the European market. Neither water-baptism nor Calvinist election might seem relevant in this thinking: infants are infants of whatever stock and condition and oughtn't be denied salvation to heaven.

Arminianist John Wesley came to more or less hold to this infant universalism. Though if infants don't choose, does it not conflict with Arminianism's control belief of individual faith-choice? Does Arminianism only kick in with the age of accountability, a faith-choice only needed for repentant sinners?

Some Calvinists heed Zwingli's hunch, that all who die in infancy were in fact among the elect. Mightn't their death in infancy prove God's especial love for them, by sovereignly removing them from the anguish of facing a sinful world? Moreover, it might seem, they have

---

and unbelieving spouses equally holy and equally not guaranteed heavenly life Did Dort wish to prove what it wished to believe?

[126]   A polydirectional song with polytheism and soft unitarianism, it contrasts lesser and greater treasure: after death all will (in a positive sense) bow the knee, fine, but "still those who gladly choose...now" receive the "greatest treasure". *Now*, as presumably better but not imperative for gaining God's treasure.

never rejected God, so have no need for repentance. One way or another, Calvinism can nicely deal with infancy death: God elects some people for ultimate life; of these, some he transfers to heaven from their human infancy, either all or some who die in infancy; the rest he transfers from their more mature years. It seems to me to be a fairly logical, even if a little heartless, system.

For Calvinism, a general question of dual election remains. Namely, does God select some to damn (or even leave damned), when those he elects to save are all as totally depraved at ensoulment,[127] with no distinguishing characteristics? Is salvation a lucky dip? Also, does God's sovereignty determine which infants will die through the malice of others? Did the psalmist's itch to bash babies to death (perfectly understandable as a verbal letting off of steam) indicate Yahweh's especial blessing of Babylonian infants?

As regards human preborn and infants, this fuzzy kind of universalism appears to be established thinking in the West, but is it mainly held for sentimental reasons (Sanders 303)? Luther asked that if the pope was able to release souls from purgatory, why not release all for sheer benevolence, rather than charge for the privilege (Thesis 82). A similar question is raised about God's unopposable election to life—if all are equal with absolutely no spiritual difference, why not equally save all if he saves any?

---

[127] There are four main ideas about ensoulment. Origenism suggests that God had created every soul before he created Adam, and since Adam has been putting these bodiless souls into bodies as bodies become available. Creationism holds that as each body is procreated, God creates its soul. Reincarnationism—not a Christian option—suggests that souls are filaments of God, perhaps in an endless cycle of leaving and rejoining him, like Earth's water supply is a unity but molecules go through cycles, cloud, rain, river, ocean, and cloud. A constant cycle of contamination and decontamination. Traducianism holds that souls are—as the Greek term *psychē* is handy for—psychological packages making the essential you and me. Our personalities reflect our human progenitors: procreation *creates souls*. Tertullian argued *tradux animae, tradux peccati*: that is, the propagation of the soul involves the propagation of sin—imperfect personalities? That is, we are conceived with sin, a personality disorder hardwired in, and as Augustine put it, *non posse non peccare et mori* (unable neither to sin nor not to die—we cannot escape sin and death).

In God's Lap?

From almost all infants damned, to all saved, in one fell swoop. Most have forgotten that most Christian generations thought the opposite to be axiomatic! Some simply say it's a blessed mystery: it seems that God will be damned if he damns and damned if he doesn't, but he is Goodness, so his dealings must be comprehensively good—he alone can square the apparent circle, or at least show our geometrical thinking to be faulty.

And what he is as transcendent, he also is as immanent. For instance, he is always good *in* time and space because he is Goodness *beyond* time and space. Martin Luther threw C9 Hincmar of Rheims at Augustinianism: though best water-baptised, to die as an unbaptised infant is OK, so long as your baptised parent(s) *desired* your water-baptism. Luther's concession still restricted the idea of ultimate life to sacramentalism, and he wasn't happy to go beyond this. What he thought about the death of water-unbaptised infants of unbaptised parent(s), I do not know, and perhaps he did not know, but of infants open to water-baptism he held that they could have faith in some mysterious way, sufficient perhaps for his argument that since they could have faith (its creation puzzled him), it was justified to baptise them though they neither spoke nor understood.[128]

Following him the German humanist Philipp Melanchthon—the quiet meadow stream to the wild mountain torrent of his mentor Luther—backtracked, feeling that Hincmar was a step too far, undermining actual water-baptism as being an essential sacrament. If such essential grace flowed through water-baptism, to allow that it could flow without water-baptism—simply an assumed desire for it—opened too wide the door to the possibility that grace didn't need water-baptism as its instrument after all, but simply a core desire to be with God. Is grace bound to a rite? If abounding grace undermined sacramental water-baptism, it would undo an entire soteriology,

---

[128]   He was at least right to consider the possibility of such faith. Sadly in dispute with the Anabaptists, he also coupled reflection on precognitive faith with a noncanonical idea that unless water-baptised we cannot be saved, and used the right idea of infants' faith to bolster the wrong idea of baptising them to ensure their salvation (Bernhard Lohse' *Martin Luther's Theology*, 1999:301).

causing a radical reformation. In short, Lutherans should keep pretty much close to the Augustinian camp.

Most Lutherans formally prefer Luther here, and accept that at a pinch essential grace can be given in extraordinary circumstances, if parents intended water-baptism. But while paying lip service to the idea of baptismal-regeneration as the ordinary means of salvation, they tend to hope that all who die in infancy, even unbaptised, will receive God's blessing of ultimate life (Infant Universalism).

However, it's a hope, not a belief, a midway position. Melanchthon's concern was valid, for "if all (or even most) infants who die are saved, then [water-]baptism must not be necessary for salvation in an ordinary sense, much less in an absolute sense, since most [who die in infancy] die unbaptised" (Sanders 297). In short, logically their blessed hope is death to the idea of water-baptism as ultimate-life-giving.[129] But why cut off your nose to save face? Many Lutherans, if asked about water-baptism being normally needed for infants, would simply say that it's in God's lap, a position of uncertainty and hope, but not of *sola fides*.

Evangelism Before/At/After Death?

Is individual choice/faith (and/or water-baptism) fundamental to ultimate life? Does the early stage of human life preclude individual choice (and/or for some, water-baptism)? Does God neither grant nor withhold ultimate life from anyone, without their consent (and/or being baptised): are heaven and hell not consensual? If the basic answer is yes, then will not all who die in infancy have an immediate or later chance to get right with God? Might it not be that if water-baptism and/or individual choice is essential, that those unevangelised in one life, and/or unbaptised, would have an opportunity to eventually be born again (in the Nicodemean sense) into a Christian household? Alternatively, in another incarnation to hear missionaries and (if essential) to be baptised?

---

[129] If the distinction of immediate and ultimate salvation was factored in, there could be grounds to say that infant baptism at least saved the infant into the church (immediate), and thus ensured heaven (ultimate) even if they lived into sinhood, whereas unbaptised, if dying as infants would gain heaven (ultimate) but would not have the salvation (immediate) of church life, nor of heaven should they live into sinhood.

Heb.9:27 doesn't rule out exceptions to the rule, such as Elijah, and those Christians who will not have died when Jesus returns. It was not intended to cover every base, but to underline Christ's death as relevant to those who experience death. His death "once to take away the sins of many" (NIV: v28; see Is.53:12), offers ultimate life to all retrospectively and prospectively, unlike the Sinaitic cultus life that covered part of humanity for part of human history. Even so, perhaps Heb.9:27 rules out even limited reincarnations.

I see no good reason to ever warrant reincarnation. But even if we totally reject reincarnation, can't we accept that there could be special evangelism by God *at* the point of death, or even special evangelism by God *after* death once the person has entered into mental maturity? Of imaginative interest and countering William Blake's hell-will-marry-heaven universalism, C S Lewis' dream romance, *The Great Divorce,* pictured a wider hope dream, wherein some borderline unredeemed were able, after death, to crystallise into creatures of heaven or creatures of hell, but unable to indefinitely remain on the doorstep of either.

I think Lewis reflected on a kind of purgatory idea, when the inner voice needed to grow loud enough to speak for heaven or for hell, is purified from heaven or from hell. Lewis certainly held that every opportunity would be granted to everyone, and that everyone eventually crystallises for or against God, who will then confirm their ultimate choice eternally.[130] Supporting the idea of conversion after death, from Clement of Alexandria's basic thesis that 1 Pt.3:18-21 (with or without 4:6) speaks of Jesus visiting hell to preach to humans who in Noah's days had perished, some advance a full-blown idea that Jesus always preaches the minute they die, to any human being who hadn't heard the gospel.

Peter was probably perfectly plain to those he wrote to—they shared his culture and talked his talk. Ironically, Peter wrote about Paul being a bit complicated (2 Pt.3:16), but without sharing his cultural background, Peter's bit here leaves us scratching our heads: "even the usually dogmatic Martin Luther [said that he]...still did not know for sure what the apostle meant" (Jobes 236). We've dug deeper than Luther.

---

[130]   His *The Problem of Pain* covers this well.

Clement's idea of merely to those who disobeyed in Noah's days, doesn't explain why Jesus would have selected so limited an audience, and overlooks a lot of lexical data. We should be careful with prior thinking. Even the Apostles' Creed is fallible. It was begun about AD 200. In 390, Rufinus of Aquileia substituted "was buried" with the more graphical "descended into hades"—today some note that the Hebrew *sheol/hadēs* could mean *grave*, and in some cultures, bodies descended into graves. Did Rufinus really intend to unofficially change an official catholic creed? Most overlooked Rufinus until the creed was standardised in 650. At that point, "was buried" and "descended into hades", were assumed to be two distinct apostolic phrases, and both became standard as if there was a *descensus* after the burial (see Grudem 586-94).[131] Even Calvin assumed that it was biblical theology.

Yet the idea that Jesus visited hell is easier to read into Scripture, than to read out of it. Let's consider these Petrine texts another way—and other options exist. Picture demon spirits living on the joke that humanity lived on tsunamis and sin, unable to escape. Then picture Jesus, moved by death from his mortal limitations into the spiritual dimension, proclaiming their joke over, that since his death (visualised by re-enactment baptism), he had been established as lord, not merely another Noahic rescuer from sin into sin. "After his resurrection, Christ proclaimed his victory to the fallen angels in the 'prison' where they were awaiting their final punishment" (Marshall 1992B:272).[132] This would have been a welcome insight to persecuted Christians. The

---

[131]   Grudem 1994 takes on the five primary proof-texts for *descensus* thinking. *Viz*, Ac.2:27; Rm.10:6-7; Eph.4:8-9; 1 Pt.3:18-20; 4:6. Let's remove *descensus* from the Apostles' Creed, and *filioque* from the Niceno-Constantinopolitan Creed.

[132]   D A Carson rejected this idea, but marshalling support Jobes (247-8) explained that Noahic legends were once strong among Gentiles in Asia Minor (Peter's audience) and that a crucial Jewish writing of a story (*1 Enoch*) was seemingly lost between the C2 and C18, without which the church had to struggle to understand Peter. She commended Augustine for coming up with a rival idea to deny postmortem evangelism, but rejected his idea of a pre-incarnate Christ preaching in Noah's days before Noah's sceptics became spirits in bondage, as having being a theory of desperation based on poor Greek and a lack of Peter's background. The Ransom Trilogy (C S Lewis) also worked on the idea that such spirits were imprisoned within earth's bounds.

demons that had kept the *Genesis* cycle of sin were now a defeated foe, their cycle of power broken. There are certainly better ways of interpreting Peter than of picturing Jesus as having preached to human spirits in hell.

Descensus thinking often extends beyond mortal humans of Noah's times (either Mesopotamian or global), to all humans who died beyond Sinai and before Golgotha. It only covers infants by extension. Some suggest that deific preaching is a special grace for those who died mentally unable to personally choose, and assume that mental maturation after death brings such folk to that choice. Other than postmortem evangelism—ideas to cover core ideas of everyone having personal choice and personal choice requiring evangelism—have included the idea that at the point of death the unborn, infants, and the mentally infirm, suddenly have their intellects raised to a point whereby also hearing God direct, they are immediately able to make their choice. I don't believe that any need preaching after death.

Death Ends Existence?

Traditionally the idea that death ends human existence hasn't been widely accepted—as Sarek said, "only the body was in death, Kirk." Whereas traditionally church graveyards posted the idea that only the 'mortal remains' were buried, nowadays they post the idea that actual people are buried: aioniology is a fascinating study, requiring careful wording. Abolitionist John Brown's body, not John Brown, might lie a-mouldering in the grave, yet hopefully his soul is marching on upwards! That's glory. Sometimes bad traditions change; sometimes good ones. The current is not always correct.[133]

Before looking at some texts cited for the main positions above, it is worth noting that while Sanders 1994 gives fair weight to universalism, it gives little weight to annihilationism or conditionalism, which has had an upturn after the C18. What are they? Both offer a logical resolution to the problem above, removing the question of whether upon physical death, unredeemed souls must

---

[133]   On this it is good to read *The Funeral of a Great Myth*, an article by C S Lewis in *Christian Reflections*.

live eternally in some dimension (limbo/hell). By different routes they terminate at the same point.

Annihilationists hold that ensoulment is immortal, and when immortality is removed—as being or after punishment—then what was a nonredeemed person, was removed from existence.

Conditionalists hold that ensoulment is mortal, not immortal. So, any who have lacked (or rejected) a chance to get into heaven, are simply not converted from mortality to immortality by God's gift: by death the 'they' has ceased to exist in any dimension—there is no *them*, but no immortal was annihilated.

Are they akin to IVF methods that have implanted several fertilised eggs to improve pregnancy rates, then have aborted any surplus embryos (ensouled or otherwise) to order? Will God abort excess life which does not fit into his family? Or, to use a nicer picture, if we would put a suffering animal out of its misery, how much more would God end all suffering, one way or the other? Or, preferring passives to actives, neither aborting nor putting out of its misery (annihilationism), simply not extending mortal life into immortality (conditionalism), not allowing people to live and to suffer? The seeds that never germinated are no more; those that did are immortalised fair flowers of paradise, which extend their fragrance ever sweet.

Proof texts include Rm.2:7-8, 1 Cor.15:53, and 1 Tm.6:16. However, though our physicality is mortal, and God alone is immortal in a non-derivative, intrinsic, sense, we shouldn't too quickly assume that these texts deny that we, as distinct from our physicality, are born immortal *in God's image* (derivatively immortal souls). Another debatable factor is defining *aiōnios*—eternal/everlasting/decisive? Conditionalism and annihilationism make for interesting debate, and there are proof texts used against them.

If I have read John Stott aright, though some may claim him as an annihilationist/conditionalist, he "hesitantly...tentatively...[believed] that the ultimate annihilation of the wicked should at least be accepted as a legitimate, biblically founded, alternative to their eternal conscious torment" (Edwards and Stott 319-20).[134] Annihilationists/conditionalists

---

[134] Stott's own position was Inclusivism: "I have never been able to conjure up (as some great Evangelical missionaries have) the appalling vision of the millions

can happily vary as to whether automatically God gives or does not give infants ultimate life—why should he if they haven't accepted him; why shouldn't he if they've haven't rejected him? Yet why intervene, if without intervention they will simply cease to exist as if they had never been?

Some Biblical Texts

Let's look rather at some texts used for the more traditional approaches above for special treatment of human death their infancy.

Some think that 2 Sam.12:23 clearly implies "that [David] would be with his son in the presence of the Lord (sic) forever" (Grudem 501). Besides the bad practice of putting God's name as *Lord*—fuelling Sabellianism[135]—I would question whether David meant heaven as his destination. Is it not more likely that he simply expressed his expectation (justified or not) that whereas he himself, David, would eventually join the other person in death, that person could not join David sooner, so continued praying for healing was futile?

Some think Jesus' talk about young children, means that God has a bias towards them, even fitting them into his eternal kingdom if they die without sinning.[136] This could be influenced by sentimentalism. Does God goo-gah at babies, and put up with the infirm and crotchety? People is people. God cannot be squeezed into our image. Somewhat similarly, some think he has a bias towards the socio-economic poor. God has no biases. Jesus, as a rabbi, showed that he would be as much for the children, as he had been for their mothers, as he had been for their fathers. To enter God's inbreaking kingdom

---

who are not only perishing but will inevitably perish. On the other hand, I am not and cannot be a universalist. Between these extremes I cherish and hope that the majority of the human race will be saved. And I have a solid biblical basis for this belief' (Edwards and Stott 327).

[135] Sabellianism is the thinking of Sabellius that God is one person who manifests himself under three different guises (modes): a father, son, and helper. They who sing, "you alone are God, Jesus", for instance, sing in denial of the father and spirit being separate persons yet deific, so sing with Sabellius. The Logos was *with* deity, not *alone* deity as if defining out the father (Jhn.1:1).

[136] http://s3.amazonaws.com/tgc-documents/journal-issues/12.3_Kvalbein.pdf is a very illuminating 1987 essay by Hans Kvalbein.

---

even adults needed the dependency attitude of their youth. He also used the child-motif to warn against side-tracking new converts from his message. Christians begin as infant believers (1Jhn.2:12?).

Some think that 1 Cor.7:14 guarantees ultimate holiness to children of Christians (page 38). In fact, ① it only guarantees to the unbelieving children, ② what it guarantees to the unbelieving spouses, who ③ aren't guaranteed ultimate life. Some overlook that second bit about spouses, because they automatically squeeze Paul into their existing theology of infant-salvation. Some don't overlook the second bit but assume that spousal salvation is also guaranteed—they overlook the third bit, Paul's express denial of such guarantee.

Paul's meant that in maintaining family unity, any Christian would remain a live-in evangelist to their unbelieving family, giving their family proximity (holiness as 'setting aside') to Christ. You are set aside (*sanctified to sin*) whenever you watch an immoral movie—bad films can corrupt good character (1 Cor.15:3), just as good films can inspire good character. Just as ultimate life wasn't guaranteed to their unbelieving spouses, it wasn't guaranteed to their unbelieving children. Sure, God might give individual spouses and parents assurance that their spouses and children will take his offer of life, but hoisting Paul's text for everyone is just raising the old flag of infant regeneration/family salvation, on the pole of shoddy hermeneutics.

Is water key?

What of water-baptism? It is important not to put biblical weight on inauthentic text, and not to Christianise Sinai. I bypass Mk.16:16 as inauthentic text. I deem Mk.16:9-2 to be non-Markan. Why? Its link with water-baptism/belief/salvation, is unusual and uncharacteristic. Nor does 16:12-3 easily fit with Lk.24:33-5. At best it is one of the possible endings for *Mark*. I would bypass Mk.7:4 too, even though Wesley—perhaps unaware that his text was insecure (see NIV and NKJV)—proof-jumped from the idea that we don't immerse couches, to the idea that water-baptism must include sprinkling or sponging![137]

---

[137]   If the text is Markan, good hermeneutics asks if the semantic range of *baptismos* in that context, carries to talk of Christian baptism: illegitimate

Regarding Jhn.3:5, I've already argued that it isn't Christian baptism (page 99). Some sacramentalists, arguing that water-baptism is for kingdom entrance what physical circumcision was for Sinai entrance, overlook the fact that, though Ethnic-Israel had physical circumcision, so too did various non-covenant peoples. Augustine claimed that it meant both water-baptism and the ultimate kingdom, so in line with his idea—*contra* Pelagius—of all having volitionally sinned in Adam (Rm.5:12), he said that if water-unbaptised people died in infancy or not, they all went straight to hell.

Let us also note that within the Sinai-covenant community, it was never for girls and so never affirmed them ultimate life with Yahweh. It was a community act for the male-line, a token symbolising the community dedicating all their children to Yahweh. And as the individualism of *Ezekiel* underlined, male sinners, all physically circumcised, would *die* for their own ungodliness: godly grandfathers would be spared, ungodly fathers would not, and godly sons would be—three generations of physically circumcised (Ezk.18:4-14).

Ezekiel also picked up that folk could switch sides midgame (33:18-9): Yahweh kept his finger on each pulse. Under mortal skies each Israelite/Judahite would walk under God's smile (life) or frown (death) according to their covenant loyalty, irrespective of ultimate life. No wonder that Paul could say that spiritually physical circumcision didn't cut it with God (Gal.5:6; 6:15)—it never had, it never could. The latter verse dismissed the previous physical distinctions as old creation distinctions no longer significant in the new age long foretold by the prophets. Hence ethnic-Gentile Christians were as much a part of God's Israel without Sinai's trimmings, as were ethnic-Jewish Christians with all the trimmings: all equally in messiah (6:16).

Is water-baptism salvific? "Countless hordes of babies have been baptised without ever coming into living membership of the covenant community of Christ" (David Wright: Themelios 2004:29.2.36).[138] Perhaps as

totality transfer? And even *baptismos* as *sprinkling* does not justify it beyond sprinkling believers.

[138]   The rite of confirmation has sometimes been claimed to justify the idea that infant baptism inoculates folk from infancy up to an age when they may in medical terms get the booster to see them through. *Pace* King Henry 8's *Defence of the Seven Sacraments* (1521), I see no biblical grounds for

much could be said for Sinaitic boys *apropos* Sinai—both rites are externals and neither has gotten anyone into God's covenant kingdoms. A whole raft of cultus practices were set up through Moses to deal with the removal of sins, in themselves allowing people's continuation within the earthly community, but also symbolic of the ultimate and heaven sent sacrifice which would supersede them as the true atonement for ultimate life itself. Sinai circumcision was also a community affirmation that the covenant was limited to them, a way for parents to opt in their sons in token of national vassalage.

Yet some insist that water-baptism is the gospel equivalent to entry into the church, even if only for symbolical membership into the visible church, some added protection preceding Confirmation. Now obviously, babies cannot show us any belief in Christ. And it's easy to think that if we can't see such, such can't exist, and then if we believe belief to be essential, to look elsewhere to see such faith. Paedobaptism is one such theory, but can parental faith give spiritual salvation? Well, if third-party faith can bring deific healing (physical salvation), could third-party faith not bring ultimate healing (ultimate salvation)?[139] If so, might we have babies favoured by parental faith, favoured by ultimate life, but babies not favoured by parental faith, damned for eternity, similar to the idea of baptismal-regeneration in infancy (Augustine)?

But isn't all this theory about ultimate life/damnation, a Jonahic leap into superstition's belly to rescue a sinking ship? Weren't all the true circumcision of the true kingdom, first party believers (Rm.2:29; Php.3:3; Col.2:11)?[140] Some say that in fact the silence in biblical accounts of

---

confirmation. That it can be a significant act of wilful dedication, I happily accept.

[139]   Actually, neither first nor third-party faith brought salvation, merely asked for salvation. Moreover, some examples surely imply first party faith—was the paralytic hosted onto the roof *without* his consent?

[140]   On Col.2:11-2, "Paul was certainly not asserting anything like...[the idea] that the rite of water-baptism 'makes someone a Christian'" (Wright 1986:107). He argued that for Colossian believers, water-baptism was a public step that cut them off from the people of their race (*tou sōmatos tēs sarkos*), we might paraphrase as *their fallen society*, rather than *their fallen nature*. Their water-baptism was a salvific declaration of their pre-existing identity with messiah—

household water-baptisms, assumes that infants were included (eg Ac.16:15,33; 1 Cor.1:16). Similarly, I know the cat is there; I don't see the cat; therefore, the cat is obviously invisible. But *The Four Loves* (C S Lewis) reminded us that we must not predicate invisible cats simply because no cats are visible.

Implicitly Ac.16:32,34 says that all were old enough to understand Paul and to individually rejoice, and 1 Cor.1:15 specifies that this household all got involved, which surely doesn't assume babies. The entire household of Crispus *believed* (Ac.18:8)—would babies *believe*, and would we know it if they did? The only household description that doesn't implicitly rule out babies present is of Lydia's household—why assume it had a baby or so and assume that Luke would have assumed that any babies would count? I invite a family around for the evening. The parents arrange for a babysitter, but come with the older children. Why the babysitter? Because they naturally assumed that the invite excluded such as were too young to be included. Even if all Luke's households had infants, may we not allow him the same leeway in his reportage?

Other than *a priori* reasoning—an arguing from silence—where is the positive scriptural justification for infant water-baptism,[141] indeed for baptismal-regeneration? The first adults Christians believed (and thus were regenerated) before they were water-baptised. So why suppose that water-baptism, which didn't regenerate them, now regenerates babies? Is not the meaning of Ac.2:39 simply that immersion is simply specified for all whom God has called in this age, and doesn't v41 lock

---

visualise the entrance—though it can be a dangerous and decisive public declaration to come out for Christ. Nowadays there are many unbaptised sheep, and many baptised wolves/goats. As about the earliest of Paul's letters— perhaps written in jail in Ephesus in the early 50s to a church founded by his teammate Epaphras—it's extremely unlikely that his audience were baptised in infancy!

[141]   *Infant baptism* (a.k.a. pedobaptism) is a valid term where infants are immersed. However, there is a technical argument that where they are only sprinkled or daubed, the term should be rhantism (sprinkle/daub), not baptism (immerse), so that we should speak in such cases of pedorantism/ paedorhantism/rhantising. For simplicity I use the traditional terms throughout.

the meaning into those who individually received the call?[142] Is not household water-baptism related solely to household *conversion*, as in the case of 18:8? *Acts* shows the pattern of conversion, followed either by water-baptism then spirit-baptism, or followed by spirit-baptism then water-baptism.[143] If we say that spirit-baptism comes after baptism-conversion, how come it can come before? Or if we say that spirit-baptism is conversion, how come Christian water-baptism can come before? Is not the whole *infant-water-baptism* edifice massive wish fulfilment, an ancient theory that seemed to make sense and became a juggernaut taking us for a ride?

For my money, I would need to see both that regeneration requires literal water-baptism, and can be biblically bestowed without a recipient's wishes. Should I throw a bucket of holy water over Richard Dawkins, to bring him kicking and screaming into God's kingdom?[144] If we don't assume that all adults wish God, why assume that all babies do? OK, you might say that we can't consult them but can give them the benefit of the doubt. I ask, is it actually a benefit if they didn't want it, and are we really saying that for the lack of some water, God can't save some babies ultimately? The church may claim to be his hands, but does it presume to bind his hands?

If buying into infant baptism, I would wish to know whether countless hordes of Salvationists have been ultimately damned for following General Booth, for by dying water-unbaptised haven't they died unregenerated? My reading of Scripture is that immersion in the primitive church was raising a flag *after* joining the ranks: "be immersed, every one of you, on the authority of Yeshua the messiah,

---

[142] Peter spoke of prophecy (17) and repentance (38). "In neither case are infants obviously included", Peter's point (39) being that God's new age mercy embraced "the hearers and subsequent generations.. and in addition *all that are far off*"—maybe at that time Peter only had Jews of diaspora in mind, but probably it refers to Gentiles (Is.57:19; Eph.2:13,17): (Marshall 1992A:81-2). Babies need not apply.

[143] Conversion/water-baptism/spirit-baptism: Ac.2:38; 8:12,17; 19:5-6. Conversion/spirit-baptism/water-baptism: 10:45,47.

[144] I don't really concede that the term *holy water* has spiritual reality.

---

with reference to the [prior] forgiveness of your sins" (Ac.2:38).[145] Elsewhere the Greek εις (eg Mt.3:11) could relate immersion to prior repentance—it was not to *gain* repentance. On Mt.3:11 the CEB/ERV/ NCV/NLT are best; the CEV is straddling; the LEB/NABRE/NIV/ NKJV/NRSV are way behind. As said, salvation accounts in *Acts* show belief followed by water-baptism *before spirit-baptism*, sometimes by spirit-baptism *before water-baptism*. Does this not show both water and spirit-baptisms to be consequent and potentially immediately subsequent to conversion—their order and status being secondary?

While any book on ultimate salvation must consider the baptismal-regeneration idea, it gets me that if infant water-baptism is redemptive, it only redeems a small part of the infant population worldwide: God is good, but is God fair, or simply too limited? More could be said from different sides, on this framework. This book is not the place for a definitive rebuttal, merely to critique, to challenge, and to offer its alternate framework. Any theory that is restrictivist, in the sense of denying that ultimate life has always been globally accessible, hits character reference texts that state that God does not wish any to perish, even if he permits them to (1 Tm.2:3-4; 2 Pt.3:9).

---

[145]   One must search long and hard to find a Bible translation that breaks ranks with tradition by rendering *eis* along the lines of subsequence. The ALT speaks of water-baptism "in the name of Jesus Christ, to [or, for; or, because of] [the] forgiveness of sins". And commendably the CJB has the first part as "be immersed on the authority of Yeshua the Messiah". Even better, the ALT opens up the big thought that the immersion might be 'because of' the prior forgiveness of sins.

Chapter 8   Inexclusivism: A Hypothesis

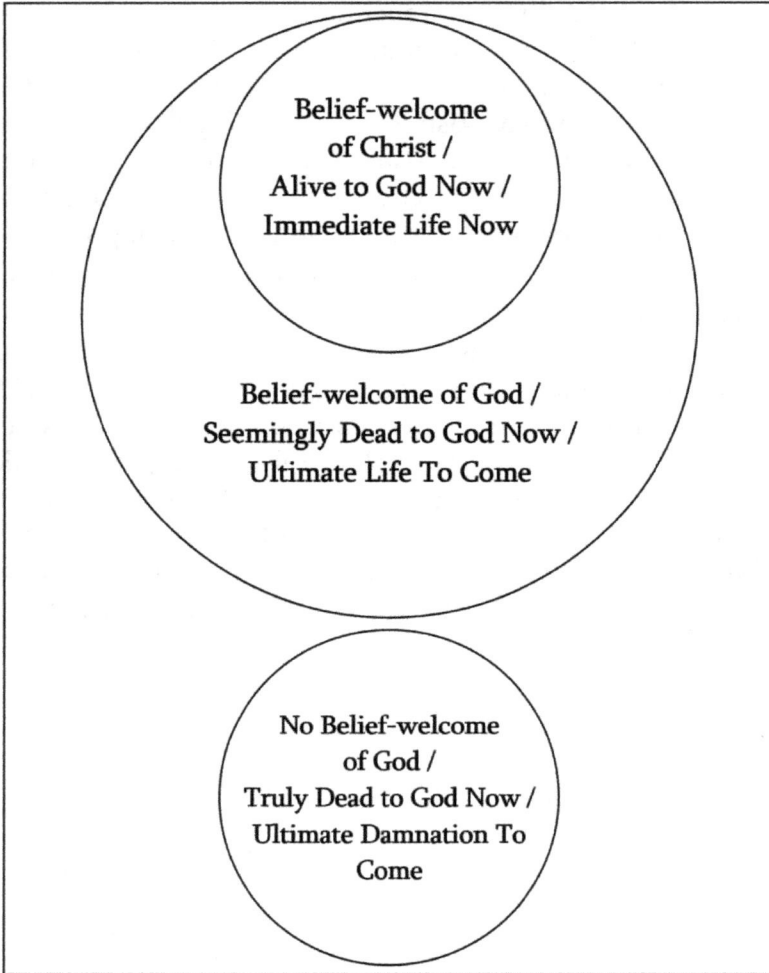

Belief-welcome
of Christ /
Alive to God Now /
Immediate Life Now

Belief-welcome of God /
Seemingly Dead to God Now /
Ultimate Life To Come

No Belief-welcome
of God /
Truly Dead to God Now /
Ultimate Damnation To
Come

Arminianism, Calvinism, and Inexclusivism

Has God desired the ultimate salvation of all, without offering
ultimate salvation of all—them making up their own minds?[146] In fact

---

[146] How free is human free will? If the girl says no, Calvinists tend to say, 'Ah, in
the background (concealed will), he'd always intended not to let her choose
him,' while Arminianists tend to say, 'Ah, in the background (concealed will),
he'd always intended she should, without bully tactics, be free to reject him if

making up our own minds is part of exclusivism; not making up our hearts is part of inclusivism. Let us look at inexclusivism, an inclusivism and exclusivism, a salvation doctrine not based on water-baptism, combining an ultimate access point from each soul's inception, with fundamental personal choice (*fides necessaria est*),[147] and with real personally chosen doors to heaven or to hell. It is restrictivist in the sense that one option restricts the other—the law of noncontradiction—and in one other sense.

On inexclusivism I advise scepticism. Some parts of this package have been tested through millennia; some are Soft, or Radical, Reformationism. To these elements I make some tentative and untested links in the hope that Christians will weigh them up, either finding them biblical or discarding them—either conclusion can be helpful. I write for reflective, not for gullible, believers.

But by inexclusivism I suggest that for everyone the ultimate decision will be clear: to be with or without God, abundant life without end. I do not think we need to postulate a *limbus infantium* where people might ultimately be partly happy that they died before being able to choose hell, and partly unhappy that they died before being able to choose heaven, thus living between heaven and hell—hot feet, cool sky? I suggest that we are conceived towards deity or against him.

---

he wasn't a heart desire.' As an Arminianist lass, you openly yearn for him to marry you (your revealed will), but you wouldn't force him for the world (your concealed will): force kills love. As a Calvinist, I openly yearn for her to marry me (my revealed will), but I jolly well will make sure she won't (my concealed will): my secret aim outweighs my open will. Could the difference be between one target (free will) allowing another target (marriage) to be thwarted, and one target (my reputation) deliberately thwarting another target (marriage)?

[147] I reject the five *Solas* (Onlys)—which the Reformers didn't come up with (though Luther spoke of 'faith alone': Rm.3:28)—partly because they can sound as if they each stand alone, rather than only together as a package deal (as all being needed), and partly because some do disservice to trinitarianism, eg, saying *Christ alone*, discounts the father and the spirit as saviour. I replace them with the five *necessaria*: Scripture is necessary: *Scriptura necessaria est*; grace is necessary: *gratia necessaria est*; faith is necessary: *fides necessaria est*; the cross is necessary: *crux necessaria est*; giving glory to the trinity is necessary: *trinitatem glorificare necessarium est*. I will tackle the question, Necessary for what?

I call my paradigm, inexclusivism, which for its inclusivism side, holds the idea we could call predilectionism or predispositionalism. For simplicity I will sketch it out as I see it, aware that variations could and perhaps should be made. It does qualify—but far less so than does Calvinism—the premise that ultimate life has always been globally available, even if this ultimate life is hidden by the slumber of spiritual sleep, a deadness to deity in mortal life. It combines fixity with fluidity, and exclusivism with inclusivism: it is inexclusivist.

Classical exclusivism teaches the rule that ultimate life is not available to any adults who, by no fault of their own, have always lived outside of a salvation zone, effectively outside the evangel: postcode salvation. Inexclusivism is only exclusivist regarding the biblical theme of immediate salvation, and inclusivist regarding the biblical theme of ultimate life. Fluidity is believed by some to allow individuals to be in constant flux between ultimate life and damnation, irrespective of whether proponents believe that each individual begins with a ticket to heaven or a ticket to hell. Arminianism is particularly open to this criticism. I hold that fluidity only effects our eternal life in mortal years, as our thoughts and interests are subject to ebbs and flows.

Calvinism's Once-Saved-Always-Saved (OSAS) teaching has the value of fixity, based on the premise that the blessed Elect from conception, have tickets for heaven (even if preaching is somehow fundamental, a kind of confirmation), and the damned Elect from conception, have tickets for hell. Calvinism stresses that we joyfully dwell on the idea that God's sovereign grace extends only to those he selects to redeem from the equally damned, and justly dwell on the idea that God's sovereign punishment extends only to those he selects to remain as equally damned—none merit his mercy. Thus, Calvinism goes back to Augustine's reply to Porphyry,[148] of all deserving to die yet grace

---

[148]   This it calls grace. Luther likewise sided with Augustine's theological determinism, indeed had been an Augustinian friar, though his successor Melanchthon eventually accepted the idea of human free freewill: "God draws, but he draws those who are willing". A fun but silly reply is in the Hornet Song: "God does not compel us to go against our will, But he just makes us willing to go". True, I don't physically drag you out of the room, but merely send in the hornets and you willing vacate, but much of life either lacks

rescuing its selection irrespective of positive or negative deserts. Like Calvinism, inexclusivism has fixity for ultimate life (OSAS), but allows fluidity to the immediate life of the evangel.

A long hard look at salvation

Inexclusivism examines the word *salvation*, connects evangelism to certain definitions of salvation, looks at the term *belief*, and justifies the phrase, 'globally accessible ultimate life' (GAUL)—if we colonise Mars this term will need updating. *Salvation* is a wide-ranging word, and a wide-ranging reality. It's not simply a case of looking at etymologies, as if the units of words make up their meaning (as if merging a fly with butter create a butterfly), though some words have been created by etymology. Nor is it simply a case of 'first mention', as if whatever one decides is the first biblical use must determine every successive use, and as if systematic theology was second nature before Aristotle.

Inexclusivism to some extent is conveyed through many a word and many a biblical setting. A rescue package was promised in *Genesis*. To some extent this was unpacked by the Scandal of Particularism, selecting an individual, then a few, for the eventual benefit of all who wished in to the messianic kingdom. We must never think that that plan automatically excluded any from, or included any into, ultimate life—whether Balaam or Moses, Nadab or Eleazar, Haman or Esther. *Genesis* had a hidden undercurrent of global and unfocused salvation that eternity will clarify.

When Ethnic-Israel was told that Yahweh "was concerned about them and had seen their misery, they bowed down and worshipped" (NIV/NLT: Ex.4:31), that was salvation. When Ethnic-Israel begun the exodus,

---

hornets or comes with a fly-swat. Did hornets drive Demas into God's house then out again? Were the lyrics about election to salvation or election to mission? *Miracles* (C S Lewis) argued that the Imago Dei lives in an orb of both cause/effect (causation) and ground/consequent (reasoning), therefore above mere determinism—a touch of God. While history is established (and our future and history are equally always known to God beyond time), history is partially shaped by free freewill decisions of our now, becoming fixed once made. See William Hasker on "the doctrine of divine timelessness" (Hasker 55).

that was salvation. When Ethnic-Israel began to take over Canaan, that was salvation. When Ethnic-Israel had its borders secure, yes that was salvation. When Ethnic-Israel met at the Tent or Temple, that was salvation. When Ethnic-Israel heeded Yahweh's prophets, that was salvation. Yet it was *covenant*, not *ultimate*, salvation.

R E O White spoke of the common word group around *yāša'*, covering ideas such as "salvation from any danger, distress, enemies, from bondage in Egypt (Ex.14:13; 15:2), exile in Babylon (Is.46:13; 52:10-1), adversaries (Ps.106:10), defeat (Dt.20:4), or oppression (Jg.3:31, etc). Metaphorically, in salvation from social decay (Hos.1:7) and from want, the meaning approaches moral and personal welfare ('prosperity'; Job 30:15); in Ps.28:9 religious blessing in general" (Elwell 967). The keyword has covered so much, but this quote gives a general summary of its uses under Sinai.

We could look at other Hebrew salvation-type words, such as *mālaṭ*, in its niphal form *to slip away, escape*, in its piel form *to deliver, save*. "In the LXX *sōzō* translates no less than 15 different Hebrew verbs" (VanGemeren G5392 [sōzō]), and it's good to look at the range of meanings in the NT from the noun *sotēria* (salvation) and its verb *sōzō* (save). The NT has a big tie-in with the OT by the very name *Jesus*, besides themes such as exodus/eisodus. The OT was the prophecy; the NT was the fulfillment.

Contexts for the salvation word group include such as saving from sin's power (Mt.1:21), saving from physical death (14:30), ethnic deliverance (Lk.1:71), physical healing (6:9), protection from torment (Jhn.12:27), getting biblical sight (Ac.2:40), and spiritual health (Rm.5:10). Salvation has an ongoing aspect of development, christification, *theosis*. Brought into his family, we should grow into family likeness. Too easily the evangelical mind—at least mine—can read into any salvation text the idea of *ultimate* life.

Take Pr.18:10: "the name of Yahweh is a strong tower; the righteous run to it and are protected" (HCSB).[149] It meant that there was safety in the Sinaitic Covenant. This includes the land theology of safe borders, within which to grow together in knowing Yahweh. Next, take an evangelical remake, such as Clinton Utterbach's 1989 *Blessed be the*

---

[149]   Sadly the 2017 update, the CSB, discards God's name.

Name of the Lord, and, ignoring its other problems, see how that song exudes more the idea of getting saved, even if it's somehow the already righteous who "run into it and they are saved". So, *salvation* is a big wide word requiring big wide glasses. And we all need glasses.

When was Cornelius saved?

Looking at a broad meaning of salvation words can show us that human evangelism can have a saving purpose, even if its beneficiaries already and unknowingly have ultimate life. R C H Lenski asked a good question, *viz*, if Cornelius' pagan convictions had been enough for salvation, why had he sought the synagogue, and if the synagogue had been enough for salvation, why had he sought Peter?[150]

Both Martin Luther and John Calvin held that "since Cornelius was a 'God fearer', he would have been saved even if he had died before Peter arrived" (Sanders 65). They meant *ultimate* salvation, and I agree. What they missed was that the type of salvation available through Peter was *immediate* life, which included assurance that God's forgiven us into his family in the here and now (Jhn.17:3).[151] Like Abel, Abraham and Aaron, Cornelius lacked *that* particular type prior to the evangel, a blessing for which Peter was summoned. As Calvin put it, "man's acceptance with God is twofold" (Calvin 3.17.4).[152]

---

[150]   Sanders 65

[151]   Mark similarly picked up Jesus' teaching that before the cross, eternal life was for the next age: Mk.10:30. We easily overlook that that next age began by the cross immediately after the cross, ie what was to come has now come.

[152]   Correct, but I disagree with Calvin's presuppositions that Cornelius had bought into Sinai and that *ultimate* life was a gift of Sinai. Calvin badly wished to believe, and no doubt did believe, that limited atonement had at least incorporated Sinai before the cross, extending back even to Abraham. But to argue that circumcision was entry into Sinai both ignores that females were not circumcised (yet in) and that God-fearers, unlike proselytes, were not circumcised: no wonder the Circumcision Party was annoyed (Ac.11:1). I welcome Calvin's support simply for him having been open to the idea I share that ultimate life could precede the evangel which brought some form of salvation (Ac.11:14). He wrestled with the puzzle but the needed exegetical key was hidden under tradition.

The step from paganism to Yahwism was a blessed upgrade but unnecessary for ultimate life, even as the step to Yeshuism was a blessed upgrade but unnecessary for ultimate life. For humanity, ultimate life is only possible by the cross of Christ, even if it doesn't come through hearing the evangel, specifically the evangel by human evangelists. Yet there is a salvation upgrade that only comes through hearing the gospel, as with Cornelius, and Nicodemus too.

Thus God has instituted evangelists (specialists) and evangelism (each Christian is part of evangelism). The speciality is listed as a Christ-given task (Eph.4:11), all facets of himself, whom every Christian has. The saving role they play is fundamental in folk calling for the lord's salvation, for "how...can [people] call on the one they have not believed in? And how can they believe in the one of whom they have not heard? And how can they hear without someone preaching to them?" (NIV: Rm.10:14). An exegetical key required here is to see that the *they* being spoken about to Gentile Christians, are the *they* of Ethnic-Israel, whom Paul desperately yearned to enter the messianic community (1). See the expression *they* in vv2-4. "Not all the Israelites accepted the good news" (interpretively, the NIV: 16). Grammatically, v14 is about hearing messiah, not simply hearing *about* him (Morris 1988:389-90): even Abraham had only heard about messiah's *day* (messianic hope). Yet Paul's context being about preaching, we can conclude that he meant that in true preaching, anyone listening can hear messiah.

Is hearing key?

Let's not be too literalistic. Paul did not expect every convert to hear an audible voice from heaven (*bath kol*); probably Wesley did not expect every convert to feel the feel-good factor, the strange inner warming which a happy psyche can produce. Nor by mentioning the *spoken* message did Paul exclude *written* evangelism—a minority method in the C1 Roman Empire. Nor did he exclude God speaking directly through other means—for instance God can give direct witness about Jesus to Muslims through dreams, though I don't believe that any faith group is off-limits to evangelisation as if they're not in the Great Commission.

Paul himself was converted through a vision, even if it followed Stephen's sermon. And human evangelism can follow a vision, as in the case of the Roman centurion Cornelius. God seeks Christian interconnectedness. With the prophecy of Joel ringing in his ears about a Yahweh Day, what did Paul believe to be at stake? He knew that his people before messiah never had the opportunity to hear messianic preachers, yet could enter deific life on an earthly level. Did he not also believe that without Christian preaching, they and Gentiles had been able to enter into deific live at the ultimate level: heaven being their home though living elsewhere? He was saying simply that a new aspect of the big term *salvation*, of *knowing God*, was only possible through the messianic message. Since a new and living way was intended, then Paul was not ruling out ultimate life accessed without direct human evangelism. Read Paul in his context.

Are we damned if we don't?

I used to hear warnings that we Christians who didn't evangelise would have the blood of the damned on our hands—it could even seem that we'd be ultimately damned if we didn't! A bit like "I am doomed"—the CEV's take on Paul's woe if he preached not the Christian news (1 Cor.9:16). The guilt trip was especially keen from *Ezekiel*—out of context. Fear not. Ezekiel described his prophetic job as being like a solitary soldier on sentry duty at the main gate, whose warning could save folk (Ezk.33). If a guard didn't warn them and villagers died, their blood would be on his hands. If he warned but they ignored, he at least would be spared.

Sadly, Ezekiel has been misused to urge evangelism by literally putting the fear of God into lackadaisical Christians. However in Ezekiel's context, surely the loss was not ultimate but covenantal? Would Ezekiel lose ultimate life by failing in a task? Would Yahweh permit any Judahite to lose eternity simply because a prophet failed to warn them that international punishment would follow national disobedience? Would all non-Israelites lose ultimate life because no prophet called on them to repent? By adjusting their lifestyle, making good wrongs committed, Judahites would be kept from punishment, kept within Judah, and her borders kept safe. It was a covenantal choice, not an ultimate one. She didn't heed and so faced the second and final wave of Babylonian captivity.

We sometimes confuse the here-and-now-immediate, with the yet-to-be-ultimate. Unlike Atlas holding up the skies, others' ultimate destiny does not rest on our shoulders—phew, what a relief!

Are they damned if we don't?

Sanders 1994 begins with the sad story about Mrs. Rachel Lynde. Her head was a little lite, and she preferred the idea that the countless unevangelised will waste in hell since evangelism is essential, to the idea that countless dollars are wasted in evangelism since evangelism is nonessential. Would we also write off people rather than write off money? But God rest her soul, may she rest assured that even *if* ultimate life has always been globally accessible, gospel evangelism is not wasted, since evangelism adds unique content in this life even if nonessential for the next.

Inexclusivism holds that human evangelism acts as the only door into knowledge of the now greatest kingdom level, pictured elsewhere as spiritual birth into an individualism unknown among the righteous even of Ethnic-Israel.[153] A knowledge base, identification, insight, joy. But at its most basic, if human evangelism is the essential door to ultimate life, then prior to human evangelism there was no such door. Yet in fact even in Isaiah's day, the *good news* (*evangel*, as in Rm.1:16),[154] a Yahweh Day, was proclaimed, and Isaiah lamented its low uptake (Rm.10:15-6). This had not been the message of the cross, and though

---

[153]   If for some it functions as their door into ultimate life itself, then we would again be in the puzzle about fairness for those circumstantially outside of its range.

[154]   Incidentally, in *To the Jew First or to the Jew at Last* (2014), Antoine X J Fritz, a former *Jews-for-Jesus* worker, argued that Rm.1:16's *prōton* meant 'initially', not the ambivalent 'first'. Covenantally, the embryonic gospel was initially to the former twelve-tribed Israel. But Paul probably had in mind the birthed gospel in C1 evangelism being tactically aimed initially towards ethnic-Jews, who had a covenant-background offering ingredients ready to bake the formative Christian cake (as did Paul: Gal.5:11), though some sought to bake it into a Sinai cake (Gal.2:12). Like Paul focusing church-planting in big cities not rural villages, it made tactical sense to develop the church with insights already in place within the tanak, apostles presumably content in the knowledge that not hearing the evangel did not mean ultimate damnation. The strong "evangelise ethnic-Jews before anyone else", is traced to London, 1809.

in an immediate context of cultural rescue, was surely a call back to Yahwism, the then highest level of deific life (which *Hebrews* says don'; go back to), besides prophecy of the true evangel. For our part we might lament how many Christians seem uninterested in Christ!

"They that have understanding in themselves are best. They who walk with the wisdom of the wise are good. They who know neither, nor will be taught by the wise, are naught" (Hesiod's *Works and Days*, lines 293-7, c.700 BC). Some don't know and don't know they don't know: they are fools, shun them. Some don't know and know they don't know: they are open, teach them. Some know and don't know they know: they are asleep, awaken them. Some know and know they know: they are wise, follow them.[155]

Not speaking about ultimate life salvation, it was reasonable for Paul to say that the salvation of *knowing* Christ, Christian revelation in the Yeshuic Covenant, was only enabled through those who had already come to know him: "...it is a beautiful sight to see even the feet of someone coming to preach the good news" (CEV: Rm.14:15). Postcode salvation dependant on the posties.

Release from the penalty and power of sin was a big possibility opened up by Christ.[156] Good News indeed. A big theme of covenant was knowing it—You shall know that I am Yahweh. *Salvation* carries many aspects and levels, such as the joy of *knowing* God's forgiveness, and the direct *knowledge* of him by each who bows before him (Jhn.16:27). To Paul, as it had been to Isaiah, the evangel was a focusing lens, yet many (as in Isaiah's prophetic eye on Babylonian Release) prefer the blindness of their imaginations, their idolatry, the short-sightedness of their culture's religion.

At kiddie level, George MacDonald's *The Princess and the Goblins* made the point that it is unreasonable, merely on the basis of someone being your mother, to believe your mother, since not all mothers are truthful. Judge people as people, not as relationships. At another level perhaps MacDonald was saying that, whatever our mother denomination, it being ours does not make it true. How

---

[155]   C12 Arabic proverb

[156]   I have been saved from the penalty of sin, I am being saved from the power of sin, and I shall be saved from the presence of sin.

eagerly do we defend what is ours, irrespective of logic! As with church prophecies, "examine everything carefully, and hang on to what is good" (CEB: 1 Ths.5:20-1).

Semipelagianism and alternatives

Before I chart the main theories on the market alongside inexclusivism, I must say something about semipelagianism since its fluidity doesn't fit snugly into the chart. Semipelagianism—very similar to Arminianism—opposes the deific monergism of Augustinianism (ensoulment totally depraved within Adam's guilt; God alone choosing which individuals get ultimate life). It also opposes the human monergism of Pelagianism (ensoulment totally unaffected by Adam's sin; individuals alone choosing for or against God). It favours a deific-human synergism (ensoulment partly affected by Adam's sin; God offers everyone, and everyone must individually decide). It is the majority idea within Eastern Orthodoxism, Roman Catholicism, and Protestantism.

Some semipelagians, especially in the East, prefer the idea of Ancestral Sin, to the idea of Original Sin and consequent guilt. That is, they prefer the idea that adverse consequences, but not guilt, are passed on at ensoulment—we're born bad (attitude) but not guilty (act), rebellious (attitude) but not rebels (act). Adam's was not *our* original sin, but we share Adam's attitude! Semipelagians divide over whether there shall be some form of damnation because of sin's infection, or some form of salvation in spite of contamination. Some think that water-baptism decides. Because of its variations, I exclude it from this simplified chart, which seeks to show some main idea about ultimate salvation even for people who die in the womb.

	Can people who die in infancy...				
	choose God...		be damned for...		
	in infancy?	after death?	sinfulness?	sins?	Destination at death?
Augustinianism	✗	✗	✓	✗	If baptised, heaven, otherwise mild hell
Annihilationism	✗	✗	✓	✗	Extinction
Pelagianism	✗	✗	✗	✗	Heaven

	Can people who die in infancy...				
Limited Reincarnationism	✗	✓	✗	✓	Human rebirth
Postmortal Evangelism	✗	✓	✗	✓	Heaven or Hell
Universalism	✗	✓	✗	✗	Eventually Heaven
Predilectionism	✓	✗	✓	✗	Heaven or Hell

The baptismal-regeneration idea fails to exceed restrictivism, and human evangelism is allowed to be subservient to it, filling something of the gaps. In the beginning, converts-through-persuasion, began the uptake of the conversion-through-water-baptism idea, as perhaps under pagan influences converts began to meld ideas of baptismal-regeneration with pedobaptism consecration, reshaping their ideas about conversion: the new idea seemed to fulfil their wish to ensure that their children became Christians. Children grew up believing that "the sacrament worked more or less magically" (Berkhof 248).

Still, both the engines of evangelism and water-baptism have, throughout their history, been minority engines, serving at best the outskirts of God's desire to redeem all. Of the theories above, only inexclusivism's predilectionism holds that personal choice is possible throughout and before infancy, and that personal faith-welcome is necessary for ultimate life. With Augustine, somehow sin must be dealt with in infancy in order to guarantee ultimate life. *Contra* Augustine, ultimate life is not accessible just for the fortunate few of Christian parents, but has always been globally accessible for each and every human being having a core desire to be with God. It's a Godward predisposition, and at death we forsake our sin bias.

Inexclusivism

In itself, inexclusivism neither adopts nor rejects Augustine's hope for deceased infants (influenced by Mt.10:15/Lk.10:12?), that those not *water-baptised* would not find heaven but would find hell less hostile than some of the symbolisms of hell might suggest to us. Various people have argued that what for the redeemed would be the anguish of fire and wailing (as Jesus' cry of dereliction), might for the unredeemed seem bearable, even if drab and meaningless. Perhaps what Augustine postulated was as good as damnation gets, that the top end of hell— with some dim Imago Dei—might in fact be as bad as it gets.[157] Richard Adams' *Shardik* portrayed this idea by the deep darkness of *The Streels of Urtah*. How hellish hell is is not central to predilectionism. Technically inexclusivism could be subsumed under annihilationism, but it does not lead me there.

Predilectionism agrees with Augustine: a sin bias infects our personalities from our beginning (ensoulment). Predilectionism disagrees with Augustine: some individuals' defining/intrinsic bias, is *towards* God, and some individuals' defining and intrinsic bias, is *against* God. Those born friendly to God have ultimate life; those born hostile to God have ultimate damnation, even if a tolerable damnation. All will get what they really seek—their hearts' choice.[158]

Inexclusivism doesn't put great weight on the idea of constant church rites for forgiveness of personal sins. When it comes to Christianity, "whoever believes in [God's son] is not condemned, but whoever does not believe stands condemned already because they have not believed in the name of God's [unique] Son" (NIV: Jhn.3:18). I take *believe* in its 1:12 sense of *welcome*, *name* in the sense of *person*, and assume that John's context was limited to those who willingly accept the new covenant— not an option for infants nor for those who have died beyond the call of the cross. Those who have heard but not heeded are unlikely to seek the church save for social reasons. They are self-condemned to here and now exclusion, but not necessarily to ultimate damnation.

Predilectionism holds that the cardinal sin is excluding God and is a defining and intrinsic sin-attitude at ensoulment of those of its predilection: they are closed to God. Yes, they may find aspects of

---

[157] Perhaps Jesus intimated that 'hell' had layers of unhappiness (see Mt.10:15).

[158] It is possible that there is a gradation of bias, even as there is a gradation between day & night. In which case there could be a twilight zone of people who would have real choice of whether to veer to ultimate light or ultimate darkness. Or it might be that the analogy is more of a light switch being on or off, or computer code being a one or a zero, allowing no real choice to switch desires, and the heart desires of the dark will be the night, and of the light the day.

God to their taste (even as a merciless murderer might welcome mercy from a judge), but they fundamentally reject him from their very beginning. Contrawise, some may find aspects of God to their distaste (Jonah disliked Yahweh's mercy to nasty neighbour Nineveh), but fundamentally accept him from their very beginning: they are open to God.

Mere socially interactive sins, which flow from our sinful infection, can perhaps show the depth of our predilection (and there is always some inner battle). But *pace* Augustine, the deciding factor is not about punishment for mystical involvement in some Original [Human] Sin. The deciding factor is our inbuilt spiritual rejection or welcome of God. Evangelism can tune into and crystallise the latter into Christian life. Christ's cross has enabled God to ultimately remove the infection of sin from those who seriously desire him. But the only true/ *alēthinos* healer, can only heal now those who enter his surgery.

Inexclusivism and belief

I've suggested both a now and a future level of condemnation, but I need to relate these to the idea of *belief*. The evangelical mindset in which I have lived over 50 years, tends to focus on belief for ultimate life, so *unbelief* as ultimate damnation. I approve its long-distance glasses for eternity, but disapprove its poor short-distance glasses for immediacy. Many of my fellow evangelicals would thus quote Paul's words to the Ephesian jailor (Ac.16:31)—and similarly Rm.10:9—as bespeaking ultimate life, of belief in Jesus as the only way to avoid future damnation, rather than simply to avoid now damnation.

But there are several senses in which *belief* is biblically used. Ac.15:11 speaks of belief more as mental conviction of a fact as a fact. Jas.2:19 ridicules those who boast a hidden, private Christianity that's detached from Christian community and duty. And if "we *believe* in God", is merely on a verbal level, is it any better than what demons affirm? They encourage the blindness of atheism yet they *believe* in God—but don't reckon on them being in God's good books: Hitler believed *in Churchill*. Belief in Mt.9:28 is about Jesus having checked out confidence levels in his ability to physically heal. Some claims should not be *believed* (24:23). These things are beliefs of philosophy and of intellect.

As we turn to Jhn.1:12, we see something like typical Jewish poetry, which rewords a point for emphasis and remembrance, an explicative 'that is'. The better versions see *lambanō* and *pisteuō* in this context as being one and the same; the worst take them as different actions, or else drop a term.[159] The CEB has a particularly nice touch in putting *lambanō* as *welcome*: "but those who did welcome him, those who believed in his name...".

Incidentally, although 'his name' sounds odd in English, it does carry a little more than a mere 'in him', and invites a study into his identity and what he represented, so is worth living with. In some contexts, Jesus spoke about us doing things in his name, contrasting what he had done as having been in his father's name. Inexclusivism holds that the fundamental belief or unbelief, is our background welcome or unwelcome at ensoulment, the point when human personality begins, and that biblical evangelistic belief is always, or most often, the point when one is born anew (not 'again') into Christian revelation and lifestyle opportunities with God. Evangelism offers the now-ness of immediate life, the way into messianic life now. So, belief can be foreground as well as background welcome, indeed a background welcome of God enables a foreground welcome of Christ. Some who dislike the unique selling point of Level 4 (ultimate) life removed from their gospel, might be guilty of myopically underselling the daily blessings of Level 3 (gospel) life. Is Christian life not worth far more than a life insurance policy beyond the grave?

Salvation's Back Door

So far, I have concentrated on the front door, the way into life. What about the back door, the way out into death? Some say that only and all of God's chosen come through the front door, and that any who seem to leave are only gate crashers who have been shown the back door (1 Jhn.2:19). This idea—the Perseverance of the Saints—is a logical construct, given the major premise that only God chooses who goes in (his sovereignty alone), and the minor premise that they only go in to stay (surely reasonable). Any conclusion allowing any to wander off permanently, undoes Calvinism's definition of God's sovereignty. It generally assumes that for adults, 'in' means that ultimate life is only

---

[159] ERV/LEB/NIV/NKJV (A+); CEB (A-); CEV/NRSV (B-); NABRE/NCV/NLT (D-)

accessible through the church.[160] Whom God sends into his house, he keeps inside? Whom he releases from sin's prison, he keeps free? But what about those who have seemed to be Christians, but have voluntarily renounced Christ? Were they never Christians? What of those who seemingly returned to Christ? If they had been Christians earlier, had they turned from Christ by God's sovereignty, and turned again to Christ by God's sovereignty?[161] Do we overplay God's sovereignty and underplay his grace? Some Christians are afraid of not dying 'in grace', as if dying outside of grace guarantees them eternal damnation. Does their ultimate destiny depend on living in holiness, their deathbed repentance of sins, some last rites, or even on conversion? No. Our background faith-welcome guarantees our future life; our foreground faith-welcome guarantees our now life.

Ultimate Door, Immediate Doors

Perseverance and unperseverance

As far as I have traced predilectionism, unlike the above it suggests that each person begins with a fixed attitude one side of the ultimate door or the other, an ability or inability to live happily with God. I don't think predilectionism is open to fundamental change, as it fundamentally defines us *vis-à-vis* God and selfhood from the get-go—born either fish or fowl. It fixes whether explicit human evangelism, or even the good news mediated implicitly through a religious experience—such as the stars in a pitch-black night sky, or the encounter with real human goodness that suddenly contrasts us to our shame—can bring out inner, deep buried love for God above

---

[160]   I argue that ultimate life is only accessible by Christ, and that church is a reasonable but imperfect indicator of who has it, yet carries the unique package of immediate life. Both Calvin and Luther accepted that had Cornelius died before hearing the evangel, by being a God-fearer he would have been saved.

[161]   The idea developed in reaction to the phenomenon of backsliding/apostasy (*fluidity*), that no one can truly identify anyone [else?] as a Christian (*fixity*). If so, and if we're only supposed to marry Christians, then isn't it best never to marry since you never know if the other party is one, and they can never know if you are one? I guess that the idea of provisional certainty is handy to such thinking;)

self-idolisation. This love can focus on Jesus messiah, so that a godly Muslim takes the next step and dares to call God *father*.

Inexclusivism values evangelism as a major player in immediate life, but not in ultimate life to come. Future-life is not based on a point-of-decision. Inexclusivism does not involve the stop-gap intervention of God speaking directly at or after the death of those who hadn't had human evangelism. Indeed, if God will evangelise after death those not evangelised before death, should not fallible human evangelism not zip it, thereby letting God's future evangelism give the unevangelised their best chance of eternity?[162]

For immediate life, inexclusivism involves individual welcome—*fides necessaria est*—as a necessary key to unlock now the life of God's sovereign grace—*gratia necessaria est*. For ultimate life it affirms the *Perseverance of the Saints* idea, in the sense that any born fundamentally towards God will remain fundamentally towards God, irrespective of whether they toggle between saintly and unsaintly lifestyle, or even between different religions including atheism.[163]

In short, ultimate life comes with a personality that's the right mix for heaven. I'm not talking about the five-factor model (FFM) or about *any* psychological model of personality that can nicely pigeonhole us. I'm talking about a mix from our parents, that at the spiritual dimension pans out towards God: the cake with the right mix will turn out right; that with the wrong mix will turn out wrong. This takes us to traducianism, a doctrine about birth which Augustine couldn't make up his mind about.

Traducianism

Traducianism has had some support both in the West (eg Tertullian) and in the East. On the one hand, the Bible doesn't say that God directly breathes life—as he did with Adam—into each individual human. On the other hand, do we create spirits by biology? Is

---

[162] Although Is.59:16 isn't about ultimate life, it carries the idea that when others are lacking to do Yahweh's will, he can act directly.

[163] Though this definition of sainthood doesn't fit the major and explicit new covenant biblical levels of saintliness, namely set aside as Christians (type 1) and Christian lifestyle (type 2). It is subliminal.

ensoulment the beginnings of a human personality by procreation?[164] Gen.5:3 might suggest creation in one's own image, but lest Adam's other children (4) be thought to be missing out on something vital, let it be said that it is more likely to mean that Seth was in Adam's personality type, the spitting image of his dad ("just like him—in his very image": NLT).

Setting Seth aside (speak it speedily!), Scripture shows all humans to be images/likenesses of God (9:6), which is why murder is so morally serious.[165] The fact that God rested from creating (2:2-3), might symbolise that he no longer does ensoulment, yet though it speaks of no major new development, Jesus commented that God has never stopped working in other ways (Jhn.5:17). If each new spirit has always been created directly by God, would they not be without any sin bias (Ambrose) or original sin guilt (Augustine)? Some trichotomists reply that parents generate bodies and contaminated souls, to which God adds *de nova* spirit, which becomes contaminated by the sinful soul. Maybe, but let's look at the terms *soul* and *spirit*.

Interestingly, *soul/spirit* are linked to the animal kingdom. *Nefesh*, often put as *soul*, is related at a primitive level even to aquatic life: "let the waters bring forth great quantities of creatures with living souls" (EJB: Gen.1:20). Later, "your blood which is your souls I will require; at the hand of every animal I will require it and at the hand of man; at the hand of every man's brother I will require the soul (or life) of man" (EJB: 9:5.). Russell Stendal's *English Jubilee Bible* might be neither the most functional nor the most accurate version, but it handily highlights *nefesh* (as *soul*)—which semantically links humanity with the animal kingdom—as a link word between texts. Surely parent fish create the soul of their offspring; *ipso facto* human parents likewise?

Ruach, often put as *spirit*, is related to animal life: "...who can prove that the human spirit goes up and the spirit of animals goes down into the earth?" (NLT: Ec.3:21). Now Qoheleth might have meant that on an individual level we cannot know whose fate will be distinct from mere

---

[164] Procreation is the idea that creatures (usually it means humans) create on God's behalf, that he now creates humans indirectly through us.

[165] Lacking the absolute of God, atheism cannot ground absolute ethics. We cannot create an ought from an is. The ought comes from beyond creation.

animals, and whose will not, but his focus was simply on our similarity with animals in leaving behind mortal life, highlighting thus the ultimate vanity of kingdom-building. But my highlight is our sharing the term spirit, with mere animals. Given this sharing of term, surely parent animals create the spirit of their offspring; *ipso facto* human parents likewise?

In the semantic game let's be aware that more developed meanings of *spirit* and *soul* exist in Scripture—we should use these terms gingerly. Besides Scripture often using *soul/spirit* interchangeably, it also mixes in similar expressions (eg heart, soul, mind, & strength (Mk.12:30)). If I should be a trichotomist on the basis of 1 Ths.5:23, I should be a multichotomist on the basis of Mk.12:30.[166] If 1 Ths.5:23 was a phrase of conscious systematic theology, on the basis of Ec.3:21 I should wish animals to be sanctified and kept blameless in body, soul, and spirit, until Christ's return, since they too have 'spirits', the highest element of life. Yet too strict a separation of the terms might even deny that Yahweh had a soul (*nefesh*: Ps.11:5)! It might seem that only sinful souls shall die, and that only righteous souls shall live (*nefashot*: Ezk.18:4), and that peoples' souls (*psuchai*) are saved at death (Jas.5:20). It can be safer to say that *soul* is sometimes shorthand for any complete person.

Soul/spirit are sometimes used interchangeably (overlapping meaning), yet in some contexts have been used as a contrast. For example, Paul could contrast mortal and immortal life, as soulish body to spiritual body (*sōma psuchikon/sōma pneumatikon*: 1 Cor.15:44). Scripture often uses terms in varying ways—we all do. Soul (*nefesh*) sometimes refers to an inner aspect, sometimes as a contrast between the perishable and imperishable, sometimes of individuals. 'Eternal life' likewise has variations of meaning. The major biblical distinction between man and beast is that the image of God, the *ṣelem 'Elōhîm/imago Dei*, is only and emphatically attributed to humanity. But the flexible term *psychē*—from which we get *psychology*—is a useful handle for us to consider man's overlap with the animal kingdom.

C19 Theophan the Recluse, took the idea of human parents creating ensouled human animals, and God raising the level of existence by imbuing the conception with reason/spirit. While this to me makes

---

[166]   Less so if I follow Mt.22:37: the evangelists weren't too persnickety.

sense for Adam (as a sub-human animal selected by God and raised to a new order), I don't think the idea of an exaltation pattern repeated for each human, best covers the facts. Some animals have enough intelligence and personality for us to bond. So, some people keep a dog or cat, though some people prefer pigs, because dogs look up to people and cats look down on them, but pigs treat them as equals. Is there not enough linkage to the animal kingdom to suggest that the image of God was a spiritual wavelength that he attuned mankind to, perhaps a personality upgrade? If so, we need not argue that God must directly plant his image into people at their conception—procreation suffices.

I suggest that personality transmitted in human genes carries the wavelength of God, the ability to bond with God. In simple, I suggest that of this world the human genome alone carries the psychological capacity to 'do God', and carries beyond death. If you study this further, do look at key ideas such a dichotomy (body, soul/spirit) and trichotomy (body, soul, spirit). Believe me, there are many hoops one can jump through! Like me, Theophan has made a suggestion.

Well, that's traducianism, or at least my take on it. The Western part of the church prefers the ensoulment idea called creationism, and argues that the soul—or at least the spirit—is created directly by God when each person begins life. Such creationism is more limited than the current Creation/Evolution/ID debate/dialogue, and perhaps should be renamed to something like direct ensoulmentism, as opposed to indirect ensoulment, procreation. Some hold that Ps.127:3 means that each individual child is directly given by Yahweh—at least its spirit.

Was any child of rape and which at birth dies and causes its mother's death, created by Yahweh's *direct* will. Should we blame the holy one for unholy rape? I'm more likely to bewail two victims of sin, rather than to thank God for such a *blessing*. Ps.127:3 and similar covenant texts probably meant that Yahweh would bless the covenant nation with generational continuity—his people would continue. Similarly, Jesus promised that Global-Israel would never die away (Mt.16:18). That's in line with Is.38:10 ('the gates of sheol'), "that the powers of death...shall not prevail against the [messianic] community [...that is,] that it will not die and be shut in by the 'gates of death'" (France 255). And that Yahweh weaves each individual within the womb (*in uterus*:

169

Ps.139:13), need not mean that he does so by direct rather than indirect means. Are we not knit by procreational, God-given mechanisms, random combinations of the human genome? As Grudem put it, "God usually acts through secondary causes" (Grudem 485).

Free Flowers?

It's from traducianism—the idea that we are only mixed by our parents—that I suggest that some mixes are from Day One pro-God, and that some are anti-God.[167] But wider than the merits or demerits of predilectionism, the idea, *free will*, perhaps has an inherent question about *fixed* will: I can do within reason (free will) what I am (fixed will): fluidity, compatibilism. Is there a backdoor out of ultimate salvation? This question can take us back to the daisy oracle game, *effeuiller la marguerite*. Just like plucking petals with 'loves me, loves me not', so Christians can go through a 'saved, not saved, saved, not saved' cycle, hoping to die in a 'saved' position.

I guess I've been a bit of a daisy for many years of my Christian life, wondering at times if I've lost it or might lose it, yet rejoicing that love both permits conversion and controversion. The greatest love of all, love himself, sovereignly allows love to be trampled in the dust, rather than violating human freewill choice. And all Flowers are by the grace of God. Tulips[168] will sometimes ask themselves if maybe

---

[167]   At a time when Anthony Flew could still commend Richard Dawkins' atheism, he nevertheless debated with Dawkins against Dawkins' "major exercise in popular mystification", *The Selfish Gene* (Anthony Flew 78-80). I am not following Dawkins' contradiction—that determinism makes selfish genes and totally maps our lives (effectively our every action and reaction), though Dawkins begged us to exercise free will (denied by determinism) in order to resist the resistless tide. Ch.3 *Miracles* (C S Lewis) explains the differences in philosophy between cause & effect (determinism), and ground & consequent (logic/non-determinism). Genes are deterministic, do not totally define the Imago Dei, yet perhaps can produce both heaven shaped and hell shaped personalities, the norm and the abnorm.

[168]   Two conflicting doctrines of salvation (soteriologies) use the acronyms DAISY and TULIP. Molinism offers us ROSES, emphasising Luis de Molina's point about God having middle knowledge, knowing how each of us would (and would have) react in given situations (subjunctivism), for example that God knows which among the ancients would have become Christians had Christ

they've not been elected (God's fixed will). Some plants wither in the frost or the drought yet spring again through their underlying tenacity for life. Even God's children can do a roundtrip prodigal now and again, though it's a dangerous journey without guarantee of return. I suspect that, at the end of the day—irrespective of the fall-outs and fall-ins with God—only those who from birth have that deep itch for God, will be ultimately redeemed. Because of *agapē*, Demas left the church but did he really leave *Agapē*? I don't think that apostasy from Christ necessarily means apostasy from God.

Those Damning Chapters

"After people have left the way of Christ, can you make them change their lives again?.... [They] are nailing him to the cross again, shaming him before everyone" (CEV: Heb.6:4-6).

"...if we deliberately continue sinning after we have received knowledge of the truth, there is no longer any sacrifice that will cover these sins. There is only the terrible expectation of God's judgment and the raging fire that will consume his enemies" (NLT: Heb.10:26-7).

Can you enter and leave?

On the one hand, according to some the warnings of Heb.6 & 10 are best explained as warning that any genuine converts who reject Christianity, won't be able to return. A bit like thinking that a divorced adulterer may not remarry their former spouse. Donald Guthrie reckoned that Heb.6 reckoned that "those who could taste the goodness were well immersed in Christian experience" (Guthrie 1986:143), that is, Christians. Howard Marshall likewise reckoned that Heb 10 spoke to a Christian audience perhaps not too near the edge, but "at least...[who should] not proceed further on the downward track away

---

died before their time and had they heard the evangel (none of which happened). Predilectionism is based on knowledge, not middle knowledge but agreeing with it to the extent that seeing each heart God can sovereignly arrange situations which lead naturally to acceptance or rejection according to human freewill. But that relates only to the spiritual advantage/disadvantage of the now. Ultimately it is not what folk would choose (based on what they are), but what they are that decides: God judges each heart. Molinism might press inclinationism too far.

from belief...the particular sin in mind [being] rejection of Christ as savior" (Marshall 2004:610 rearranged).

Angels have turned their backs on God unto ultimate damnation. Can't Christians? The term *God's son/child*, now best kept only for the Logos, was used biblically of Adam (Lk.3:38); Ethnic-Israel (Hos.11:1); Solomon (1 Chr.28:6): angels, including the satan, might have been called his sons (Job 1:6). So, to say that God's children can't be damned, overlooks the fact that God's sons/children have been known to reject him. And once left, is there any guarantee they would wish to return? Is it ethical for God to compel back the unwilling?

Can you enter but not leave?

On the other hand, according to some the warnings of Heb.6 & 10 are best explained as simply warning that any bogus or borderline converts who reject Christianity, will be damned.[169] They underline that the words used in 6:4-6 could carry either strong meanings or loose borderline meanings in that context. They opt for the looser meanings. Besides the wider discussion on whether genuine Christians can lose salvation (tulip), they note the context of thorns and thistles folk (6:7-8), and invoke Jesus' words about bogus believers being like weeds, and saints being like wheat.[170] They can say that sanctified but unsaved—indeed according to the lesser meaning of *sanctified* in 1 Cor.7:14-6—could describe these folk.

John Bunyan's *The Pilgrim's Progress* paints this idea in story form. (1) Christian (prophetically named (elect) before becoming one) heard the evangel and repented unto salvation, so becoming a true Christian. (2) Christiana his wife (thus sanctified), played the fool at first by ignoring Christ, but eventually repented unto salvation and walked the Christian walk. (3) Christian's early companion Pliable almost became a convert, but repented unto damnation. (4) Formalist from

---

[169]   Grudem 796-802

[170]   Eg Mt.3:8-10; 7:15-20; 12:33-5. The first incidentally was John's warning dressed in sarcasm—he knew they were coming to challenge, not to comply. True, folk can deceive and we should check character references when prophets & politicians offer significant change. But I'm not sure that Jesus was saying that Christians would always and only be good, or that non-Christians would always and only be bad. He certainly begged people to be honest (12:33).

Vainglory (form/appearance without deific power), walked the walk without conversion.[171] Perhaps other NT scriptures speak of the impossibility of Jesus losing his own, and some say it's downright silly to speak of us losing him. Perhaps the Writer meant that the borderline way could damage without damning Christians?

Can Christians be damned?

It might seem a little strange as to why the Writer should switch (twice?) from encouraging and cautioning fellow Christians, to talk about damnation threatened to the Pliables (borderline) and Formalists (bogus) of this world—if that is what he did. Why should I switch from directing you within Yorkshire, to talking about someone's journey to Yorkshire in order to prevent you from leaving Yorkshire if you can't leave it anyway? If you can leave God's Own Country, then my warning makes sense. Indeed, the warnings were to remain as one was, so if to the nonconverted would they advise against conversion?

I do not buy the idea that folk will be either all and always thorns and thistles, or all and always rye and roses. The impossible in nature can be possible for human nature (Jas.3:10-2), the Imago Dei factor of compatibilism. And if we can change from bad to good, can we not change from righteous to unrighteous (Ezk.33:12)? And by Heb.10:26's we (hēmōn), didn't the Writer identify himself with those he warned? Yet he was neither a Pliable nor a Formalist.

I think that he wrote to ethnic-Jews, possibly Levites, being pulled back into Sinai as a safer lifestyle choice than messianism/Yeshuism.[172] He reminded them that the Levitical cultus (Nb.15:30) excluded highhanded sin—covenant defiance—from its forgive list. Under Sinai, highhanded sin opened the exit door from immediate

---

[171]   This story is Bunyan-shaped, of course, reflecting his journey alongside the Bible plotline. The storyline seems to be that Christian (Bunyan), having been formally a Christian, truly became a Christian at the wicket-gate (Mt.7:13; Jhn.10:9), but needed a later revelation of the cross for his guilt complex to fall off his back (Rm.8:1). For some the wicket-gate is cross-shaped; some Christians may never see the cross this side of the celestial city.

[172]   There were two forms of Yahwism, viz Yahwism via Moses, and fulfilled Yahwism via Yeshua, whose very name meant Yahweh saves: Moses handed over to Yeshua.

life, whether by literal death or disgraced exile (Heb.10:28; Dt.17:2-7): the deadly OT term *kārat* (*cut off*) often meant *life excluded from the community*. As life outside Sinai had been symbolised as hell on earth—Gentiles were unclean, dead to Yahweh—so *Hebrews* symbolised that life outside the messianic community (excommunication) was immediate damnation, the life of the unclean, the new Gentiles. Worse than having left Ethnic-Israel under Sinai, leaving Yeshua was exile from true Israel, the true covenant. Some deliberate/intentional sins under Sinai were deep, such as murder (King David), yet forgivable. However, the unforgiveable highhandedness in Dt.17 panned out as refusing the covenant authority—Dt.13:8 links with this (Beale & Carson 979). Sinai's defiant sinners blasphemed Sinai's covenant lord, and were to be cut-off from the covenant people.

If this is truly hearing the Writer, then *Hebrews* effectively says that those who through apostasy have cut themselves off from Christ, are in turn cut off by Christ. Perhaps it hints of grace, that only as long as such sinners don't care to be reinstated to the royal covenant they defy, they can't so won't be, but if these prodigals repent, they will be restored: an open two-way door. Heb.6:6 is about an ongoing state—"What they are doing is the same as nailing the son of God to a cross and insulting him in public!" (CEV). Stop with the nails, and return.[173]

This would be *apropos* the messianic community, not necessarily about ultimate life. Heb.10 does not withhold grace from any people who sincerely repent, but simply majors on the self-destructive and self-exilic nature of violating covenant lordship. I think that spiritual

---

[173] The C4 Donatists—a bit like the C3 Novatianists with the *lapsi* in general—formed around the idea that church leaders who had become *traditores* by caving in to Roman persecution, should not be allowed back into leadership: the specific issue was about church priesthood/sacraments. Sadly, Augustine's part in quelling these ultra-strict believers involved undermining Christian reluctance to use police tactics to quell freedom of religion, invoking his idea of Lk.14:23 and Saul's conversion in the process (Letter 93 to Vincentius). This idea has led to misusing religion as a weapon against human freewill and binding church and state. However, even these debates allowed apostates to return, howbeit as substandard Christians penalised as to spiritual giving and receiving.

darkness is lived by many self-willed Christians who don't bother any longer with messiah and his church. Some wave the Christian flag in support of Zeitgeist—the immoral spirit of the age—thus sacrificing Christ on the altar of Equality. They might be the *traditores* of our generation, burning scriptures unto the new Rome but nevertheless heaven bound in spite of all their folly and betrayal of Christ's word.

You may say that in contrasting Yeshua to Sinai, *Hebrews* speaks of apostasy now being worse. In what way could it be worse? Obviously physical death under Yeshua would be no worse than under Sinai. You may say that ultimate death is far worse than physical death, so must be what's intended. It is indeed worse, but I think that the meaning of Heb.10:29 is exclusion from Yeshua's community, which is far worse than merely leaving Sinai's.[174] Under Sinai they were excluded from its immediate life (Level 2), and under Yeshua are excluded from its immediate life (Level 3): Sinai was better off without the ideologically disloyal; the church is better off without the ideologically disloyal—as prodigals let them sort out their position and then return.[175]

Likewise, when Paul told the Corinthian church that they needed to excommunicate their big name convert—who displayed gross disloyalty by his antisocial sexual sin—both for their sake and for his (1 Cor.5:1-6).[176] Let our language be covenant language. Heard as C1

---

[174] Perhaps all Christians find annoyances within their Christian communities, personality clashes, folly, betrayals—the list is long—even obnoxious 'worship' pop songs which can be such a fiery trial! But shyness, as in once-bitten-twice-shy, is not the best solution to even multiple bites. There are dangers in abandoning church attendance, and difficulties in getting back into the loop, although Heb.6/10 aims more at wilful rejection of covenant.

[175] Identifying as a *broad-church* Anglicanism isn't a 'church' and is morbidly 'broad'.

[176] Garland 3841-4369/28028 took a similar line: they had to risk offending even Roman patrons who might shield them from persecution, for the sake of their holiness and that of their patrons. This man, already snubbed by his peers and also his church, would in Satan's zone (the *kosmos*: 2 Cor.4:4) hopefully come to his spiritual senses (see 1 Tm.1:19-20)—his *sarx* (old life orientation) destroyed—and so be saved in the lord's day. Garland assumed the latter to be Christ's age-end return. However, might the context of Passover—and excommunication for destroying the symbolism by using yeast (Ex.12:15)—

ethnic-Jewish Christians, we can see ourselves warned in old words for new times, not of ultimate damnation—that would depend on our relationship to God as God—but about the loss of messianic identity: post-Christians are sub-Christians until the eschaton. Leaving the church offered a wasted life. Like wasted harvest fields, an Israelite life outside Sinai was a waste, but a Christian life outside of the church is a bigger waste since a bigger loss, no matter how productive they might be in worldly ways.

Under Sinai's vine (Is.5:3-7), by not remaining in it, the Omrides (Omri–J(eh)oram 1) were a powerful international dynasty, but useless to Sinai and spiritual wastes. Under Yeshua the true vine, not remaining in him would spiritually be as useful as wasted vine branches that were incinerated—not the burning of ultimate hell (Jhn.15:6). Heb.5:12 had lamented the audience's wasted opportunity to teach and its need of a refresher course. Heb.10:35 urged readers not to ditch their Christian security—which offered great spiritual reward (Mk.10:30)—for mere social security. It was an exhortation to stay with the immediate life of knowing messiah as brother (2:11-2; 3:1,12; 10:19; 13:22), rather than self-excluding from that blessing into the comparative hell of nonbelievers. Falling back into Judaism would damn Christians to immediate hell, goyim status, but not to ultimate hell.

How Hellish is Hell?

Many have wondered about ultimate hell, especially as a dimension awaiting all those who have never had a chance of Christ. The C13-4 Italian poet, Dante Alighieri's *Divina Commedia*, divided his idea of spirit life—both human and angelic—into *paradiso* (paradise), *purgatorio* (purgatory), and *inferno* (hell/gehenna). Its idea of purgatory is as redemptive, angels correcting Christians from their remaining

---

modify *hēmera tou kuriou* talk? Did Paul fear that the way they were going, unless they (and their Roman friend) repented, there could come a Lord's Day—like Sinai's Yahweh Days—when the lord could step in in punishment (Rv.2:5)? The NT uses *Lord's Day* in various ways—see Ac.2:20; 1 Cor.1:8. Following Garland, if the man accidentally died in his sin, he would be ultimately damned; I suggest that he would have died spiritually dishonoured (3:15), but not ultimately damned. If any Christian dies in any sin, are they doomed for eternity?

sinfulness in preparation for heaven. Above there were levels (concentric circles) of heaven (ultimate life), which could accord with the biblical idea of rewards. Below there were levels (concentric circles) of hell, based on how evil spirits had been:[177] limbo, the top level (hell's outer circle), had the virtuous such as Saladin, Seneca, and Socrates,[178] who had really never heard of Christ, and who would probably live forever in a green and pleasant land.

Dante had not been the first to suggest levels of hellishness, though his lower levels became ever more hellish. As mentioned, quite a few have suggested that ultimate hell itself might be bearable by its citizens, howbeit unbearable by heaven's. The tidy freak cannot bear the slum; the slum dwellers can. Will the fate of those who are simply not born towards God be a no-fault separation from God, even as in Sinaitic Israel where those who failed symbolic standards of wholeness were doomed, at least while below standards, to form their own outskirt community (note 224)? "To enter heaven is to become more human that you ever succeeded in being on earth; to enter hell, is to be banished from humanity" (Lewis 1972:113). Might that banishment extend to banishment from the good life they knew before death, banishing our jokes about friends in hell? Any reigning in hell, within the moral void of goodlessness, would be a reign of terror—dystopia, not utopia.

Against the charge of taking the hell out of hell, William V Crockett said that "Jude took the hell out of hell because in verses 7 and 13 he talked about hell as being both eternal fire and the blackest darkness... clearly metaphorical expression.... Jesus also took the hell out of hell because he used opposing images of fire and darkness.... The truth is that these incompatible images were never intended to be literal..." (Carson 1996:531). Of course, by their extreme imagery, they were intended to make extreme points: the issue is extremely important.

---

[177]   The idea of bearability levels.

[178]   The Swiss reformer Zwingli believed that Socrates would be in heaven, as had C2 Justin Martyr. Justin's Logos Christology held that the preincarnate Logos had always been globally and savingly accessible, but I disallow his use of the term *Christianoi* before the Logos became the christ: Socrates wasn't a Christian.

Jesus and Immediate Hell

However much I seek to tidy up ideas under one roof, if Jesus' warnings don't fit under that roof it's the wrong roof. To those born to perdition, did he offer the false hope of an impossible escape? Calvinism faces the same question—why discourage or encourage what your inescapable fate decrees?[179] In Norse mythology, Odin gladly plucked out one of his eyes to gain wisdom. Probably many a Norse warrior boasted an eye lost in battle, drawing comfort from the idea that the chief of gods was similarly monoptic in a good cause.

Jesus spoke in the hyperbolic language of his people of parting with an eye rather than losing heaven and gaining gehenna (Mt.5:29-30). A vague vision of heaven is better than a vivid vision of hell; limping into heaven's better than running into hell. I don't believe that Jesus urged the impossible, but he did speak in hyperbole. I think that in the Gospel sayings, hell (sometimes *hadēs* as *separation*; sometimes *gehenna* as *rubbish*) sometimes at least means the immediate lot of those who refuse to convert into the messianic kingdom, those who would stop others from entering messianic life. That is, hell in the same sense that *Hebrews* sees for those who revert from the messianic kingdom into the likes of mere Judaism, a goyim gloom.

When the rabbis spoke of the later life (*olam ha-ba*), sometimes they meant life as after death, and sometimes the now present messianic age. Christ's warnings were not flippant, but warning those under Sinai that wrong attitude to fellow covenant people threatened *ultimate* gehenna might have seemed over the top, especially since those before hadn't been so warned (Mt.5:22). Likewise Jesus taught that Sinaitic inclusion was not ultimate inclusion, and that Gentile exclusion was not ultimate exclusion: many Gentiles "will come from east and west and will eat with Abraham and Isaac and Jacob in the kingdom of heaven, while the heirs of the [ethnic] kingdom will be thrown into the outer darkness, where there will be weeping and

---

[179]   It upholds all true preaching as good, but—like seed cast willy-nilly on different types of ground (Mt.13:1-9 reflected Palestinian culture at that time)— producing or perishing according to the hearts of those who hear it, their hearts being thus fixed by God's sovereign decision. I suggest they're fixed by traducianism.

gnashing of teeth" (NRSV: Mt.8:11-2). Yet Sinai to the rest world had been as immediate heaven to immediate hell.

I suggest that from this context,[180] Yeshua's wider context was of the new covenant kingdom which even the Baptist promised/threatened (Mt.3:2; 5:10), though at that stage his people didn't realise that Christianity would terminate Sinai, even as wheat supersedes husk. Even as the Baptist had begun, so would Jesus go on. He called upon his ethnic/covenant people to prepare their hearts and minds for the immediate life of the new age, when missing out would be hell: bad trees would be cut down and burnt; the unrepentant baptised in fire; the husks burnt (Mt.3:10-2). Mark's account is slightly fuller than Matthew's: far better to enter God's kingdom life incomplete (one-handed/one-footed/one-eyed), than jump or be pushed complete into gehenna and be burned (Mk.9:43-7).[181]

And v42 is linked. It speaks of non-Christians tripping up (skandalizō: 43,5,7) immature Christians, and has the same word 'thrown' (ballō) for the drowning image, as was used for the burning image (45,7). So, again we find a contrast in mortal life between the devil's kingdom-death (hell on earth) to God's kingdom-life (heaven on earth). When Isaiah spoke of the undying worms and fire (66:24; see Mk.9:48), he spoke poetically of the messianic age when those who opposed it would be like the slain of Yahweh, a dead contrast to global kingdom life centred around Jerusalem. At least opposition in the main are really able to reconsider their opposition and repent. Jesus urged the possible escape from Egypt's hell into Canaan's heaven. This then is inexclusivism: ultimacy is determined at ensoulment, but the option of immediacy, whether of salvation as immediate life or of immediate damnation as hell, is only unlocked by the evangel.

---

[180]   For other contexts, with hadēs see Mt.11:23/Lk.10:15; Mt.16:18, and with gehenna see Mt.10:28/Lk.12:5; Mt.18:9; 23:15,33. I presume that the devil was never going to become a Christian and that the eternal fire (note that fire is linked to gehenna) of Mt.25:41 is for after Christ's return. I suggest an immediate fire and ultimate fire (both prefixed eternal/aiōnios; see Mt.18:3), counterbalancing immediate life (Jhn.17:3) and ultimate life (both prefixed eternal/aiōnios).

[181]   The parallel of entering the kingdom being entering (the) life is clearly made: eiserchomai eis tēn basilleia (47) with eiselthein eis tēn zōēn (43).

Paul and Hell

Some who heard Yeshua believed that both their eyes were fine—yet they were blind. Unwilling to be directly helped (Jhn.9), were they not rejecting the messianic kingdom, so headed into immediate hell, namely exclusion from his church? If Lk.23:34's "forgive them" is authentic, it was asked not because otherwise ultimate hell awaited them, but that if forgiven they'd immediately become heaven-bound, and was prayed aloud (Jhn.11:42) to inform them that they were invited to the immediate life his cross would open up. In short, they could still become Christians. Pharisees had come from a spiritual holiness movement, yet could be hell bent (Mt.23:15), closed to the gospel of immediate life.

Saul of Tarsus, better known by his Gentile nametag *Paul*, came from their ranks and as a Christian still self-identified as a Pharisee (Ac.23:6). Having heard Stephen's prayer, he became a Christian. Wasn't Stephen's prayer (Ac.7:60) not for ultimate life, but for immediate life? Had he believed that had he not asked for God's mercy, their ultimate doom was sealed? Or had he believed that had he not asked for God's mercy—and asked in their hearing—their immediate doom was sealed? It is short-sighted to think that forgiveness only refers to ultimate forgiveness from ultimate hell.

Nowadays, some Judaists disparage Stephen's defence as being a wild concoction misrepresenting them (Ac.7). Have they a case? When interviewed by Gentile historian and team colleague Luke, Saul admitted he'd initially been furious over, but later accepted, Stephen's speech, and encouraged Luke to document it. No, Luke's account was validated by an onsite high-ranking insider. Stephen was a diasporan Jew. His reasoning was soundly based on the organic method of interpretation then used in ethnic-Jewish circles, especially among the diaspora. Initial reaction motivated Saul to proactively attack Christianity. Saul felt his fellow Pharisees' blind unwillingness to see (Jhn.9:39-41).

By revelation, Saul saw conversion worth living for, worth dying for. Yet I suspect that, though he might have shared the same boat with his fellows condemned as blind, because of his predilection towards God, the only hell he knew at the time was its meaning as separation from God's will on earth, broken off from the olive root. I think such uses of hell warned against missing the way in this life. It was ethnic-Jews who formed the brood of vipers warned to flee from the wrath to come, the inbreaking of the messianic kingdom (Mt.3:7; 23:33). They formed a messianic contrast in this age. Gentiles who died before the cross had no such warning, perhaps no such need, but could align to God as best they knew how.

Yet I also think that such teachings contain inklings of ultimate cutting off from God. Paul, having experienced immediate cutting off from God by the cross, also spoke of an ultimate cutting off from God for those who did not know God, expressed as refusing to obey messiah (2 Ths.1:9).[182] He himself had once refused to obey messiah, but only as a conscientious objector (1 Tm.1:13), so the ultimate cutting off would likewise be qualified: refusal—if faced with messiah—based on inbred hatred of God would have been Paul's meaning. He didn't speak much in hell terms, though he connected *hadēs* and *thanatos* (1 Cor.15:55). Likewise, John saw both being thrown into the eternal fiery lake—the second death/*thanatos* (Rv.20:14), showing that *hadēs* can be used as a temporary dimension (v13).[183]

Summary

We've looked at various ways to juggle how faith features in ultimate salvation: Rm.10:14. For their part, exclusivists can be too tied up in individual texts that seem to speak of salvation only possible through the work of the church, that they miss the general grace of Scripture. For their part, inclusivists can be too carried along by an inclusivist feel from the general evangel of Scripture, that they miss the weight of individual scriptures—proof-texting must be with a careful eye on levels/types of salvation.

Some exclusivists define water-baptism as potentially conferring ultimate salvation through the faith of one's parents, while allowing

---

[182]   I would locate the *anathēma* texts as for the church and its mission, immediate—not ultimate—exclusion: Rm.9:3; 1 Cor.16:22; Gal.1:8-9. "The malediction is probably intended to apply to any headstrong provocateurs within the church.... 2 Ths.3:14 (1 Cor.5:9); Tts.3:10-1" (Garland 17688-91/28028).

[183]   Mt.25:41 describes this fire as eternal/*aiōnios*.

that adult evangelism at the fringes of the 'Christian' world must catch adults before their infants can be protected.[184] Some throw out the water and the babies. Exclusivists who reject the pedobaptism idea—even if they accept the idea of baptismal-regeneration—tend to fall back on the idea that ultimate salvation flows from saved parents, like receiving an adult entrance ticket allows accompanying infants in for free. Alternatively, that if deific sovereignty chose them, it has also (or hopefully also) chosen their infants, at least if their infants die before an 'age of personal accountability'. Or maybe that deific sovereignty might redeem all who die in infancy on the consideration that although born (indeed conceived) into sin's domain they have been unable to endorse sin.

Some of these ideas uphold God's grace—particularly the idea of infant universalism—but shelve the Reformation given called *sola fide*. A greater part of church history has held to a basic damnation of infants, usually promoting pedobaptism as the exception that at least would save some from ultimate hell. My position takes exclusivist texts to refer to the level of eternal life available in mortal life—no one can come to God *as father* except through knowledge-welcome of his proclaimed son. I have taken inclusivist texts to refer to the fourth level, the highest level of God's offer of life, based not on the revelation of God's son, but on faith/welcome of God *as God*. The third level, the Christian level of salvation, has been impossible for most of humanity, but does not affect the ultimate level, Level 4. Both levels require personal faith/welcome.

The ultimate level of life has, in my opinion, always been open to all who have had a basic predilection for God, a yearning for the skies even though born into the mud of sin caused by Adam's fall. The hell of this life can end with the heaven of life's next step. Thus by inexclusivism I embrace and define exclusivism and inclusivism, affirm personal faith as always required for eternal life, and affirm a wider grace than exclusivism ever can. This wider grace can be seen in the global reaching out to God that can be seen in the major world religions, which I have briefly surveyed.

---

[184]   Some think that water-baptism seals the deal for adult believers too, even as they think that weddings seal the deal of engagement. Neither is biblically true.

Chapter 9   <u>Christian Salvation</u>

First sadness: picture a Western non-Christian couple, once bubbly in love, now fading apart: "home late, he mumbles of traffic and rain / She smiles at him as she covers her pain / 'We had so much, now so little remains. / Can we ever be Adam again'"?[185] Thus Michael Omartian sang of hope that, yes we can—love can be made new. It's a good song, but why seek to be Adam *again* since the last Adam came to give love a name and a way as *new* Adam to reign (Rm.5:17)? "..if anyone is in Christ, that person is part of the new creation. The old things have gone away, and look, new things have arrived!" (CEB: 2 Cor.5:17). That's the glory now.

Paul pictured a new creation—a new *Genesis*, alongside a new Adam, a new Eden—and each Christian as incorporated as a full member of the new race of new humanity, having a new future without need of future redemption. The new outlook is one of having died to the old *Genesis*, and risen to new life in the new *Genesis*. John likewise began his Gospel with this true genesis. Paul often spoke of this, and you must admit it all sounds good. But if you don't have to be a Christian to have ultimate life, and in this new age you may well suffer for such belief—as the NCV well puts it (Mk.10:30)—is it worth being a Christian? If we do get hooked on its truth, Jesus junkies, is it not immoral to get others hooked, to evangelise them, if the good news is net pain over gain?

Perhaps Karl Marx was right to warn that Christianity was like a potentially dangerous drug. While he feared it was a painkiller dealt out by the bourgeoisie to keep the proletariat under control, its real danger might be that it is the most addictive truth drug. To go with the flow is protection from the flow, and so long you get off before it flows into hell, does the journey towards hell really matter? Jesus went against the flow, and look what happened to him! Of course, that was an unavoidable one-off, if humanity was to know eternal life. But must *we* take up a cross? What is truth worth?

Is it worth death? Islam can demand execution for any born into its community who turn to Isa (Jesus) as to a better. Judaism holds that

---

185   www.invubu.com/music/show/song/Michael-Omartian/Adam-Again.html

ethnic-Jews who turn to messiah Yeshua, die to their families and communities. Atheistic Communism—or England, for that matter—can threaten imprisonment for those who do not comply. Why annoy those who wield the sword? Why disturb the hornets' nest? Judaism, though it began after Christianity, certainly got the popular vote of ethnic-Jewry—*national* messianism remained the hope. While it is different from Sinaitic Yahwism, lacking temple foci such as forgiveness, isn't it better for those within it to remain within it? What price messiah? Death?

Many have paid the conversion price with their blood; evangelism is a dangerous gift. For me, well, I've been hooked on Christianity from my early teens. With hormones kicking in, I sometimes wished it hadn't been a chain of truth that bound me to decent behaviour. Ah, the urges for autonomy, freedom, unaccountability. 'Jesus is lord' is, to many, anathema. Sadly, the hippy dream which post-modernism remoulded, of our own *bag*, doing our own *thing*, all being relative, there being no sin, is but wishful thinking. Jesus is lord, and redeemer, and highlights God. Escape for the intellectual is difficult, but the heart can learn to enjoy captivity.

Mk.10:30 adds to what I've just said of it. It says that you lose A, but get A × 100 + persecution, with immediate life in sight. God didn't consign to damnation all before who didn't, indeed couldn't, give up such things. 'If you do this, you will get that', does not necessarily mean that 'there is no other way to get that without doing this.' If I ask the neighbour to feed the cat, the cat will get fed, but the neighbour might feed it anyway. Jesus said that siding with him risked excommunication from one's community, even one's family, even the geographical Promised Land. The challenge was to change perspective in the light of eternity. And before eternity, we can join others and together form his *alēthinos* community, his family, his land—messianic blessings in this age now dawned, as distinct from the age and the ultimate promised land still to dawn.[186]

---

[186] Theology often has this four levels approach: common land (Gen.1:28—before language: a pre-alpha level); promised land (Sinaitic—the alpha level); promised land (Yeshuic fulfilled—the omega level); ultimate land (postmortal

True Land

"Firstly, compared with the OT portrait of the Israelites' time in the land of Canaan, the modern State of Israel clearly lacks those elements which we have noted as prominent in *Genesis–Kings*. There is no temple to provide a sacred location, the population cannot be viewed as the covenant people of God, and there is no rest. Secondly, the NT writings look beyond the limited fulfilment of the promises associated with land in the OT to a much greater fulfilment" (Johnston & Walker 49). Land was basic to identity. Ethnic-Jews had covenantal right to ancestral plots of land, such as an Ahab would have to kill to get. Since our hearts will always be where our treasure is (Mt.6:21), Jesus challenged his audience to let him have their birthright and become outsiders, as they travelled to eternity, the penultimate exodus. It was a command to spiritually relinquish, though the spiritual can impact the social. Persecution would soon force the issue. Abraham had been prepared to give up his ultra special son (Heb.11:17).[187]

Within years of messiah's death, many would happily give up the old land claim, downsizing to help the socio-economic poor among them (Ac.4:34-7)—they saw that land's spiritual meaning had transferred to messiah. Jesus wished his audience to attitudinally wave goodbye to the geographical Promised Land, to embrace him as messiah. Those committed to him are neither to idolise the land as hajjis, nor defend it as land he had walked. Justice remains justice, and biblically the land has become irrelevant theological chaff. When the Sinaitic Covenant ended, Ethnic-Israel's spiritual stake in the geographical land lapsed: all that land is now simply common land, desacralised. There has always been spiritual land linked to land levels.

Empires come and go. "'They were a powerful people, and rich, and great builders. They built to last, for they thought their city would last for ever.' 'But what became of them all?' asked the Mole. 'Who can tell?' said the Badger" (Grahame 87). "Abraham was confidently looking forward to a city with eternal foundations, a city designed and built by God" (NLT: Heb.11:10). As the Complete Jewish Bible says, "It was because

---

universe/heaven—post omega: beyond language). Ultimate land has never been tied to levels 2 or 3.

[187]   The MEVV fail: it's not *only*, *one & only*, or *begotten*, but *unique* (HCSB/ISV).

of him that I gave up everything and regard it all as garbage, in order to gain the Messiah" (Php.3:8). The true land, and all it means—not the shakeable land of shadows—is ours in Christ. Abraham himself lived in common land. However, with an El Shaddai relationship—between the Gentile Elohim relationship (Level 1) and the Sinaitic Yahweh relationship (Level 2)—and Level 2 land promised, interfacing levels 1 and 2 he shows how by putting God first, Gentiles could as Abel be deemed righteousness. That same faith joined with the evangel opens up Level 3.

Jesus' kingdom was not of this world. He taught them attitude, not necessarily literal exactitude. Whatever their ethnicity and roots, the NT letters would address Christians as wanderers, the diaspora, unsecured by social identities, their true treasure and identity heaven-based, and thus, we may add, of most earthly good, since not socially competing for positions of identity. Not all would be expelled from their families, communities, geographic Israel, etc. But an inner leaving of such ties, a putting himself and his teaching above their other aims, was called for.

A literal abandonment of connections and responsibilities is not in itself commanded, even as Abraham wasn't literally to kill Isaac, but we might find that we are cut-off by others. "Jesus said, 'Truly I say to you, there is no one who has left house or brothers or sisters or mother or father or children or fields on account of me and on account of the gospel who will not receive a hundred times as much now in this time—houses and brothers and sisters and mothers and children and fields, together with persecutions—and in the age to come, eternal life'" (LEB: Mk.10:29-30). In loss and abundance, rejoice!

Kingdom Individualised

In line with Evangelicalism, I have argued that fundamental individual response to God is required by God and cannot be given by any third-party: not *sola fide*, but *fides necessaria est*. In line with Jesus' talk with Nicodemus, I have also argued that the blessings, once on a community basis, are now individualised in the messianic kingdom which we can only join in messiah. Yet mere individualism is a serious error. 1 Cor.12:27—"all of you together are Christ's body, and each of you is a part of it" (NLT)—combines individualism and togetherness. Indeed, we have received much, and much is required from us. There is much teaching about discipleship. Failure at the individual, or the community level which Jesus spoke of as blessing (Mk.10:30), is serious failure, and both deserve consideration and commitment. But here I'll focus on glory at the individual level.

Kingdom kids

In the ethnic kingdom, Israel was Yahweh's son. For some it might seem strange, but the term son/child didn't have to imply genetic paternity: King Saul called David his son (1 Sam.26:25). Saul's genetic son Jonathan had a covenant brotherhood with David (brotherhood closer than marriage), but they weren't genetic siblings. Adam was God's son (Lk.3:38). In some cultures, older generations sometimes refer to young men as 'son', perhaps related to the extended family idea. Within Sinai, the community was Yahweh's son (Hos.11:1), an honorific term, and when individualised was only to highlight a few individuals whose special tasks were for the community (1 Chr.28:6).

Nowadays, by entering the new revelation, people instantly become individually children of God—but it's wrong to say or sing that 'I am God's son', since that's a special term for Jesus only.[188] It is about spiritual birth, entrance insight about messiah and his mediated covenant. Patterns which were community assets within the Sinaitic community, are internalised in Christ, globally and individually. The covenant is a familial covenant, each individual being precious, and the father loves and knows each of his children. As I've gone into in my *Singing's Gone Global* book (ch.4), for us it should be the father first, yet nowadays it's too often Jesus first and last. *Jesus Onlyism* cheapens the blessing of being kingdom kids. If it's only he on our brains, our brains are too small.

Here's a medley from various Onlyism songs. "Only Jesus can satisfy your soul; only Jesus brings redemption; only Jesus satisfies; Jesus only is our message; Jesus only will we see; Jesus all in all we sing; Jesus only is our saviour; Jesus only is our healer; only Jesus can our every sorrow know; you alone are God, Jesus!; [Jesus] alone can truly help us." Are God the father and God the spirit redundant and insignificant to us,

---

[188]   See my *Singing's Gone Global*, 2016:ch.8.

complications we can well do without? Onlyism songs sound very far away from the biblical position and Jesus' teachings. Abba might not be in fashion, but Jesus was never the destination—he himself is the Way. He is the permanent temporal mode of the eternal second person of deity.

As I cover more in my *The Father's Gone Global*, Thomas Smail described God the father as the forgotten father! And James White, perhaps with an eye on that, wrote *The Forgotten Trinity*. Here's three daily prayers to develop and maintain trinitarianism. ① Father, I love you; brother, I love you; helper, I love you. ② Destination, I love you; way, I love you; navigator, I love you. ③ God, I love you; lord, I love you; spirit, I love you. Regularly thank the father for sending his son; his son for becoming one with us; the spirit for living with us. And, to disengage from the common 'the LORD' workaround for God's name and go with Paul, try this as a daily catechism: Who is God? The father is God! Who is lord? Jesus is lord![189] To whom should we pray? To God, not to the lord! OK, these suggestions might shock some, and they could be more nuanced. They are but blunt pointers in the biblical direction, to help reverse the West's slow slide into Sabellianism. We are kids of the father, not the son.

The paternoster looked beyond Jesus to the father. He and his son *are* one, yes, but the Greek neuter gender here implies a oneness of purpose, not of personhood (Jhn.10:30). The father was and is greater than he. Of course, in international management, a queen is greater than I, yet we are both human. God the father is greater than God the noncarnate son, but they are both deity, and God the son incarnate, is deific. Jhn.14:28 should be looked at contextually for its missional meaning. Before the cross, his disciples would look to Jesus for help. Just before the cross, he looked a little forward (prolepticism). Whether or not 16:23a refers to them soon not needing to ask himself *for* things (NLT), or *about* things (ERV), 23b makes it clear that from then on their requests should go direct to their father because of the direct contact Jesus was just about to establish.

The same applies to us. The rule of thumb already given: the father is God, Jesus is lord, ask God, not the lord! What of Jhn.14:14? Some

---

[189]   1 Cor.8:6

might say it was only valid until the cross. I disagree. Some would say that the text isn't a problem—go with the simpler KJV/NKJV! I disagree. Even with the complicating word 'me', if Jesus will respond indirectly by the spirit (though the text says *directly*), need we say more than that Jesus is indirectly asked? That is, we ask the father and the spirit responds. However, why would Jesus have spoken in direct terms if only an indirect party?

I suspect the answer is that he wished to link himself vitally between the one asked (the father) and the one answering (the spirit). He is the coordinating motif, God the son, and it's about the messianic mission. After all, it's the Holy Spirit who directly does it, not Jesus. It's a case of reading the wider immediate context, in order to get the meaning. Even in Western society, a building contractor can say that they will build you a house. This doesn't mean them personally. It means a dozen or so people of different skills (bricks, electrics, plumbing, etc) will be hired to do the work. What literalist would sue contractors for not doing it all by themselves *as promised*? As kids of the father, let's ask him direct.

Nevertheless, some Christians prefer mediated prayer. Asking deceased saints to pray for us helps us identify with them. That can be good, a kind of "you've been where I am, Saint Joseph, so it's you— rather than Saint Joanna—I'd like to pass on this request." It's good to do biographical studies, as a reading of *Prayers and Meditations of St. Anselm* shows, and identity with previous saints. It's good to show solidarity with others in prayer (eg Phm.22). I cover this in more depth in *Prayer's Gone Global*. So, if we build up rapport with Christians who have died, doesn't asking them to join us in prayer make some sense, even though it lacks biblical backing and can mislead? The trouble is, whatever blessings might come from the above reasoning, asking Mary, Jesus, saints who have died, or fellow priests (all Christians are priests), to ask the father on our behalf *as if he won't hear us directly*, misses the point that we now have a one-to-one family link with him. It's not such a problem if we also ask our father directly. May neither fear nor any sense of unworthiness, hold us back.

So, it's fine to ask others to, like us, directly ask the father about our needs: both Paul and Philemon would have asked the father for the same thing. I'm not against another asking Saint Joanna, once of

Herod's household, to pray with me, but that's really not my thing. But my father's love is so deeply ingrained within me that I must go beyond this. One of my few revelation days (epiphanies) came through reading an article by an Australian pastor, Leo Harris, on Jhn.16:27. I suddenly saw that the father of my lord was himself aware of me, one who had waited long for me to speak, who himself loved me. A bit like the Great Lion waiting patiently at the pool for Jill Pole to begin a conversation, or walking alongside Shasta in the mist (*The Silver Chair*, and *The Horse and His Boy*, respectively: C S Lewis). Picture young teenager me, cautiously kneeling at my bedside, apprehensive lest I be blasted (were Harris wrong) for the sheer audacity and wonder of speaking to God *as my father*. Each Christian is a child of God the father, free to love him and to be loved.

Kingdom assurance

In the ethnic kingdom, there was one site for forgiveness. Do you know the one about Adam passing the blame? He blamed his wife, she blamed the snake, and it didn't have a leg to stand on;) Adam's sin corrupted interpersonal relationships upline (with God), sideline (with each other), downline (with nature), even intraline (inner disharmony). Humanity, fallen out with God, disintegrates, since "sin, while it involves acts, is at its base relational failure" (Martens 55). In Ethnic-Israel, Yom Kippur (*Atonement Day*) was intended to repair the national drift (Ex.34:7; Ps.32:1-2) and to reinstall the community's operating system, while patches were applied individually throughout each year at point of need. As said (page 146), forgiveness through rites was about keeping the temporary covenant link, rather than a matter of the heart or ultimacy.

With the new covenant, assurance of eternal forgiveness became internalised, individualised. The whole covenant is individualised. Each member now has God's love placed inside (Rm.5:5): from the KJV's 'shed abroad' and ignoring its 'in', funnily enough I thought we shed it abroad by evangelism! Though ultimate life (thus ultimate forgiveness from sin) is not exclusive to Christianity, understanding its inner workings certainly is. In Christ we are made right with God. Since ultimate forgiveness can come through outside of Christ but because of Christ, the distinction *in Christ* is one of assurance. This connects to kingdom entrance: it was after Peter had mentioned Moses, David, and Jesus as the messiah, that he urged his ethnic people to repent so as to enter messiah's kingdom (Ac.2:36-8)—that was salvation. In short, immediate forgiveness was a way to say that you are in and know it.

Forgiveness-now, is also assurance that we are forgiven-future. Christianity has the only sacrificial site where the sacrifice was made once, a sacrifice potentially effective for all humanity since creation. God is outside and inside the timeline. If we're in his son, we can know that we're not slated for ultimate condemnation (*katakrima*: Rm.8:1). Unbelievable? Well, those who added to Paul thought so.[190] Indeed, any who welcome the son by their will, have welcomed his father in their womb.

Paul flagged up that the ultimate deliverance from sin's dominance, which the Anguished of Rm.7 so desperately sought, meant moving into solidarity with Christ and the spirit. Those with an eschatological turn of mind, might identify this with John's picture of the Mega White Throne (*megan thronon leukon*) judgment, which arguably judges only and all those who throughout human history have died internally aligned to the Beast (Rv.20:11-5).[191] Whenever a Christian sins, they are guilty and should feel guilty. It does cloud their daily fellowship with God, but it does not change their ultimate destination —ultimate condemnation doesn't apply to Christians. How come? Because of the new solidarity, the workings of the spirit.[192] We are assured God's kingdom-now, and God's kingdom-future. "Sinai's law had right but not might; Sin's law has might but not right; Salvation's law has right and might" (Morris 1988:301). What of daily sins?

---

[190] Rightly or wrongly, the CEV focuses on punishment as a corollary of condemnation. The NCV footnotes the KJV addition. The NKJV puts the addition as if canonical, but points out that the NU rejects it. The CEB/ERV/ LEB/NABRE/NIV/NLT/NRSV are best, not even footnoting the addition: release from condemnation doesn't depend on our daily holiness.

[191] This judgement would thus be a foregone conclusion, a true and just showcase trial, the universal revealing of their spiritual rebelliousness.

[192] Presumably *the Holy Spirit* rather than a principle, for this section is about as full of the Holy Spirit (20 times) as it is short of looking at human egos (30× in ch.7).

The paternoster (Mt.6:9-13/Lk.11:2-4) wasn't sourced from *Mark*. It was perhaps one of those dominical sayings (sometimes called Q) that Matthew and Luke felt that their target audiences should hear. Possibly Luke simplified or reported it into a less poetical, more Gentile style. Matthew possibly structured it for Jewish congregational praying (*our* father); Luke possibly for individual (father). I could talk of Markan Priority, of deuterocanonical additions, about translation, about the great teaching about prayer (who to, what about, etc): lots of interest here! But to our purpose is the bit about our forgiveness being based on our forgiving.

This puzzled me for a long time. Though an aficionado of Lewisian writings, I have long thought his *Forgiveness* (Lewis 2002:3.7) and, incidentally, *Petitionary Prayer* (C S Lewis' *Christian Reflections*, ch12), misleading. On the former, in spite of many gems, such as "all killing is not murder, any more than all sexual intercourse is adultery", and Lewis rightly hating his sinful actions yet loving himself the sinner (do thou likewise), he failed to analyse the context of daily forgiveness. I say again, that biblically we are assured that all in Christ are ultimately forgiven: ultimately sin is rejection of God, and Christians have shown their inner Godwardness by their Christwardness.

Ultimate forgiveness isn't the focus of the daily paternoster. Indeed, its original audience were ethnic-Jews, not the church. They had long understood that God could forgive without immediate sacrifice. For instance, dated about C3/2 BC, Sirach 28:2 says that those who forgave others, would themselves be forgiven when they prayed.[193] Yet that forgiveness would have been based on doing *Leviticus* so far as able, so Yom Kippur and the regular five offerings (in desire) would have been the anchor for forgiveness (Heb.9:22). "In consideration of sacrifice, which generally by the very act itself indicated willingness to comply with God's provision, God in grace extended his forgiveness to the guilty" (Martens 65).

God was also already father to the people *as a people*—basically their corporate father. So short-term the paternoster supplemented *Leviticus* under Sinai, though soon gained a deeper meaning when the cross left Sinai behind. Deific forgiveness in fact predated Sinai,

---

[193]   Our acts don't force God to forgive, but can allow him to.

though some kind of sacrifice was common. "Your kingdom come" would soon be answered, and a new application begin—in fact the expected messianic kingdom was stirring even as Yeshua spoke. We will get our fullest answer by the lord's second advent—in fact the kingdom is growing among us.[194] The answers to this prayer will have varied according to which side of the cross it has been asked. Well, what about for us praying "forgive us"? Is that based on Sinai too?

Our human relationships get a hammering daily. Offence is given and taken, toes trodden on, feelings hurt, plans upset, and damage unkindly done. God joyfully offers forgiveness to those who have rebelled against him. His nature is within us, and he wishes it to take root and develop. In order to develop, it must be allowed to go his way, and we like him to offer forgiveness to those who sin against us. Being like him, our relationship with him will flourish, and the daily sins we commit against him he'll happily brush aside, wash away.

God's willing but unable to forgive those who won't accept his forgiveness. If we're unwilling to forgive others, he's unable to happily walk with us. "Walk happily with us, as we would happily walk with others", is the inner meaning of that prayer. The paternoster focuses our attitudes towards being forgivers, fellowship builders, and our minds towards the daily need to be readjusted at the fellowship level: even Sinai had an optional fellowship offering (Lv.3). James urged Christian sinners, the double-minded who were toggling between living towards God and living against God, to repent their sin. He probably spoke of significant drifts away from the father. He even threw in some Greek aorist tenses to underline the decisiveness needed in getting back to God the father.

But even pleasing James, won't achieve sinless perfection in this life.[195] For daily walk with God, we still seek his daily forbearance, as we cultivate his attitude of forgiveness towards those who sin against us.

---

[194] It is like the growth like wheat, like waves of the incoming tide.

[195] Seeing some Bible versions using the word *perfect*, and that a major *Holy Spirit* upgrade is available to Christians, has led some folk into the idea that a decisive coming into holiness is available for Christians. I argue that gaining Christ gains holiness (type 1), into which Christians ought to grow by the spirit (type 2).

But it's neither to gain, nor to guarantee, our ultimate forgiveness. That is already assured us.[196] That is the big point: we stand forgiven by the cross into God's kingdom and should know it. Be assured.

Kingdom priests

Ethnic priests had special access to Yahweh, and acted as mediators between him and his people. A variation on the priestly theme likens us to priests. Do I believe that women can be priests? Yes, whenever they become Christians—all Christians are priests. As regards ecclesiastical jobs, if they can do 'em, let 'em, I say, within the courtesy of not damaging toes. Same goes for men and children. I don't say that all people are interchangeable, or even that the genders are interchangeable in function, but that all those in Christ are equal vis-à-vis the father—and it's this level I'm focusing on. "We...have access to the father through Christ by the one spirit" (CEB: Eph.2:18).

In fact, Christian access precludes any priestly level within Christianity—Christianity is priestly. The term *priest* is, like *minister*, somewhat misleading, even if the office holders do fantastic work. All Christians are ministers, *diakonoi*, servants, even though some specialise as servants/deacons (Php.1:1), a specialisation not applying to the term *priest*, but applicable to those called elders/*presbuteroi* (Ac.15:22)—not all who were older were elders.[197] All Christians have priestly access to the father.

The term *priest* has been rather abused. In tracing the modern word *priest* back to its roots, one Roman Catholic scholar admitted that the

---

196 It is that decisiveness that Jesus actually implied by footwashing (Jhn.13), rather than daily cleaning: aorist tenses imply a one-off. Before the cross, the Eleven were clean as preconverts, but lacked the final touch, likened to the end of journey footwashing. For them, that came by their master's death to complete the deal, so it is not a pattern for us—Jesus doesn't wash Christian feet but made Christian feet. The total bodywash illustration supersedes the preconversion bodywash-with-an-end-of-journey-footwash. Conversion makes us totally clean before God—which water-baptism symbolises—and daily sins are dealt with as we walk in the light (1 Jhn.1:7—present tenses, unlike v9).

197 A good case can be made linking them with the spiritual oversight as *episkopoi* of local congregations—what some call *bishops* (eg Ac.20:17,28). The logic would be that for church oversight only the mature (age based) should apply.

Greek term *presbuteros* meant elder: "the term priest as used today is not identical in meaning with the word presbyter as it was originally used." Welcome back Erasmus! And as regards Sinai, *Hebrews* "made it unmistakeably clear to any who...hankered after the ritual of the past, that Christ has...fulfilled, superseded, and abandoned...the priesthood of the OT" (Küng 364-5—rearranged). As for the church, the real word for priest, *hiereus*, "is not used...anywhere in the NT for someone who holds office in the church" (Küng 364).

Küng didn't mean that no office holder was a priest, but simply that since all Christians are priests, it was biblically misleading to use that tag for any specialism. That said, not all ecclesiastical office holders are Christians, even if called priests/bishops—plenty of wolves cross-dress as sheep, and some sheep transition outside the flock, gamekeepers to poachers! Küng contrasted the old to the new: sacrifices yes, but now mediated through Christ and offering thanksgiving and praise; not the giving of external gifts, but the giving of external gifts of ourselves (Küng 369; Heb.13:15; Rm.12:1). All Christians are priests—thank God.

The individualisation of priesthood is amazing. In the Yeshuic Covenant, priesthood is based neither on one's paternity nor on subsequent election. Yeshua bypassed the priestly tribe of Levi/Aaron, and based his priesthood on that mysterious character Melchizedek, a royal priest and type/pattern of priest to whom Ethnic-Israel's priests bowed. Electing for Christ elects to that priesthood—conversion is consecration. We need no mediator other than messiah, nor is the former Sinaitic duty of mediating for sinners our duty, though evangelism now is. In Christ we have God's attentiveness—within the royal priesthood we're priests unto God (Rv.1:6), priestly service being worship: "John used images of [Ethnic] Israel to describe the...church" (Smalley 36). If you are a priest, are you playing your priestly part?

Kingdom temple

Are you a temple? In the ethnic kingdom, the holy tent/temple became the very orb of national worship. Indeed, in crisis some felt that all they needed to do was to invoke the temple for total protection: "Yahweh's temple, Yahweh's temple, Yahweh's temple", they chanted (Jr.7:4). Yahweh heard, then demolished his temple by his Babylonian army. Whereas Christians often go first to *Genesis*, Judaists often go first to *Leviticus*, which is very much based around the tabernacle/temple theme. Bear in mind that Judaism began as a rethink over how to operate after Yahweh demolished the *second* temple by his Roman army. It differs from the multi-stranded intertestamental Jewish religion, into which Jesus was born, and is itself multi-stranded and ethnocentric. Yet some ethnic-Jews still hope for a temple rebuild, a red heifer sacrifice, reinstitution of cultus sacrifices, and a sense that Palestinians (unless Judaists) have been cleansed from their land, their borders secure. Should we back them?

No. Sadly the temple, once the pivotal community asset, is still longed for. When they had Herod's stone temple complex, some imagined that Yeshua dared them to demolish it, their very hope to precede the messianic temple predicted by Ezekiel—an irony there! Herod the Great's temple enlargement plan had been going on for forty-six years (dating this dialogue at about AD 28), and the temple compound was only completed in AD 63, seven years before its demolition.[198] Even his literalist disciples didn't understand at the time that Yeshua was God's true/*alēthinos* temple: "some things 'predicted' in the [OT] were not set out as verbal predictions, but as pictures, events, peoples, institutions" (Carson 1991:182).

Miraculous signs (*sēmeia*) given in Jerusalem (Jhn.2:23), were generally unheeded by its leadership: Nicodemus was an exception (3:2). Jesus had declared himself the true place where God's glory was, and even his close disciples didn't make sense of it until they had witnessed his resurrection. The NT puts much weight on Christians being 'in Christ' as their point of identification. In line with this, they can say that while messiah is the light of the world, they too are that light (8:12; Mt.5:14). Yahweh's Servant would be the light to the Gentiles (Is.49:6): the messianic community took on this messianic role (Ac.13:47).

---

[198]   Some say that the term *naos* carried its narrower meaning of *most holy place, inner sanctum*, note that that was built in under 2 years about 46 years earlier, and reckon that the Greek aorist verb must be consummative—as if "it was built 46 years ago." This would allow dating Jesus' death at AD 33, but I think it's more likely that they would have used the wider meaning of *naos* to contrast 46 years of building to Yeshua's presumed nonsense of 3 days.

Likewise, Yeshua was the temple which the physical buildings had predicted: we are temples individually (1 Cor.6:19), communally (2 Cor.6:16), and globally across the generations (1 Pt.2:5-7), the loci of the Holy Spirit. A cosmic temple is yet to be.

And yes, a temple upgrade awaits as well. Paul spoke of all being subjected to Jesus (except God his father), the supreme commander until the point when his father, the king of the king over all human monarchs, takes over (1 Cor.15:27-8):[199] his father appointed him lord (Php.2:11). Like J R R Tolkien's story in which Aragorn entered Minas Tirith to be its king, God the father shall ultimately take his place among us, as if the true glory has only just come (Rv.21:22)—but oh what tasters are ours!

Interestingly, Scripture speaks of the church—both globally and represented locally—as being messiah's *bride* (Eph.5:32). Yet this is before the wedding—he's making arrangement for her to be ready for the wedding (not 'marriage'). Oh, how badly Hollywood yearns to brainwash us by its idea that a hero is only happy to die for a heroine if he's ~~fornicated~~ slept with her! It was as if the Christian congregation at Corinth was Paul's daughter. It was as if he had betrothed her, with her consent, so she was a wife, but being a wife should remain a virgin until her wedding (2 Cor.11:2): Paul feared spiritual adultery. Likewise our *marriage* to messiah is glorious, yet we yearn for the *wedding* feast when we may fuller enter our true home (Rv.19:7: CEB/CEV/ERV/LEB/NABRE/NCV/NIV/NLT).[200] Theologically, *engagement* is a poor word, and sacerdotal talk of the church 'marrying' couples is vain.

Anyway, all that's to come. Back to this age as God's temples. It's good to recap the movement from tabernacle/tent to fixed temple, then to

---

[199] "..all in all" (1 Cor.15:28) in context is metaphysical, not soteriological: "it is not the absorption of Christ and mankind, with consequent loss of distinct being, into God, but rather the unchallenged reign of God alone, in his pure goodness" (Barrett 1986:361). Once the irredeemable is subjugated by Christ, the redeemed will be joyfully presented to God, who will then be "utterly supreme over everything everywhere" (NLT). Paul's setting was of the true Adam authoritatively bringing harmony to chaos, and abundant harvest gratefully to God. One could also think of the true Joshua/Jesus, and the true conquest of Canaan allowing for the harvest.

[200] The MEVV get Lk.14:8 right; the NKJV/NRSV get the significant Rv.19:7 wrong.

Jesus (who is God's son's pitched tent: Jhn.1:14). He was what they typologically prophesied as God's glory among us. He in turn enables humanity, through transformation by his spirit, to be as individuals temples, as congregations temples, and together over the Christian millennia, God's temple on earth, until the father ultimately pitches his permanent tent site (*skēnē*) with us (Rv.21:3).[201]

It's good to recall that the tent was where Moses alone would meet with Yahweh, and come out with a glowing face. Once Aaron took over as high priest, only high priests in his line were allowed to enter into central tent/temple area (the shrine/most holy place, *naos*), and then only once each year, as national servants to deep-clean the nation. If we're Christians, we too were prophesied, and we are prophecies of the cosmic temple still to come. In this age, we are individually worship sites, mobile tents that signal God's nearness and the knowledge of forgiveness. Each of us has become a shrine, a most holy place, a *naos* (1 Cor.6:19), which God indwells in covenant. At times we come into a local worship site, a local congregation (1 Cor.3:16-7),[202] as part of a bigger thing. At times, as assemblies, we reflect on the bigger picture again, the church worldwide and spanning millennia (1 Pt.2:5), that is, on Israel gone global.

In the ethnic kingdom, Jerusalem was geographical. Is it too much to ask if Jesus' talk about us being like a city on a hill (Mt.5:14) had in mind Jerusalem-Zion, home of the temple? Is.60 spoke of Yahweh's light going to the Gentiles (3), with Jerusalem being the obvious imagery. She would be called "Yahweh's City, Zion, of the holy one of Israel" (CEB: 14). Paul used the illustration of ethnic Jerusalem. Having been God's focus in salvation history, by clinging to that past once it had moved on ("Jerusalem in its present state" (NJB: Gal.4:25)), she had become as much a slave as Hagar had been, spiritually a Gentile, the pre-alpha, pre-Davidic level of common humanity (Rv.11:8).[203] The

---

[201]   For a really in-depth cover of the temple theme, see Beale 2004.

[202]   Compared to the pagan temples in Corinth, and the wonderful one in Jerusalem, their disunity would have made them seem a poor relation: Is.53:2.

[203]   Douglas Moo noted how in Rm.9:7-8, ethnic Israel could be contrasted the Christ as Ishmael to Isaac, Abraham's seed *kata sarka* but not God's true child, not Abraham's child according to the promise (Scorgie, Strauss, & Voth 370).

Snake, which had been a blessing in Moses' time, had become a curse in Hezekiah's (2 Kg.18:4)—an instance of Level 2 (Sinai) reverting to Level 1 (pre-Sinai) of the Snake.

Hagar's child was in Yahweh's will, but in his common noncovenant plan. Egyptian-born—like Jacob's people had been just before the exodus—Hagar settled with Ishmael in Midian (now Saudi Arabia), which incorporates Mount Sinai. By ignoring the call to move onto the messianic land (True Canaan), Ethnic-Israel had, by and large, theologically settled alongside Hagar in Sinai—common land. The true Joshua had indeed given them the option of true covenant or reversion (Jos.24:15).

Meanwhile, Global-Israel, beginning with righteous remnants of Ethnic-Israel, has moved on towards the next stage of promised land, wherein is the city of true/*alēthinos* peace, though even spiritual Jerusalem now is but a shadow of spiritual Jerusalem future—the ultimate level. We have shalom-harmony with God now.

The definition of *Israel* had moved on; the definition of *Jerusalem* had moved on; the definition of *temple* had moved on—much had moved on and left many behind, cut-off from the root plan. The New Jerusalem was to be the temple radiance from God's hill, shining to a hostile world God's love and redemption offer, covenant entrance. If a Christian, a mobile messenger of Yahweh's shalom, you are a Jerusalem. Let your light so shine—and rejoice.

Kingdom prophets

In the ethnic kingdom, prophets were major players. Now, the prophetic spirit is individualised. When Jesus spoke about the most honoured of OT prophets, he named John the Baptist (Mt.11:11). John fitted the Elijah role as messenger. Moses had set up Sinai, and Elijah had played a crucial part within Sinai, but John directly prepared for what had been the ultimate goal of Sinai, the passing of the baton to messiah when Sinai bowed out gracefully before the new *berith*. This was history's crux, more significant than even Abraham becoming the faith pattern, or Moses mediating the Sinaitic Covenant, or Aaron heading up the cultus or the great prophets who directed Ethnic-Israel. And to think that some have said that the NT church was an afterthought or at least a subtheme in an ethnic master plan!

Mt.11:11 contrasts the words *micro* and *mega*, and context refers to advancement. The least (micro) Christian probably isn't as holy in lifestyle as John had been, nor as dynamic in God's kingdom, yet is more enviable than John was, for unlike John they are within the messianic community. It's a position beyond John's dreams. Each Christian is better placed than the greatest person of Ethnic-Israel had been. Christians, suffering social intimidation and exclusion in Asia Minor, were told that "they were more privileged in the perspective of redemptive history than they could have known—more privileged than either the great prophets of old or angels above" (Jobes 105).[204] The Sinaitic Mountain (salvation Level 2) dwarfed world religions, yet even the Yeshuic foothills (salvation Level 3) dwarf Sinai's pinnacle. Under Sinai, Moses wished that all would have Yahweh's spirit (Nb.11:29); under Yeshua, all may prophesy (1 Cor.14:31).[205]

John the Baptist's generation waited for what has now come. His prophetic insight now pales alongside entrance level Christianity— which boasts not of itself but of its lord. By comparing the former with the now, we do but acknowledge Christ's facticity; to dismiss comparisons is but to deny Christ. Either he is as he claimed, the way, the truth, and the life, or he is not.[206] The basic level insight of each convert is likely to be something like the key to the kingdom, redemption, the newness of the kingdom, its joy, peace, love, meaningfulness, or cleanness. Different people see the doorway differently, but the prophetic vision was of Jesus who is the door.

It may be significant that John expected community rescue more than salvific individualisation, his national hopes trying to interpret his prophetic feelings: Israel-Judah had long deemed itself to be the

---

[204] C S Lewis' *Out of the Silent Planet* pictured the idea that angels are universal creatures, undying photosomatic beings that cross the galaxies yet stand amazed by God's redemptive work upon earth—how marvellous, how wonderful.

[205] Paul taught sensible deployment of this non-preaching ability. Glossolalia was an option for all, but not all should publicly practice it in meetings.

[206] Jhn.14:6 specifies God as father, not God as God. Maybe Hinduism accesses God as God, but Jesus is the only way to God *as father*, Christianity's unique selling point. For Jhn.14, think 123—1 mention of God, 23 mentions of the father: significant?

global hub. God had given John specific help to prepare for and to identify messiah.[207] Some of the righteous remnant became his disciples, and when he identified Jesus as messiah, some switched from prophet to messiah. But even then, not everything was clear to John. He had earlier misunderstandings, too. He had long known that his cousin Yeshua was exceptionally holy. So John was shocked when Yeshua asked him to immerse him. After all, John's baptism ritual was linked to national repentance, yet obviously his cousin didn't need to repent so he had tried to talk him out of it.[208]

Having given in, he saw the sign that God had spoken to him about, and realised that his cousin Jesus was messiah. Yet wearing national glasses—like Pontius Pilate—John still thought that Jesus' kingdom (as heir of King David) was ethnocentric/earthly, not christocentric/heavenly (Mt.11:3; Jhn.18:36). Thankfully, prophetic vision now comes with free heavenly glasses for all—and what a vision!

John was a prophet. In each local church, each Christian may prophesy as part of the charismatic skills base. Of course, as Paul taught, to keep things on track others should weigh up what's said, and correct any glitches. Of course, this can be hard, especially when the clouded vision is a prophetic song with pleasing content, a thrilling tune, and a high woo and wow factor. And funnily enough, charismatic churches seldom encourage their members to critique songs anyway.[209] Christian revelation is far beyond the best insights of the ancients. Charismatic prophecy is in fact a minor though blessed sideshow. All Christians are in the prophetic school: we might not all foretell/predict, but we may all forthtell/proclaim as prophesiers of God, low level prophets.

Paul taught that Christ established Christian prophets and also Christian evangelists: both should work side by side (Eph.4:11). I

---

[207] John was, like Abraham, a link between salvation levels. Like Abraham, he had a message of righteousness. Level 2 had immediate righteousness for its covenant; Level 3 had immediate righteousness for its covenant (Mt.21:32; 5:20).

[208] And indeed Jesus hadn't needed to repent but had needed to identify with John's work so as to affirm it by reduplication and fulfilment.

[209] For some issues, see my *Singing's Gone Global*.

suspect that evangelism has taken on part of Christ's prophetic message. It proclaims the new message, and gets on well with the element of predictive prophecy. The latter functions at various levels as messages in line with Scripture and geared to situations where we need to hear what God is saying to the churches and to us. To some extent even this spirit of prophecy, this hearing ear, is open to us all though some specialise in it. But let us judge with caution. Each of us can hear from God and speak for God.

Chapter 10 <u>Ultimate Salvation</u>

<u>The Best is Yet to Come</u>

"O resurrection body, young, radiant, vibrant, free / with powers unthought, undreamed of—how rich your joys will be! / Through endless years to marvel, design, create, explore / in resurrection wonder to worship, serve, adore!" (Margaret Clarkson's *In Resurrection Bodies*, 1987, stanza 4).[210] OK, it's a bit weird to sing to a body, especially one not yet existing, but her terms of wonder make the song. The study of aioniology (study about eternity) is looking beyond death's door: "because of the joy awaiting him, [Jesus] endured the cross" (NLT: Heb.12:2).

Let's wax Lewisian. C S Lewis touched a little on this: Reepicheep joyously went over the crest of the permanent wave (*The Voyage of the Dawn Treader*); to someone who had not died, Aslan pointed out that he himself was in the majority who had died (*The Silver Chair*); at last, all Narnians divided themselves into seeking and finding Aslan, or disappearing into his shadow to be lost in darkness (*The Last Battle*). To those who used the pie-in-the-sky taunt to jeer him out of belief in heaven, Lewis replied that there is either pie in the sky or there is not (Lewis 1972:132).[211] Facts are facts, whether nice or nasty, and we should pursue truth in its own name. Be open to God. Imprisoned in their unbelief, the Black Dwarfs ate decay instead of...pie. God can even give pie to those who seemingly seek it rather than seeking himself the baker—the deific humility.

The heavens declare the glory of God, but let's not be too quick to think of heaven as a bait or bribe. Some seek the glory of marriage and look for someone to marry; some first see someone and then yearn to marry them. Both approaches are far different from mercenaries who seek to marry a wealthy person to gain their wealth. In fact, since the heavens declare his glory, to accept God in order to

---

[210]   www.hopepublishing.com/html/main.isx?sitesec=40.2.1.0&hymnID=3236

[211]   And "if there is not, then Christianity is false, for the doctrine is woven into its whole fabric". Yet that's not to be our aim as if mercenaries (Lewis 1972:132-3). John spoke of our wedding feast in heaven (Rv.19:7)—why not some pie?

---

get heaven, might not be so much amiss. After all, isn't loving his creation tied in with loving its creator?

In *The Last Battle*, once Emeth (a pagan with the Hebrew name 'truth') had died, he found heaven, but meeting Aslan was wholly a holy surprise. Though now in his true home, his mind was uneasy. He had consciously sought to please Aslan's enemy, Tash the inexorable, the irresistible. Yet Aslan assured Emeth that Tash was so untruthful that the truthful Emeth, mentally misguided by false teachers, had at heart always sought Tash's enemy, Aslan, and always rejected the demon that Tash really was. Emeth's heart and head had travelled different paths, and Aslan straightened out the head. We don't always know what we seek, until we find. Heaven is the rightful reward for those who have truly sought God, even if their heads have been misguided. Likewise, the joys of marriage are for those who have truly sought their spouse, even if their heads have been misguided.

Sadly, some Evangelicals put so extremely negative a slant on Lewis' writings, that they'll be wholly amazed to find him holy in heaven. When Lewis became a Christian, he deeply felt his sins. His mind hadn't desired God, though had long felt atheism to be a useful but increasingly shallow defence. In the early part of 1930—probably in the Trinity Term of that year[212]—and already beginning to fear that God might exist, on what should have been a safe bus journey home, he fell off atheism's safe cliff. "Amiable agnostics will talk cheerfully about 'man's search for God.' To me, as I then was, they might as well have talked about the mouse's search for the cat" (McGrath 138). Indeed, he had been delighted when his atheist teacher Kilpatrick had confirmed his teenage atheism, a bit like confirming that debt collectors don't exist—there is no debt. Yet when the cat came for the mouse, the collector for payment, Lewis was surprised by joy, the serious business of heaven, and repented the moral mess he'd lived.

He had long walked under a basic umbrella of atheism in denying a creator and lord, though dabbling in a number of pagan philosophies and romanticism for heart's ease and for the distant call of joy. In such lawlessness he had been "a zoo of lusts, a bedlam of ambitions, a

---

[212] Departing from the standard dating of Trinity Term 1929 (McGrath 138). Oxford term-times were Michaelmas, Hilary, and Trinity.

nursery of fears, a harem of fondled hatreds. My name was legion."[213] As a Christian he developed a purgatory concept. In his daily diet he avoided aphrodisiacs like the plague, fearing least his libido led to sexual sin. Quite possibly his landlady Mrs. Moore, whom he had taken on as a duty of care, had once been a lover. Quite possibly his love for Joy Davidman (from fellow Christian, to friend, to wife) had had to undermine his defences built to maintain a bachelor life as some kind of penance, even some kind of protection by celibacy against a perceived vulnerability.

In *A Grief Observed*, we can see that marriage released his libido, and that sexually he had had a whale of a time. But though he was by nature a jovial man, I think his concept of purgatory—not the Roman Catholic concept—was established long before marriage, in which he spoke of his shy reluctance to enter the throne room of God unclean. Whereas Johann Eck had charged people money to let souls out of purgatory, C S Lewis would have paid good money to get in.

As a Christian he saw that his spiritual pride was a war in which sexual misconduct (still deadly) paled to the level of a child's game. His heart cried out for purgation, which he hoped would begin in earnest once he died, and continue for some time. Here I think he underestimated God's tolerance over messed up minds, and God's power to free us from sin's presence upon death. In his chapter on heaven (Lewis 1972:ch.10), he unfolded his idea that self-surrender—like a peeling off of layers like Eustace's dragon scales—might well be an eternal operation. Discordia, goddess of the Trojan War, continues to laugh whenever we continue to look towards our pleasures, our vanities, our selfhood, our our-ness. But does she live in heaven?

Lewis, I think, felt so, imagining heaven as a gradual shedding off of sin's scales, which leads to our becoming more what we are: decreasing contamination, increasing joy. And this I quite like, without agreeing with it. He well noted that heaven, not hell, is humanity's natural destination: "the saved go to a place prepared for them, while the damned go to a place never made for humans at all" (Lewis 1972:113–citing Mt.25:34,41). He also combined individualism with corporality here, along the lines that in heaven each is a soloist, each

---

[213]   www.gci.org/history/lewis

has their particular insight into God, yet together form the choir, each fully enjoying what each other sings. Indeed, that each has their own instrument, together playing the great symphony—the "communion of the saints" (Lewis 1972:138). The *Music of the Ainur* without Melkor, we could say.

Paul applied some of Isaiah's sentiments to the unimaginable having happened (1 Cor.2:9; Is.52:15; 64:4), namely the opening up of Global-Israel, but I think we may extend it into the future unveiling. Let's discount as naive the picture of a gigantic campfire circle of harpists, whose only job *ad nauseam* is to praise God who's sat in the middle (Rv.5:8 and 15:2 are more Picasso than Photo-realistic). We're not going anywhere, we're not learning anything...boring. I think of *A Little Princess* (1995): Lavinia's harp and boredom, versus Sarah's fun and joy! If the harp is heaven's best, well, God could do better.

J R R Tolkien reminded us that those created in the creator's image are subcreators. So, if our imagination can do better yet at best is a mere shadow to God's, his surprise for us must indeed far exceed our wildest imagination. In *The Silver Chair*, Puddleglum faces the idea that perhaps his belief in Narnia is a mere child's imagination. Yet, says he to the queen whose sweet magic seeks (like Political Correctivism and 'shame on you' lobbies) to overcome better sense, it's better dying for that imagination than living in her unimaginably dark and dreary kingdom. An eternal camp singsong to an eternal egotist? No thanks. *Revelation* has broader imagery—city, river, etc. In imagination, let's explore its city, its river! Its aim is to be suggestive of deeper realities. Literalism isn't the endgame. Prose will give way to poetry in motion.

The word *heaven* covers a number of concepts. For example, it's Earth's sky (Gen.7:11), it's the cosmos (Ps.8:3), metaphorically it's God's home (Rm.1:18; 1 Cor.15:47)—though philosophically speaking he *is* his home, our ultimate surround. We are each a soul integrated with our body. Jesus rose with his physical transformed body to maintain his physical connection with us—so where is he physically now? Surely neither in a space suit nor flown to some class M planet!

Science fiction, often uneasy with Christianity, plays with the idea of phasing between dimensions, and might sometimes have more truth than it knows. What begins in time and space must continue in time and space—but has space hidden dimensions, like a mansion with many rooms? The apostles were behind sealed doors. Did Jesus pass through those doors by *phasing* his physical body? We are to become as Jesus is. Perhaps our glorified physical bodies will be under the protection and use of our spirits made perfect under the father of spirits? Bodies immortal, able to eat and drink for pleasure, not for need? Glorified, Jesus was still able to eat and drink. Enjoyment value, not survival value. Exploring eternity is part of exploring salvation.

Job is something of a detective story. The big question was why such a good man had such terrible suffering. Unlike his readers he didn't see the first act, which showed that at one level Yahweh possibly sought to teach the satan, humanity's ultimate sceptic, that humans were capable of unselfish loyalty. Yahweh allowed the common calamities of life to reach Job. Many contemporaries of Job asked the same basic question—should the deities be worshipped purely for advantage and protection? And what if the deities, far from benefiting us, allowed or even sent overwhelming suffering? Is suicide not the logical escape (curse God and die)?

The dialogues carry certain presuppositions, wheedling out whether or not only sin leads to suffering, and whether the depth of hidden suffering reveals the depth of sin. If the man wasn't at fault, was the deity at fault? Yahweh was named. Was he a cosmic sadist? Job finally bowed to Yahweh's overwhelming wisdom, with a "your will be done", and the drama ended with superabundant blessings for him and humble pie for his well-intentioned but misguided friends, who hadn't understood God well enough to help Job. Job was blest to meditate on wonders concealed from his peers, and some of these wonders we can enjoy by scientific instruments. What if one day we will enjoy them better, without instruments? Does that glory await us? Job was encouraged to think about the microscopic (38:22), the ornithological (41), the astronomical (31), and the mathematical (33). Clues, I think, to heaven.

But, you may ask, isn't nature to be destroyed? For "...the day of the lord will come as a thief in the night, in which the heavens will pass away with a great noise, and the elements will melt with fervent heat; both the earth and the works that are in it will be burned up" (NKJV: 2 Pt.3:10). Reformationism isn't as happy as Lutheranism to take this as being literal, perhaps being more nature affirming. The Bible speaks of removing the dross, burning the fields of weeds for a fresh start. Yet it's as Smalley said of such talk in Rv.21:1, "the removal of the sea does not mean that the physical universe has been completely destroyed, but rather that it has been completely transformed, and that there is now no threat from Satan" (Smalley 524).[214] And Isaac Watts sang of thorns no longer infesting the ground.[215]

It is because Scripture affirms the universe to continue and to be glorified (Rm.8:20-1), that I think that 2 Pt.3:10/Rv.21:1 speak poetically of fallen governance/society ending. The old washed away like at the Noahic Flood, but with a new and blessèd intoxication to follow. The animal kingdom will, I suspect, continue in some way liberated from the impact of sinful man, and Paul poetically spoke of it looking forward to new management, not terminal maelstrom.

The psalmists, rejoicing in the shining stars, were awed that Yahweh cared far more for mankind than for stars (Ps.8), a destiny that Jesus began to unfold as the first of the new humanity (Heb.2:8-9).[216] Glorified, Jesus could move between dimensions, ignoring walls, yet eating food (Lk.24:36,42-3). Is space God's gift to us of a universal playground? In *Out of the Silent Planet* (C S Lewis), Ransom felt surrounded by life—what we call angels—in Deep Heaven, once he left our silent planet. Decontamination makes room for true joy.

I'm not against the planet of my birth, nor the town of my birth. I have long left that town, but can happily revisit. Glorified by our heavenly father, will we fly from Mother Earth's nest? Will we planet hop, star hop through space, captaining our glorified bodies, safe from harm to revel in exploring both God's creation and God the creator? Glorified eyesight, glorified hearing, seeing in infrared the 'snowflakes' of other worlds, hearing the whale songs of other planets, feeling the pulse of quasars? Will we be at liberty to phase in and out with dimensions we cannot yet see or touch? Will we hover over universal history without TARDIS or Internet? It's a mighty big universe, but then, we'd love a mighty big playground.

---

[214]   *Sea* had long carried the idea of chaos and mythological horrors.

[215]   www.hymnsandcarolsofchristmas.com/Hymns_and_Carols/joy_to_the_world-hakes.htm

[216]   Level 3 salvation is also proleptic of Level 4.

In *The Lord of the Rings*, Legolas is able to adjust the curvature of his eyes to focus them as binoculars. Will we not have more control over our physical bodies, once glorified? Will we not be able to communicate astronomically without communicators? Will we not be able to adjust our eyes to the telescopic and to the microscopic? Will we not be able to see endless colour combinations beyond the rainbow? Will we not be able to revel in creaturely life? Will we not be able to behold the inner life of the atoms? To explore the deepest oceans of worlds unexplored, even their very cores? To explore more taste buds than a Ratatouille Rat? To zoom around the universe without needing protective suits and spacecraft, where kryptonite holds no fears? Will we not have abilities far beyond that of angels?

And will not our spirits, once purified, be able to totally share with one another, redeemed humanity without shame or fear—what release and what joy! Earth is a wonderful planet. It's so anthropic that some atheistic scientists even create a multiverse in their imaginations, to blind their followers from the idea that Earth seems rather God-shaped for man to live in and to thrive. So amazing is our planet within the amazing universe. Will we be confined to one planet? I think not. Amazement awaits beyond death when we meet our risen lord, who has bodily gone where no man has gone before.

In a local graveyard somebody—perhaps pompously selfish—put a plaque that boasted that if possible, they'd drag the deceased kicking and screaming back from heaven to this woe begotten world—shades of Persephonē. Did their folly imagine that heaven was hell, and hell (or this fallen world) was heaven? One feels for Lazarus, the proto-martyr who was summoned back only to die yet again. With a Pickwickian smile, we tell the youngster that if we could we would drag them back from their marvellous holiday camp, where all are friends, back into dull old school where many are bullies. Good heavens!

Romans taught that death—sorry, nowadays that's 'passing on'—opened up new possibilities. To die is not to pick up where we left off, nor to clamour for the former times. Graves that speak of reunions speak of folly. "Unless, of course, you can literally believe all that stuff about family reunions on the further shore,' pictured in entirely earthly terms. But that is all unscriptural, all out of bad hymns and lithographs. There's not a word of it in the Bible. And it rings false. We know it couldn't be like that. Reality never repeats. The exact same thing is never taken away and given back. How well the spiritualists bait their hook! 'Things on this side are not so different after all.' There are cigars in heaven. For that is what we should all like. The happy past restored" (Lewis 1985:23).

The Sadducees had a standard way of rubbishing resurrection. It would be both silly and turning the biblical law of levirate marriage into an eternal sin, they said, if a woman widowed more than once had all her husbands restored after death (Mk.12:18-23). That seemed to them to be a clincher. But Jesus contradicted their conclusion, by denying their premise that spouses were reunited as spouses. Relationship links—be it of parents, spouses, offspring, friends, or enemies—all perish on death. One who has died a father no longer stands in that relationship—they have been retired from the job, and if redeemed will enjoy richer nonbiological relationships. So she who was my mother, is no longer my mother, but is simply a heavenly sister. From family trees the redeemed fly free, disencumbered. The joys and trials of earthly life have helped shape them, but have been preliminary, at best anticipations of true life, true relationships, true unity, true human society.

Beyond this life of shame, honour, regrets, loves, failures, and satisfaction, disinhibited we shall share our joys and insights with each other, beyond mere speech, of God's goodness, of God. No longer hiding ourselves, disinhibition shall be a gift from God, as we stop to chat with one another, ranging the universe. The universe is his handiwork. What better medium to explore and enjoy for eternity, feeling his vibrancy throughout time and space, as the fish feels always its watery surround as it moves through underwater marvels. Thus, always worshipping; thus, supremely worshipping. The music of heaven—here the imagery of harps perhaps meets reality. Our fascination will be the harps. Life will have moved from talk to song, from the prosaic to the poetic, to infinity and beyond. With a nod to C12 Bernard of Clairvaux's *Jesu dulcis memoria*: "Yahweh, our deepest joy are you / As you our prize will be / Yahweh you are our glory true / and in eternity."

Summary

Some ask that if ultimate life is not unlocked by the evangelistic key, why trouble people with the evangel? This falls into the old blindness that salvation's only about pie in the sky once we die. We should not be mindful of the future at the expense of the moment. Is knowing God now as father, insignificant, a cosmetic accessory? Is the pearl of greatest price not worth selling all else we have, including our mortal lives?[217] Being under Sinai (the Level 2 domain) didn't give eternal life, but it did give a much better life than under any Level 1 (common) domain: it welcomed people in but didn't seek them. But there was no ultimate need, and Naomi actually disangelised Ruth.

Level 3 salvation is knowing Yahweh as family (Jhn.17:3), a realised, an immediate, eschatology: God is father to his individual children, an eternal blessing hitherto unknown. We have looked at a number of blessings that have been rejigged from the Sinai-communal to the messianic-individual level, and have thus been fulfilled, truly defined. For example, all Christians are priests but priests in different ways than the few among the Aaronites who had been priests under Sinai. These blessings are the glories of Christian life, which includes the assurance of Level 4 life that *Revelation* glimpses into. To dare to call God 'father' before death, is as Bilquis Sheikh realised, a life worth dying for.[218] The evangel offers something that the world can't give and the world can't take away, as we awesomely await the surpassing glories of ultimate life, what we may call future eschatology.

Scripture speaks of our physical bodies being like tents, earthly tatty tents needing to put on heavenly immortality. It also states that to die is of personal advantage (Php.1:21), but that we are not immediately to don immortal bodies. Might it be that upon death we enter a waiting and watching mode? That being released from Earth, we wait in incomplete mode in the theatre wings with the lord, and that only when the curtain comes down on this earthly show, will we in immortal bodies be released into deep heaven to fly free? A three-phase thing: on the stage, in the audience, departing from the theatre.

---

[217] Matthew's context was of a merchant spotting an incredible bargain price. And as Bonhoeffer said, free grace is not cheap grace—there is a cost of discipleship.

[218] Significantly, one of the few Aramaic words kept in the NT is *abba*/father.

Chapter 11   Ethnic-Israel; Redundant Road?

Jacob-Israel

Realising that many will zone out of this section with glazed eyes, I moved it from the opening chapter 1, to the closing chapter. Many Christians will, I guess, not be interested, nor need to know.

As already noted, the term Israel (*yisrā'ēl*) has had many layers of meaning. Let's begin with the first mention, often a good place to start, though not always the best place to end. A grandson of Abraham, named Jacob, fought his way into a new relationship with God. He was told, "Your name will no longer be Jacob. Your name will now be Israel, because you have wrestled with God and with people, and you have won" (NCV: Gen.32:28).[219] Accounts vary as to whether it was interaction with God himself (*Yahweh*) or with a *messenger* of his— elsewhere the 'angel of Yahweh' (*mal'āk Yahweh*) can very closely identify with Yahweh. The term for *messenger* can apply to both heavenly angels and human beings. The options can throw up struggles in our thinking. Is this biblical error, or biblical perspective? Before tackling Jacob, let's sidetrack to an NT example of mixing human/deific terms.

Angels, men, or God?

Did the empty tomb involve theiophany (divine appearance) or anthropophany (human appearance)? Mark spoke of a *young man* (*neaniskos*) at the tomb, while Matthew spoke of two *angels/ messengers* (*angeloi*), and Luke, to a more Gentile audience, spoke of two radiant *men* (*andres*)—radiance saying that they weren't mere humans.[220] Horses for courses, of course; images for audiences. Mark possibly spoke of a man (in white) who had been a secret disciple who, having gone to the tomb, realised Jesus had risen from death, and hastily told the approaching women. Ac.10 shows an angel (3-4), dressed up as a man (*anēr*): 30.

---

[219]   The Hebrew carried the idea of fighting/struggling/wrestling with God.

[220]   Likewise, Luke's account about Cornelius identified an angel (Ac.10:3) with a radiant man (10:30).

Indeed this was Frank Morison's take in his quite brilliant *Who Moved the Stone?*[221] He argued that a secret disciple, perhaps a servant of the High Priest and on the outskirts of Jesus' group (Mk.14:51-2), had overheard Jesus and arrived at the empty tomb before, and unknown to, the women. Swallowing the camel of resurrection, while straining out the gnat of angels, Morison—perhaps overly influenced in days when many sought a demythologised authentic text—thought Mark's the no nonsense matter of fact account, inflated by imagination into one (*Matthew*) or two (*Luke*) angels. But if this was what had happened, and this young disciple's story later circulated among the church— and why would it not?—how would any Gospel get away with calling a mere man an angel or two, and why would it wish to, knowing that living witnesses could blow the gaffe?

I suggest that for editorial/redactional reasons, Mark focused on the one heavenly angel who spoke to the women, describing its appearance (not its ontology) as that of a young man—just what the women first thought him to be. To an ethno-Jewish audience, Matthew, to clearly underline the majestic nature of the one who spoke, used *angelos*, which would more readily suggest a heavenly angel.[222] Luke phrased it in ways that Gentiles would nevertheless assume meant that divine messengers had been there. This is an NT example of stylistic changes. And it's a case of us adjusting to ancient manners of speech, able to divine that we're talking angels who could look conveniently like men.

Likewise when Heb.13:2 encourages hospitality—a wise but open-door policy. Jewish culture expected hospitality to those of the same extended family: Christian culture taught that fellow believers *were*

---

[221]   www.gospeltruth.net/whomovedthestone.htm. Some say, "too many probabilities to be possible", but proper scepticism asks whether, after reason fills the holes in our data, the result is coherent. If coherent, then at least the story is seen as possible—granted some reasonable conjectures.

[222]   I take Mt.28:2-4 to be a parenthesis after the Marys set off but before they arrived—the confused guards hadn't known what hit them, and their leaders tried to make sense of it within their denial mentality. The angel dimmed his glory so wasn't recognised. His message—along with their unease over the missing body—was immediately passed on. A return visit by Mary Magdalene also saw angels before she met Jesus (Jhn.20:14).

one's extended family *par excellence*. And some Christian travellers are special leaders, special *messengers* (*angelous*) with special blessings—see also Mt.10:41. And maybe one might even open the door to an immortal—a real live angel might be knocking at the door, but the Greek doesn't insist on this sense. We need a sense of historical culture and to tune in to how folk spoke in those cultures.

Jacob tried and tested

So going back to Jacob, from top down, theophany, huiophany, theiophany, or anthropophany? Reported one way it was as if an evenly matched man picked a fight with him in the night, testing Jacob's persistency, wondering how easily he would give up. Jacob was tested and stretched to his limits in the physical even as he would be in the spiritual. He had to hold on in great pain, and years later, his witness before Egypt's pharaoh would be of his difficult life (Gen.47:9). Yet he saw his people begin an era of blessing so profound that some would look back and say that God's particular love for Israel was scandalous, biased, not realising that this *scandal of particularism* was to develop God's dream for global blessing.

Jacob's opponent showed an ability to bless (Heb.7:7), and various other powers. It seems that he was more than human, but was he less than God? If Gen.32:28 shows that Jacob's opponent was *God*, it equally shows Jacob's opponent was in fact opponents, *men*, an illogical impasse. If it's about one event, the Aristotelian mind is left confused. However, Gen.32:28 included Jacob's earlier spiritual searching, struggling through deific and human barriers. He hadn't found his place with God or human society, but had struggled to the door that God had planned for him. Anyway, Rembrandt painted Jacob hugging a winged creature, so it must have been a heavenly angel! The Master has spoken. It is good to weave through the data, harmonising text with text within their culture. Sceptics prefer apparent contradiction and dismissal, to God's challenging message.

The message retains its inner core. Through the struggles of that night, Jacob was given a spiritually symbolic name, perhaps saying that he struggled with God (Hos.12:3-5). Jacob saw that his complex life had had meaning, and that he would significantly shape the future. Still, we do not need to picture deity as having appeared as a man (a theophany or huiophany) and *literally* having fought Jacob, like the Hulk literally fighting a flea. Nor indeed would even an angel of light, able to wipe out a human army at the blink of an eye, go all out to defeat Jacob, fail, and then cower terrified at the thought of being identified in the light of day. If a theiophany, the angel didn't fight his best. No, Jacob had been roped into a spiritual drama, an angel enrobed as a man play fighting to test Jacob, and—please excuse the pun—pulling his leg a bit. Like the enacted drama called water-baptism, Jacob was left with something to look back on, specifically a limp. Indeed, it might have encouraged him to witness to all who asked him how he got that limp.

Israel: God's Face

So, he and the angel had just acted out Jacob's life to date. Jacob didn't assume his opponent to be God and asked his name (Gen.32:29). That he named that place God's Face (*Peniel*) speaks not of the direct identity of the opponent, but of a level of revelation from God. Generations later Moses said to Yahweh, "If I have truly pleased you, show me your plans so that I may know you and continue to please you" (NCV: Ex.33:13). Yahweh affirmed his pleasure in working with Moses, showing him a shadow of his plans, a vague outline. The exodus wasn't a time for any to see God's Face (20), but Yah did affirm his covenant name, thereby affirming his covenant, and indicate that much of his plan (glory) remained hidden. In so many words, "It's classified. If I tell you I'll have to kill you!" But now the secret is out: we have looked at God's Face, going beyond the ethnic into the global. God's Face is Global-Israel.[223] Those who see this are in Israel.

Moses only had an inkling about that Face. None could fully ID it. Inspired by God, OT prophets (Moses was one) spoke of future times, yet try as they might they never saw the full story (1 Pt.1:10-2). Jesus of Mary was cousin to John of Zechariah, yet they represented different revelations. John had the final Sinaitic task of passing the mission to Jesus. Jesus had the new mission of a new covenant. Various markers show Jesus as the new Moses, but we shall not go into these here. Jesus was the first prophet of the new covenant, and John was the last prophet of the old. John was the greatest prophet of the Sinaitic era

---

[223]   We might also reflect on Heb.1:1-3 & Jhn.14:9.

because he had the greatest task to hand over the baton of that era, yet he didn't see how Jesus messiah would fulfil the prophecies.

The blindness of pride

Jesus failed John's ethno-nationalistic expectation (Mt.11:2). In 1901, William Wrede dubbed Jesus' silence on messianism, the Messianic Secret, wondering if the church later promoted their former leader to messiahship. Jesus probably kept silent simply because the expectation had become so deeply nationalistic, a warrior king who would deliver Ethnic-Israel from Roman occupation and raise it to international supremacy. Even a lot of OT prophets had assumed that any spiritual dimension would presuppose a renewed national aspect of Israel. We may question their assumption, and ask whether global grandeur was—common sinfulness aside—perhaps Ethnic-Israel's greatest problem.

Yeshua "did not incorporate into his message or mission any idea of nationalism.... [but] predicted a new community, a spiritual Israel" (Guthrie 1981:706-7). Nationalism can be great blindness. "If England was what England seems (An' not the England of our dreams, But only putty, brass, an' paint) 'Ow quick we'd drop 'er! But she ain't" (Rudyard Kipling's *The Return*). The English can see their country looking socially and economically bedraggled, yet dreamily feel that she's good at heart. Yet as good or bad as a country is, we are more likely to love ours not because it is good but because it is ours. We defend our identity and dream on, not wishing any rude awakening.

So much of our self-identity is tied into the history of our birthplace. We can be willing to die for her in battle, but what if such conflict conflicts with our spiritual identity? Conscientious Objectors have sometimes been right but seldom been praised. Consider a 1935 German man happy to kill or die for his country, but not for Hitler's Empire—praise him. And what of C S Lewis' warning that if there are spiritual mortals on other planets, human Christians might even be obliged to fight against fellow humankind to defend their alien spiritualkind—praise them? Our ultimate commitments and identities are with he whose kingdom was not of this world, not to the nationalism of a fallen race.

Opened eyes can often see the blindness of nationalism. Consider for instance the ten lepers (Lk.17). Incidentally it wasn't true leprosy (Hanson's Disease), simply skin blemishes that under Levitical law required sufferers to be treated as peripheral citizens. That was all part of teaching by symbolism. And such leprosy had potential spiritual blessing for unblemished citizens, as well as for the blemished, in understanding Yahweh's plan and love for them. It is too big to look into here, yet part of this blessing was to understand that the normal was better than the subnormal, and that life in the main community was better than life in the peripheral community.[224]

At a time when Jewish nationals resented the subnormal Samaritan enclave in the land, Luke spoke of a Good Samaritan. Of the ten whom Jesus had healed from leprosy, in order to worship Jesus only the Samaritan postponed the order about visiting his priest (Samaritans had their priesthood descended, they believed, from Aaron)—the twice subnormal welcomed grace even more. Incidentally biblical worship wasn't and isn't limited to deity. The long and the short of it is that of the ten, only the non-Jewish one put Jesus above the itch to reintegrate quickly into their community. He alone caught God's vision, whereas nationalistic Zionism sometimes relegates Jesus to peripheral leper status. Interestingly but wrongly, some suggest that Yahweh's Servant of Is.53 was a leper. Dezionising can clear our heads from glorifying an Ethnic-Israel: God's nation is messiah's church.

A sight for sore eyes

Opened eyes? On the Damascus Road, messiah zapped blind Saul, a blind Pharisee Saul. Dezionised and rezionised—healing from blindness symbolising his spiritual turnaround—and thereafter preferring his Gentile name *Paul*, he would look back to what had been a mystery face, and proclaimed at last as God's Face, revealing the depths of what *Israel* meant in God's design (Eph.1:9; 3:3-4,9). For the Greek *mystērion*, the CEB/ERV/NCV use the word *secret*; the CEV/LEB/NABRE/NIV/NKJV/NLT/NRSV use the word *mystery*. It carries

---

[224]   For more detail, see Nobuyoshi Kiuchi's *Leviticus* (AOTC), and Gordon Wenham's *The Book of Leviticus* (NICOT).

the idea of a classified secret, which when the new covenant came was declassified into the public domain—the secret is out.

Thus, the fact that Jacob saw God's Face, says much about the revelation concealed in his new name, *Israel*. For his people, the residue of that revelation had to be enough—even for Moses, that great leader, priest, and prophet. However, Moses did see that covenant with Yahweh had moved from solitary heirs of Abraham, to the entire children of Israel: covenant became ethnic and Yahwistic. There was great glory even in the partial revelation.

Let's reinforce the idea of God's Face *as meaning God's main plan*. We should remember that culturally they spoke of God looking like a human being (*anthropomorphism*), not because they believed that he did look like that, but because they could more easily identify with him in those terms. Naughty puppies, said a dog in one story, were called *boys*! Convenience terms. Ethnic-Israel even pictured Yahweh with wings (Ps.36:7), but then they also pictured the wind as having wings (18:10). Like us, they didn't believe that metaphors were literal, and being head over heels in love isn't only for gymnasts.

We shouldn't take their poetry literally. God hasn't a super-giant-size human shape, complete with beard. Islam is more prosaic, and to some extent is a helpful corrective to anthropomorphically thinking about God, who doesn't sit on a literal throne above us in outer space. If we would understand the Bible, we must understand its language.[225] While I've sketched a number of related points, my main point for now is that the name *Israel*—whether or not it means 'struggle with God'—was first given to someone as a prophetical name with a future. Let's look at its next stage, before going back a bit.

Ethnic-Israel

Spiritual life is a struggle. After his fight at Peniel, Yakob was sometimes called *Israel*, and sometimes (perhaps a name-play on his propensity to cheat and steal), *Jacob*: Esau might have been a more decent bloke. Israel's descendants were bequeathed this new name, yet a lot of weight was put on reminding them of Yacob-Yisrael. Besides a menu reminder (Gen.32:32), they were for many generations called

---

[225]   See Fee and Stuart's *How to Read the Bible for All Its Worth*.

Israel's children. Though most of my 10 Bible versions often read 'Israelites', and the NCV/NLT have a fairly consistent use of 'people of Israel', it is good to flag up the NKJV's 'children of Israel'. Rv.7:4 speaks of the sons and daughters of Israel (*huiōn Israēl*).[226]

Of the 2,000+ mentions of the word *Israel*, the Pentateuch (or *Scrolls of Moses*) covers a little over 20 per cent of the OT scriptures, and speaks of *Israel's children* about 350 times. The remaining 80 per cent of the OT uses the term only about 250 times. There are a few variations, such as *Israel's elders/sons/congregation*. It seems to me that the theme weakened as the years rolled on, and perhaps forgetting their roots in favour of their developing identity, Israel's children adopted the name in their own right: they adopted the struggle.

But even early on, Israel's children were sometimes called simply *Israel*. For instance, pharaoh had to see that Israel, not Egypt, had global spiritual inheritance as Yahweh's firstborn (Ex.4:22). Pharaoh was given every opportunity, including miraculous signs, to bless Israel on her way and in turn to be blessed. Egypt simply needed to accept a spiritual second place, but nationalism hardens. She was simply too proud of her rich myths: Roger Lancelyn Green's *Tales of Ancient Egypt* retells some nicely. They are well worth reading.

Let's bear in mind that while Yahweh prophesied pharaoh's hardness of heart, this was because he knew pharaoh's disposition, and also what to pharaoh was past, future, or present. Living on death row about 1500 years ago, the Roman administrator-philosopher Anicius Manlius Severinus Boëthius, reflected on the eternality of God. That the Eternal Is is beyond mere time and space, even though we use convenience terms of time and space to refer to him: framing the

---

[226] I bypass the Wellhausen system—the postulating of hypothetical vested-interest parties—as critically flawed, though it can offer some useful points and has been an interesting literary theory. Yet this sad idea has sadly undermined moral standards. For *pace* Wellhausen, if Scripture was supremely inspired by God then Scripture is a witness to God by God, so has objective authority. But if, with Wellhausen, Scripture merely evolved along conflicting human ideas of some greater power, we can reasonably dismiss those ideas as invalid and wrongly conceive of morality as merely a human idea, lacking absolute obligations. Moral *instincts* might exist to preserve mankind, but obligation to obey such instincts would not exist.

unfamiliar into the familiar isn't an exact science. Boëthius also pointed out that better than talk about God having prevision or foreknowledge, "it will be more correct to think not of a kind of foreknowledge of the future, but as the knowledge of a never ending now" (Boëthius 165).

Putting this into visual language, God could be pictured as a cube that has the time-space line within it, the cube seeing the whole line in its completeness, while rational creatures within the spatiotemporal line can at best look back a little, see a little of their now, and guess a little of the future. Creaturely perspective is based on lacking the future and the past, sailing the ever forward-moving present in their small corner of space. Yahweh knew pharaoh better than pharaoh knew his own self. Knowing that Yahweh did not make Pharaoh stubborn against the pharaoh's own nature, helps interpret Rm.11, a big chapter in salvation history. Ex.11:7 parallels the expression, *children of Israel*, with *Israel*. Part of the often repeated *Shema Yisra'el* is "Hear, Israel, Yahweh our god, Yahweh is unique" (LEB: Dt.6:4).[227] Since God's name was linked to his covenant, the *Shema Yisra'el* would be to remind them of their Israel identity, and of their covenant with him. This takes us back to the history of covenant. Let's step back a bit before going forward.

---

[227]   The MEVV almost always employ a capital G for God. However, I think it makes better sense in some contexts to treat it according to its original life setting and I do so. Where many of God's people assumed that he was their covenant god, a small g better fits their Popular Monotheism/Polytheism. A later stage, Philosophical Monotheism, argues more clearly that there is only one god, God, and versions should reflect this difference. The MEVV do not think like this for the OT and prefer a false 'reverential' marker. They seem happy for pagans to speak more respectfully of Israel's god than about their own—as if! Israel may speak of Dagon as Philistia's *god*, and Yahweh as Israel's *God*, though neither Hebrew nor Greek texts had such distinctions. The only glimmer of sense is having pagans speak of Israel's [god] instead of Israel's [God], as *per* the NIV (1 Sam.7:7). A risky move but it should have been riskier. Still, it's top of its class with the A+, all other MEVV being D-. For the NT, several MEVV do better. Based on the *god of* constructions in the NT letters, I grade them as CEV (A+); NLT (B); NCV (D+); ERV/NABRE/NKJV (D), and the CEB/LEB/NIV/NRSV (D-).

Covenant with Adam

I began this section with Jacob and a modification to a covenant, since with him began the name Israel. Yet to be comprehensive about salvation history, we must predate Jacob-Israel. The very name *Genesis* conjures up all kinds of responses, even among Christians. I resist the temptation to take some interesting sidetracks. It is a fascinating and an important study which I have enjoyed, with its debates on biological etiology, the age of the universe, multiverses created to hide from the creator,[228] time warps, rationality and ethics as haphazard or transcendent, etc.

All I will say for now is that if you wish to read a fair summary of a range of positions of the theme of micro/macro-evolution, you could do far worse than Kevin Logan's *Responding to the Challenge of Evolution*. And by long-term atheist philosopher turned deist, Antony Flew, *There Is a God* deserves a close read. And Perry Marshal's *Evolution 2.0*, might really crack the code. Mention *Genesis*, mention Adam, and battle lines immediately ask if you deny or affirm history and literalism. Yet our focus is theological: what does the text say about theological themes, specifically about covenant?

Genesis first uses clear covenant terminology in 6:18, which relates to Noah, but it's long been held that covenant was implicit in Eden. More recently, William Dumbrell has argued that by using a term which didn't mean *establishing* a covenant, Gen.6 implied that a covenant-type relationship—by virtue of creation—had previously been established, and was being re-*established*, reaffirmed (see Dumbrell 1983:32). "God was declaring a willingness to continue what had already been set up by action in Gen.1" (Dumbrell 1983:25-6). Covenant features, such as blessings for obedience (see Hos.2:18) and punishments for disobedience (Gen.2:17) to the overlord, were

---

[228] Dawkins *et al* have simply imagined an idea of multiverses to explain away the anthropic principle. Antony Flew noted that if each so-far only imaginary universe—divided by what?—has its universal laws (atheists trying to avoid ours), then the problem compounds, since there would be a superlaw overarching each universe's law. Atheism would replace its universal problem by a multiversal problem.

assumed prior to Noah.[229] The latter can be seen by the very fact that disobedience had led to man's exorcism from Eden, and had led to the Noahic flood's drastic surgery for drastic anarchy.

Genesis and Noah

The Noahic Flood symbolised humanity being reformatted for a fresh start, its corrupt drive wiped clean. The way that it was recorded probably suggests to us a global flood. Some scientists speculate that this was when an asteroid hit our planet, extinguished dinosaur life, collapsed a protective water canopy, and dramatically altered atmospheric conditions and the earth's tilt. However, this is not our subject. Our question is, has archaeology proved anything like a Noahic flood? The simple answer is probably, yes.

In 1928-9, archaeological excavations by Leonard Woolley at the ancient city of Ur—roughly midway between Babylon and the Persian Gulf—found a 2½ metre uninhabited silt layer between later habitation and earlier al-Ubaid habitation: Ur's flood is dated about 4,000 BC. Various similar flood finds have been discovered, such as at Kish (about 2,800 BC) over 100 miles away, and Nineveh. Ur's was perhaps the earliest. Traces of a great flood or floods, remain in extra-biblical history, howbeit written in mythological style and wrapped around ideas of divinities being involved: the library of Assyrian king Ashurbanipal (Nineveh) had such a story. Did *Genesis* use Babylon or Babylon *Genesis*, or did both come from the same memory pool, one perhaps exegeted by God? Abraham came from Ur.

Indeed, we may compare four extant Mesopotamian accounts of a great flood, namely the *Sumerian King List*, the *Atrahasis Epic* (from which came the *Gilgamesh Flood Tale*), the *Eridu Genesis* (*Sumerian Flood Tale*), and *Genesis*. They share basic ingredients, such as flooding sent by deity, a man told to build an ark, and at least he and his wife surviving the flood (see Kitchen 425). But only *Genesis* links it to man's sin, rather than man's chatter disturbing Mesopotamian gods; only the *Genesis*

---

[229]   This is also relevant to the translation of Hos.6:7, where the factor of whether a covenant existed and was known to have existed influences whether 'ādām should be held to mean Adam the person (see Jos.3:16 = Tell ed-Damiye?).

boat's design would actually float; only *Genesis* gives a natural account of repopulation. *Genesis* is also shorter and more concise.

What we may have is a shared memory of a particularly massive epochal flood, in which factual details and theological interpretation passed down through Abraham's pagan ancestors and was prayerfully reconstructed by Moses. Arguments that 'Noah's Flood' was a fantasy story, no longer hold water. *Genesis* does not, of course, teach that every flood or natural calamity is God's direct plan. The Bible does not extend the claim that he once guided a particular arrow (2 Chr.18:33), to a claim that he guides every missile. God, man, and nature, are all interactive. Allan Millard's *Discoveries from Bible Times*, covers more on the archaeological side.

A quick note about ancient writing styles is in order. Global terms might happily fit into bigger theories, but the text itself might simply relate to the Mesopotamian 'world', even as 'my world' may at times means me, my family and where we live, our orbit of activity. Theologically speaking, Noah was certainly a representative of then future man, but tracing all mankind back to Noah, may not be theologically, biologically, or historically, necessary. I will not argue towards either a global, or a local, flood. Enough to paraphrase a Richard Burton line from *Where Eagles Dare*: a flood is a flood is a flood. The Noahic Flood massively changed Noah's familiar world, and a covenant renewal word was prophesied.

Noah and human identity

Remembering the Imago

The so-called Noahic Covenant, seems to have been prefixed by guarantees of intent: population levels would increase and agriculture would be re-established. Previous *carte blanche* restrictions of carnivoranism were removed, though a symbolism of ultimate ownership was left in place alongside a particular theology against murder (Gen.9:6), which had probably been commonplace. In saying that mankind is in God's image, do we rule out the possibility of morally intelligent and self-aware life on other planets, species aware of having personal choice? No, and on this see C S Lewis' essay, *Religion and Rocketry*, since it puts some good basic thinking into place.[230] We happily affirm God's Image, the Imago Dei, and on Earth is limited to humanity.

Some people either desacralise the concept of humanity to that of merely another animal species, or sacralise the concept of mere animal species to human status. Animal Rights? Even if a shark says that fish are friends not food, when it's peckish it's unlikely to bother about another fish's right to life, nor about mine. Intrinsically animals have no *rights*; but probably neither do human beings. The legal fiction called *human rights* has both virtue and blindness. Some would so equalise the concepts of shared animality so that, if while driving I must either swerve left or right, killing either three little pigs on the left or one man (let's call him Kant) on the right, I ought to swerve right since three lives have thrice the value as one Kant. How often does political correctivism preach that to be moral, we must not morally discriminate even virtue from vice?

Discrimination is a moral obligation, which is perhaps one reason why some vilify the term discrimination. Of course, if we ought not to morally discriminate, then there cannot be any ethical right and wrong, and therefore there cannot be any *ought* to navigate by. Thus "we ought not to morally discriminate", does not compute, since if it is morally right to discriminate against the ought, it is meaningless to say that we ought not morally discriminate. A branch on the Ethics Tree, says Kill the tree, and listen only to me. But once the tree is killed, why listen to the dead branch?

If *morality* is a meaningless term, and driving my car I must swerve and head back simply if I'm not to be late for a date, I really need not concern myself with any moral notion that *any* loss of life should be avoided, unless its loss inconveniences me. So, if they wish to live, Kant and piglets must jolly well try to avoid *me*, because there is no categorical reason why I *ought* to even preserve the human race. Even the Hedonic Calculus becomes not what gives most people most happiness (and like Hitler with the ethnic-Jews, why bother about any unhappy minority?), but what gives *me* most happiness. Of course, for self-interest I might avoid Kant because the police (not for any categorical

---

230   Similarly, Hasker 122: "if..intelligent extraterrestrials..they also would bear the image of God."

imperative) might arrest me if I kill him. But if they do so, it would only be to enforce a law that a self-serving government has decided randomly to impose: and if the police overpower the government, they become the government—police state.

If morality is dead, then only power matters, as Nietzsche argued for—and to hell with compassion: said ironically, for hell cannot receive compassion. Some atheists joke that God is no longer even on the side of the big guns, and that if he appears they will fire at him, even as they do on theism. Some secularists are in the delusion of seeking moral progress, while blind to the facts that progress implies both a moral absolute (to judge improvement), and a moral destination to be progressed towards. Radical Nietzscheans realise that if Nietzsche was right about God being dead, then community wellbeing itself is a myth, and that Nietzsche was a half-baked philosopher followed by a half-baked world, telling it what he'd like it to be without God bothering anybody.

With Noah, came the affirmation that murder remains an absolute sin, since as humans we—not being mere animals—are in God's image. If we walk into the moral void we will not find any moral reason to walk out, and in our subjectivism will be damned. Without an ought, government has no moral compass towards legislating to protect others, and no reason to try and help, if their individual best interests are not served by doing so. In a moral void, why legislate morality, and why enforce it, and why expect it?

But the Ought does exist and underpins creation: it is deontological. And while Animal Rights exists no more than Human Rights, its nebulous neighbour, treating animals and humans morally but not equally (for they are not equal) is right. The concept of the Imago Dei needed a flood to restore it. It is vitally important to humanity as being human. Indeed, remove the *Dei*, the concept of God, and the *Imago* (his image, his likeness)[231] will die with a bang or with a whimper.

---

[231]   The Heb/Gk. terms for *image* and *likeness* are ṣelem/eikōn and děmût/ homoiōsis, respectively. It has been debated whether the terms in context are synonyms. It is nice to say that mortal humanity is as God and is to be like God—a moral journey from image to likeness. However, Hebrew style often

With covenant renewal after the Flood came the reminder of man's privilege and responsibility as Imago Dei, at one with, yet distinct from, the animal kingdom. Hence with Noah, *Genesis* highlighted both humanity as being God's Image (murder was not permitted), and animals as being in subject to, and protected by, man.

Noahic affirmation

A rainbow was used to illustrate the Noahic covenant—or rather, the Adamic covenant renewed. Incidentally, the rainbow need no more be taken as the first ever rainbow (after a water canopy collapse), than the heap of rocks used to witness a different covenant, need be taken as the first ever heap of rocks (Gen.31:51-2). Covenant practices in that culture included some kind of third-party witness, which could be something as simple as a pile of rocks, to a witness in the sky. There is a tie-in of 5:1-2/9:6, and 1:28/9:7, and with 6:18, using the Hebrew *hēqîm* (derived from the wordgroup *QWM*), rather than the usual word for *beginning* a covenant, *KRT* (cut). It was probably an affirmation that the humanity-wide covenant had not been, nor would be, annulled, at least while God's basic likeness remained. We can similarly see how, after a covenant was cut with Abraham (*karat*: 15:18), the idea of renewal was used (*hēqîm*: 17:7,21).

The NLT is best, speaking of covenant confirmation, while the ERV/NCV are bad, speaking of *promise* or *agreement* instead of *covenant*. They misunderstand what covenant—an opposite of contract—means. English versions from the C14 Wycliffe Bible upto and including the C16 Bishops Bible, didn't differentiate between *karat* and *hēqîm*. Enter the C16 Geneva. Its take was followed by Rome's C16 Douay and the C17 Anglican KJV, and has been kept by most of my Bible versions, simply speaking of making covenant (for *karat*) and establishing covenant (for *hēqîm*).

In short, it's reasonable to say that the first covenant was with Adam and was affirmed, re-established, with Noah. Moreover, an affirmation possibly hints that covenants were never assumed to be unconditionally permanent. Into this covenant, another covenant

---

used synonyms, and Gen.1:27's *image* seems to totally fulfil v26's *likeness/image*, and 5:1's *likeness* seems to parallel 1:26's *image*.

was made with someone through whom a salvation history covenant would bring forth messiah, the promise of *Genesis*, into the world. Let's move onto this big covenant.

Covenant with Abraham, Isaac, and Jacob

New name, new identity

The next globally significant covenant came with Abram. Stage 1: Yahweh gave him promise (Gen.12). Stage 2: Yahweh gave him covenant (15). Stage 3: Yahweh gave him affirmation of covenant (17) plus a name change. Peter was happy to relate the new name to Stage 1 (Ac.3:25); the apostle Paul was happy to relate the new name to stages 1 and 2 (Gal.3:8; Rm.4:3). The Writer to the Hebrews was happy to relate the new name to Stage 1 (Heb.7:1-2). We need not be too particular for our purposes. Although *Abram* was significant in his life, and its significance is good to understand, in general speech *Abraham* is fine, even as we may speak of the birthdate of a monarch without implying that they were monarch at their birth.

So, let's look at Abraham. At the promissory level, the term *nation/s* (*gôy/gôyim*) was used: Gen.12:2 and 17:4-6 for the Covenant People. Later this term would usually contrast the Gentiles to God's people. While terms can be reshaped with time, is this an early trace of the promise being for Gentiles? This aside, the bigger picture is that the extent of blessing was global and the particular method would be through Abraham. His half-sister, his wife (12:13-9; 20:2,12), could have testified that Abraham was far from perfect, even though we may say that technically his disingenuous 'sister' claim was correct: he was protecting her husband.

Islamic scholars have divided over whether the OT text has been degraded in any serious sense. Some Muslims have argued that since the Bible and Qur'an are both from Allah, he would have preserved his text; some have argued that some Qur'anic suras speak of textual tampering: a good book on this is Moucarry 2001. Some have gleefully highlighted what they think to be ludicrous in the Abraham-Sarah texts, as if the text is corrupt. Yet sceptics should be sceptical about scepticism, as so should non-sceptics! We sometimes find in the text what we have put into it—garbage in, garbage out.

Sister or spouse?

One C11 Muslim scholar joked that it was daft to think that a 90-year-old woman would have attracted Abimelek, and that as a prophet Abraham would neither have lied nor violated the Sinaitic Covenant. Therefore, he said, the OT accounts of Abram/Abraham letting others take Sarai/Sarah (Gen.17:15), were inauthentic text. Yet if what seems daft now seemed daft then, why was it ever written and believed—especially to Abraham's discredit—by those who claimed descendancy? Good interpretation here requires us to think about the life setting (*sitz im leben*), and rates of aging.

If Sarah died at 127, then about 40 years earlier (think say Elizabeth Taylor) she might have made a good infertile wife to show off and to discipline younger wives in Abimelek's harem. Don't women keep better figures, if they've never given birth? In addition, while 20:7 declares Abraham to have been a prophet, *'achot* covered half-sisters as well as full sisters, so was true enough even if prophets can lie. Nor should we anachronistically downgrade Abraham for not obeying a covenant that didn't exist in his days! For the Levitical framework wasn't relevant, and Levi wasn't even a twinkle in the eye. The Sinaitic Covenant came several centuries later, and Lv.18 was within a framework of symbolism—a secondary perk incidentally reduced close inbreeding thus reduced genetic malformations.

Why castigate Moses' ancestor Abraham for not obeying Sinai, or Abraham's ancestor Noah for not being circumcised centuries before Abraham instituted physical circumcision (Gen.17:12), or Canadians for not driving on the left like British drivers? Covenant stipulations can be only mandatory within their framework.

C11 Ibn Hazm, a sincere and outstanding scholar, helpfully highlighted possible objections to these accounts, but they're not quite the problem he seems to have wished.[232] Moucarry concluded that Ibn Hazm had made "no attempt to understand the underlying issues from perspectives other than his own" (Moucarry 301). He noted

---

[232] Nor need you spend much spend time on Wellhausenism and Finkelstein's low opinions of biblical inspiration, and their speculations that numerous redactors chopped and changed the text, doubled stories, and the like—though it can be useful to see and to scotch them.

that based on the principle of *tawatur*, C12 Muslim scholar Fakhr-ul-Din al-Razi argued that the OT text had not been falsified: "...the Torah is first and foremost the word of God. Just as God is trustworthy, so must his word be. Razi stated openly that he supported the...interpretation...[that only] the meaning of the [biblical] text" had sometimes been falsified (Moucarry 52—rearranged).

On this, Moucarry linked Muslim scholars Al-Baqillani, Avicenna, Ghazali, and Muhammad 'Abduh, to Razi, Juwayni to Ibn Hazm, and graded Ibn Taymiyya as middling (Moucarry ch. 4). Abraham, a man of fear mixed with faith (*iman*), might well have expected Yahweh to deliver him and Sarah both times, which is what he did do. Yahweh singled out this imperfect man (and even prophets are imperfect), to represent us imperfect humans who trust in him. He then began an individual covenant line leading to the messianic line. Recording old stories, Moses noted Abraham's fear both sides of he and his wife's name change, fear both sides of the covenant (Gen.12:10-20; 20:1-18).

A study in righteousness

If weak, was Abraham unrighteous? Do saints never sin? Paul commended Abraham's righteousness (Rm.4:9). But let's examine this English word *righteousness* (put as *justified* in some texts). The idea behind it has a number of layers. In the OT it has a lot to do with social justice, but in the history of English translation, the Hebrew/Greek root terms (*sedeq/dikaios*) have sometimes biased away from this in the interests of political correctivism. You will never read the word 'justice' in the KJV New Testament, and only 28 times in the whole KJV, whereas the Spanish RVR (*Reina Valera Revisada*) translates the Heb/Gk. 370 times as *justice*, and the more recent NVI (*Nueve Versión Internacional*) translates thus 426 times. In English, the NIV has it 130 times, and the NJB has it 253 times.

Justice is a big theme: 'rebellious sons, stubborn asses, forgetful oxen, and an unrighteous harlot, all four images were used to describe how God saw a people who had forsaken social justice" (White 17). So why was it so hidden in the KJV? UK Protestantism has preferred to translate by the word *righteousness*, even though the evidence presents "a clear indication that the Hebrew term has more of a relational and communal flavor than a moral, individualistic sense" (Scorgie, Strauss, & Voth 328). This is one reason why Protestantism has lagged behind Roman Catholicism in linking loyalty to Scripture, with social issues. The likes of John Stott have done much to redress the balance of neither social nor spiritual, but both rightly related.

The translation preference can be traced back to King James, who hoped to unite the English people by a Version neither tied to the common people (the Geneva Bible: 1560), nor to church leadership (the Bishops Bible: 1568), and one that safeguarded royalty. Once Reformationists questioned the doctrine of the Divine Rights of Monarchs, uneasy lay the head that wore the French crown—shifting power to the people helped prime Rome's anti-Huguenot gunpowder that exploded on St. Bartholomew's Day, 24/8/1572. While the Geneva Bible used 'justice' forty times for *ṣedeq/dikaios*, conveniently for the king the Bishops Bible never mentioned it: the Bishops Bible was the basic text for the KJV, though the latter was influenced by the Geneva Bible.

Those hired by King James, were specifically to remove the political threat of the Geneva Bible, ideas such as all citizens being equal to monarchy under God. Respect for monarchy, and the fear of displeasing King James, probably encouraged the KJV translators to prefer the spiritual to the social aspect of *ṣedeq/dikaios*. "Powerful words such as justice, just, rights, and communal faithfulness, were not in the king's best interests. A religious word such as righteousness, which speaks of a state of being and not of an active, intentional responsibility towards others—especially the poor and the marginalized—was a much safer term" (Scorgie, Strauss, & Voth 333).

The Puritans were a minority voice in the KJV, yet while they had an agenda for social justice (tough on the king), they also had a strong belief in internal spirituality (easy on the king). The KJV was not without its weak spots. New revisions/translations can only redirect public attention gradually—too much too soon and they will simply be ignored and die. *Romans* says much about community living. Elmer Martens argued that because it implied Yahweh's dedication to humanity, such righteousness included the theme of corrective punishment (Rm.1:18-3:20) and deliverance for those who accepted his helping hand (Martens 286).

Of course, *ṣedeq/dikaios* sometimes relates to spiritual relationship. In the NT, commenting on Abraham, Paul made it clear that *dikaiosunē* carries the idea of normal relationship with God: "God makes people right with himself through their faith in Jesus Christ" (NCV: Rm.3:22). Paul dedicated a substantial section to showing his fellow Jews that Scripture witnessed to this aspect of righteousness. Since Calvary, God can say that all who commit to his son are of the same calibre as Abraham, standing with himself as they ought (*righteous*). His courtroom (*forensic*) decision is not to prosecute. Though Christians are daily judged in God's family court, they can know that they are exempt heaven's condemnatory courtroom.

And besides being spiritually *dikaios* we should be socially *dikaios*. *Dikaiosunē* is supplemental to other aspects of the new creation act. What we have become by God's intervention, is so declared. We have been justified—put right with God—for all time. Thus, there is no condemnation for us (8:1), although at times we may be guilty and feel justly condemned over specifics. A normal guilt complex is healthy for guilty Christians. Yet being 'in Christ' offers the gnosis that beyond the skies we are 'not condemned' (Jhn.3:18).

Thus, justification/righteousness may be contrasted to daily forgiveness, which seems very much ongoing in terms of *fellowship* rather than of ultimate adoption. The latter is not in dispute. It is a welcome judgement which follows our acceptance of Christ (Ac.13:39; Rm.3:28; 10:4; Gal.2:16; 3:11), and opens believers to the benefits of right standing and to none of the disadvantages of wrong standing (Rm.8:31ff.). When Abraham was pronounced righteous, Yahweh effectively responded to Abraham's welcome of himself (faith commitment), by formally welcoming Abraham into close fellowship: those he welcomes, he sends not away. I do not say that these ways of putting it were in play four millennia ago, nor that no one can stubbornly leave heaven on earth for a living hell.[233] I do say that Paul wrote this truth large, namely that Abraham was not rewarded for any good deed on his, and that Yahweh cemented the relationship before Abraham was circumcised and in covenant (ch.4).

---

[233]   See ch.7.

Paul's example of faith

Abraham was a prime example of good pre-Christian relationship/ *righteousness* with God, but I doubt that all his friends were diabolical and totally lacking in love and trust in God within their secular world. At the end of the day God can pick one among equals for a task—Abram was one good pagan among many good pagans.[234] Was there nobody else in Galilee-Judea suitable for apostleship? No more sons of perdition lurking in the wings, vying for the Judas spot? Had the unknown archer stayed at home, could Yahweh not have easily chosen another to fire the arrow that killed the king (1 Kg.22:34)?

When Paul wished to speak of a father-figure for our faith, he chose Abraham, not because Abraham was the first righteous human being, but because for *Romans* he was an ideal choice to illustrate a point. Abraham was a prime example of faith before Sinai. A brilliant choice to unite the ethnic Jewish/Gentile factions within the church, quelling the former's exclusive and unjustified covenantal boasts. But we mustn't imagine that justifying faith began with Abraham, and that earlier folk such as righteous Abel (Heb.11:4: *dikaios*) were unrighteous. Nor was he their only faith-father/pattern. Likewise, Gal.3:7 countered the Circumcision Party's exclusive boast. The time had passed when physical circumcision was symbolically indicative of a prior spiritual transaction (6:15). Abraham was simply chosen as a great pattern for Christians from common humanity, a connective between the limited world that had had deific covenant, and the unlimited world that can have deific covenant. His was not a mystic fatherhood, but a proof that welcome-trust connects to God.

Our best isn't good enough

A new phase of human history was sown with Abraham in the ground of common grace, then germinated by Moses—Level 2 redemption. How effective was it? "He knew better, but she didn't know any better", we say, in condemning or justifying. Coming from finest Abrahamic

---

[234]   Before their conversion to Yahweh as El Shaddai, presumably Abram and Sarai had been a pagan couple of the Ur Empire in which the Moon god was a major god. The 'tower of Ur'—the 'tower of Babel' was in the same empire—was a ziggurat-temple built at Ur for this god.

stock, and given the best human chance for proper spirituality, Abraham's covenant descendants—Isaac, Jacob and his sons—did 'know better' than others, yet still walked in sin's darkness. Knowledge/*gnosis* doesn't in itself save spiritually, but spiritual salvation can come through it. Egypt would show that Abraham's covenant line could come in as saviours, and yet become slaves needing deific intervention: at a social level that was a recapitulation of man's metanarrative—Adam the saviour became Adam the slave.

Even theologically righteous Abraham, had remained a morally unrighteous man. For all its promise of hope, the human weakness in the Abrahamic Covenant showed how sin remained in the sap of even the new level of Eden, the new level of covenant that flowered with Moses: a new level of covenant would be needed for Level 3 surgery, and even that is not the final cure, so we await the eschaton for the deepest of deep healing, Level 4: the teaching about sin, precedes the teaching of salvation; hamartiology precedes soteriology.

C S Lewis said "that human beings, all over the earth, have [the] curious idea that they ought to behave in a certain way, and cannot really get rid of it. [And] that they do not in fact behave in that way. They know the Law of [Human] Nature; they break it. These two facts are the foundation of all clear thinking about ourselves and the universe we live in" (Lewis 2002:8). There is an uncreated Right, and we fail in our duty to it. Abraham walked faithfully with God (Gen.48:15), but can that walk really cure human sinfulness?

That medicine was refined then trialled among one chosen group, Ethnic-Israel; the rest of humanity had placebos. Yet Ethnic-Israelites and Gentiles remained sick; all saw that a radical new medicine was needed. When at last it came, Golgotha travelled back in time, enabling ultimate redemption of all who had met its demands, Abraham having been a prime example of how faith can result in redemption now. Abraham was made and declared right with God (Is.29:22), but his descendants who sought redemption in Babylonia, knew he'd be ashamed of them—as Jacob-Israel or Ethnic-Israel of old would be (63:16). That the covenant line had been redeemed was a given (Ps.74:2), as was the fact that they sensed that there was a prophetic level of a new level of redemption (Jr.31:33; Gal.3:13).

Revelation would pick up on the newness theme (Rv.21:5), speaking of a yet to be new heaven and new earth, to be the ultimate promised land, with its new temple and new Jerusalem. Jesus the redeemer needed no redemption from sin. He was born among corrupt descendants of righteous Abraham (sin tends to corrupt, and absolute sin corrupts absolutely), and redeemed his great great...grandfather Abraham, and such as righteous Abel, even further back in time and countless millions more, into ultimate redemption (Level 4). His atoning death enabled worldwide redemption to humanity before, at the time, and beyond.

If we waxed Augustinian, we could say that the idea that at least Abraham's people had salvation, beats the idea that everyone was or will be damned simply to please Equality, the western god. And what if rather than ensuring that all are ultimately damned, God had begun a slow yet needful process that had to begin at that time with but one person, so that while only the select few were saved in the then and there, eventually across the globe every human being conceived could be saved if they willed? Isn't even limited salvation better than no salvation history?

Well yes, but we have already explored whether this limited selection ensured ultimate salvation for *all* ethnic descendants of the Abrahamic Covenant—it did not—and ensued ultimate damnation for *all* outside of it—it did not. We have pictured salvation in even broader terms than did Augustine, based on faith not blood. In investigating what is meant by covenant, we have looked a little at Abraham, seeing a message of eventual global blessing somehow following from his relationship with God. And we have seen that in spite of his fears for his own safety, there was special merit and special blessing in trusting God.

Indeed, when asked to offer his special born son, Abraham showed his habit of thinking through the possibilities and then committing his ways to God: if God wished Isaac—to whom he had committed the covenant—to die a bachelor, well, God would simply have to bring him back to life in order to carry on the covenant line (Heb.11:19)! Abraham typified the rational believer, the look and leap believer, a true rationalist. Faith can undergird reason, overcoming the irrational fears that the anaesthetist will neither prevent the pain nor awaken us after the operation. Faith and Reason walk hand in hand, which is another reason why Abraham, combining both, was highlighted as the pattern for faith. John's Gospel begins with the word λογος, from which we get the word logic. Logic incarnate; God with us. God is love, light, and logic.

The Abrahamic Covenant wasn't national, and went from one person to one person down the family line. Had it continued so indefinitely, four millennia on there would still be one person who alone carried it. So, although slave girl Hagar—perhaps ironically given to Abram by Egypt's pharaoh in exchange for Sarai (Gen.12:16)—had according to Hittite custom birthed a legitimate firstborn son to Abraham, she was not his principle wife, and the covenant would be channelled to Sarah's firstborn, Isaac. Isaac took on the obligations of what was the vassal member of the covenant. This included a proper relationship with Yahweh as his exclusive god (to speak their polytheistic language) and physical circumcision as a pledge of lifestyle (17:1,7-8,11,17).[235]

Like Abram/Abraham, Sarai/Sarah also experienced a kind of name change (Gen.17:15,5). Probably both forms of her name meant *princess*, with the language change either simply showing cultural change—a shift from her birth culture, to her new Hebrew identity—or an extension of her royal title. Some suggest *Sarai* was an Akkadian form of ancient Sumeria's Ningal, the moon-god Sin's wife. This picks up on Akkadian residents at Ur calling Ningal *Sarratu* (queen), and suggests this as the etymology of *Sarai*. Was she transferred from her past paganism? Either suggestion implies a change of identity.

Breaking from the past life, her son would carry the covenant (19,21; Rm.9:9; Gal.4:21-31). Abraham's son by Hagar, Ishmael, would merely carry an ethnic blessing (Gen.17:20). Ishmael was circumcised when under the covenant umbrella of Abraham, but arguably once dis-established from Abraham, neither the covenant obligations nor the circumcision rites, still applied. Yet they did for Isaac, the immediate

---

[235]   The Bible neither started the practice of physical circumcision, nor ever related it to girls. The female equivalence is known a Female Genital Mutilation (FGM) and is a quite horrific part of African culture. Campaigning against this, Sicily Mbura Muriithi has a good short article in Adeyemo 2006:37.

heir. None of the obligations through Isaac would benefit Yahweh, but they would benefit Isaac's relationship with him.

Isaac

We don't read much of Isaac. Some scholars say that Isaac had been more significant, so we hear less of Isaac than of Abraham. For, they say, the ancients had a habit of downgrading the biggest names when a new name came to town—chronological snobbery? Simplified, they assert that an Isaac legend was popular, until superseded by a later developed Abraham legend. In short, that if you think characters are simply legends, always assume that the least significant now, was the most significant once upon a time. Some scholars have a credibility gap, but can sound good at first.

Fantasies aside, as a link in the chain Isaac remained centrepiece in the often-mentioned patriarchal triad, of Abraham, Isaac, and Jacob/ Israel. Yet unlike Joseph, Isaac actually saw Yahweh. Major blessings can come to minor characters. I won't linger with Isaac, except for two things. One, he used the same trick about his wife being his sister, stretching truth for safety's sake. Being in love with a beautiful woman could, in that general culture, be dangerous when you lacked the protection of being high up the pecking order. Again, Rebekah was a close enough relative to be called what we translate as 'sister'— a deceptive economy of truth, but not a lie. Two, it seems that he and his wife had only the twins Esau and Jacob.

Jacob

Nor need we linger on their stories. The heir apparent Esau, was probably the nicer guy, yet Yahweh may sovereignly bypass both the nice guys of the world and cultural norms. Rm.9:13 speaks in Semitic terms, where *hate* can mean *bypass/minimise* and *love* mean *choose*. Such hate is not an arbitrary emotional negative towards an individual, but simply forward planning, a choice for the big plan.[236] Heb.12:16 depicts Esau as godless, in the sense of ignoring spiritual values, but *pace* Philo probably not as sexually immoral.

---

[236]   He who told us to hate our own parents relative to our love for God, told off those who said that sons should support God's temple rather than their own parents.

Yahweh knew that Jacob would turn out the more spiritually minded. We've looked a little earlier at this (page 212). There we looked at the key idea of relational name-change, and at various other important points in his life. Between Jacob and his four wives, twelve sons were born. It is perhaps as well to say something here about marriage. Being a covenant—which we have looked at in-depth—marriage could have social levels. A woman on the highest level was to be simply an *'ishah* (plural, *nashim*). The next level down was the *pilegesh* (concubine). This too was life-long, but didn't give such wives the full range of entitlements.

Translation is sometimes at best a rough and ready attempt to convey the basics from one language culture into another. If we use the convenience word *concubine* for both a Hebrew and a Chinese setting, we should be aware that the mentality it represented in these cultures might have varied in important ways. In short, if you condemn the Chinese practice of concubinage, do not necessarily condemn the Hebrew practice, and contrawise: examine words in their cultural settings.

Bilhah and Zilpah were concubine-wives (*nashim*: Gen.30:4,9; 37:2). Whether or not this is an interpretative key to the biblical use of *pilegesh*, we shall not consider. But they were not "bits on the side", nor *partners* (libertine activism undermines marriage in part by engineering the concept change from *spouse* to *partner*; from *Miss/Mrs.* to *Ms*), nor mere slaves, disposable or otherwise. Marriage promoted them to junior wives, even if their husband lacked a senior wife. Let's remember that at least at that time and place, polygamy wasn't wrong.

Paul later—in line with Jesus' teaching from *Genesis* that monogamy was the ideal—taught that church leadership should positively discriminate away from polygamy. Basically in line with Adams 1980, Paul's *mias gunaikos* (1 Tim.3:2,12; Tts.1:6: one wife) pans out as "[if as most likely married, be] a faithful monogamist".[237] For leadership, adults

---

237   The Greek, *mias gunaikos* {*anēr*} (1 Tm.3:2,12; Tts.1:6) may literally be [one woman man], happily descriptive of a faithful monogamist *type* of bishop/overseer, whether married or not. Likewise, the fact that *if* they had children they were to be *good* fathers, does not rule out husbands who weren't fathers. Nowadays in some sectors bishops must neither husbands nor fathers be.

were the norm; for adults, marriage was the norm; for marriage, monogamy was the ideal; in marriage, sexual faithfulness was obligatory. Married leaders are absolutely not to stray from their exclusive beds, whether by affairs or by plural marriage: they should lead by example. The texts no more rule out divorce than they rule out remarriage. Paul approved of remarriage (within certain parameters), even as he approved of divorce (within certain parameters). The Bible urges due loyalty. Jacob did not sin by or in his polygamy. His concubines were true wives, and he was entrusted with the covenant.

There are interesting sidelights in the story of Yacob-Yisrael, such as examining the custom of regular loyalty tithing—unrelated to the one-off gratitude tithe from Abraham. From Heb.7:1-10 it is sometimes thought that every Christian ought to give only, or at least, 10 per cent of their income or earnings to their church, or at least to charities. Arguably this idea underplays both the heavy typology of *Hebrews* (and some other hermeneutical points), and what the new covenant means by a stewardship lacking both minimum and regulated options. All that we are and have is God's, and he needs neither, but our resources should enrich ourselves and others.

Wisdom, generosity, faith, love, all must go into the mix of "the grace of giving" (NIV: 2 Cor.8:7). Although tithing might insult God, he takes it with a smile. Jacob-Israel adopted this practice that traced back into Ugaritic and Akkadian times. It signalled offering his people to subsequent vassalage, buying them into covenant. He and they would pay a vassal tribute, in exchange for Yahweh's overlord protection, a vassal-tribute status taken up and ratified under Moses, a kind of tax then used to finance their religious hub. There is much to be seen by putting on the right covenant glasses.

As already seen, Jacob bequeathed his new name to not just one heir, but to all twelve sons together: it became a community investment, whereas hitherto it had been limited to one son *per* father: one son of Abraham, one son of Isaac, a pass-onto-one-per-family blessing. Jacob had had the real vision. Jacob-Israel's offer of family allegiance was more fully taken up in the days of Moses. With Moses, it underwent a major covenant upgrade, from an El Shaddai relationship, to a Yahweh relationship (Ex.6:3). Centuries down the line, Yeshua would both begin a community on the basis of a core group of twelve, and also be as the prophesied Moses (Dt.18:15). In short, the Yahweh relationship established through Moses, would become the model and baton for global blessing.

Community Covenant through Moses

A man of history

Zipporah found it easier to date Moses than we do. I have moved from defending a C15 date for the exodus, to holding a C13 date, but the debate goes on. Christian scholarship divides between exodus dates of roughly 1440 (Bimson), and 1240 BC (Kitchen). Biblical factors include reconstructing texts from Hebrew and Greek versions, interpreting them, understanding how the 'judges/champions' related to each other (eg did they overlap?), and naming the Egyptian sites and the relevant Egyptian pharaohs. Archaeology has revealed some problems with having an overly simple approach of the biblical text, and has suggested some useful ways to think in ancient ways. But archaeologically the question is not whether Moses lived, but when.

Moses was born into a history where his people had, through Joseph a son of Jacob, gone into Egypt for mutual blessing. What had started well, ended in despair (Ex.1:8). Hyksos, Semite outsiders who had usurped Egypt's throne, may have favoured Israel as fellow Semites: did Ex.1:8 record their overthrow by Egyptian nationalists who renewed Egypt's national disdain of Semites? Or perhaps the 'king' who knew not Joseph, was the incoming Hyksos pharaoh? Yet whether or not Joseph had coincided with the beginning or end of the Hyksos era, the children of Israel had overstayed their welcome. Suffering enslavement and infanticide, Israel asked where her god was, and whether he was or was not sovereign.[238] Was Gen.50:20 relevant anymore? His answer first delighted his people (Ex.4:31), then dismayed them (14:11-2): fickle faith. Indeed, their type of faith has implications for the meaning of true salvation.

A mighty man for a mighty job

The burning bush was critical to deliverance. Spontaneous combustion was fairly common in the wilderness, but uncommonly

---

[238]   True, they had no god—since God is not a god—but I put it in their terms.

Moses met a bush that burnt without burning. A real attention grabber. Again we meet the expression *mal'āk Yahweh* (3:2), one who spoke as Yahweh. It seems a straightforward rescue package, apart from Moses preferring the backseat: as Jill Briscoe loosely paraphrased 4:13, "here am I, send Aaron!". 3:11 could read as Moses protesting his inability, to which Yahweh replied that it would be himself, Yahweh, doing the job. As one song puts it, he turns our weaknesses into his opportunities.[239]

We don't know why Moses was selected for his ginormous job, but presumably it included his ability, willingness, faith, and humility (Nb.12:3), and perhaps Yahweh had planned for a Levite to become Israel's deliverer, so sent the infant Moses into Pharaoh's courts. He doesn't always explain himself, nor need we fear: "has [Yahweh] ever needed anyone's advice? Does he need instruction about what is good? Did someone teach him what is right or show him the path of justice?" (NLT: Is.40:14). Why, for that matter, did he choose Abram? Why were Saul, David, Peter, and Paul, chosen? These people were obviously suitable and subsequently selected, but surely Yahweh had had other candidates. And those elected weren't always in his kingdom or even destined for his kingdom.

For instance, King Cyrus of Persia was chosen for a messianic task (Is.45:1-4); Judas of Kerioth was chosen to betray messiah (Jhn.13:18). Sure, some given a mission might also have a predilection towards God and have ultimate life, but in itself ultimate life was neither a prerequisite for, nor a perquisite of, election.[240] Moses was an exceedingly good man, though like us he had his not so good moments. At one point he could risk his reputation and life by siding with the underdog—though whether killing the Egyptian in the process was accidental or premeditated manslaughter is moot. But at another point Yahweh threatened his very life; indeed, he would tell Moses off more than once. Moses had outstanding faith, yet because of his imperfect faith he failed to take his people into the Promised Land, a failure that can symbolise the fact of the failure of the Sinaitic Covenant to deliver God's true people into the true land of the true

---

[239]   The song mentions God's glory—he seeks the glory for our benefit.

[240]   Obviously some elections—eg Mary—required a predisposition towards God.

promise. Yet his successes far outweighed his failures. He was a spiritual giant of a man

And set aside in Pharaoh's palace, he had become talented. According to Kenneth Kitchen, Moses was probably trained like other adoptees, in jobs like the diplomatic service, and in the then current covenant conventions. Of these, we can analyse over eighty Ancient Near Eastern covenant records between the years 2500 and 650 BC. They fall into six distinct phases. The Mosaic Covenant, better named the Sinaitic Covenant (from Mount Sinai), followed a structure that was limited to approximately 1400–1220 BC (Phase 5). This nicely fits the idea that Moses was a key player in recording the covenant between Yahweh and Ethnic-Israel.

There seems no genuine reason for dismissing the account that a man named Moses, born a Semite and raised within the Egyptian ruling class, should not have led a group of about 20,000 Children of Israel, out of Egypt to the borders of Canaan, God speeding. And yes, some still assume that millions of Israelites migrated from Egypt. That's an issue of faulty translation, tradition, and fearful translation. Such a population explosion within a few generations is stretching it a lot. Recalculating, based on the entry into Egypt of 273 Children of Israel and good birth-survival rates, Colin Humphreys suggested that the exodus had 598 small units ('LP) of about 9 men in each unit, that is, about 5,500 men: this is similar to numbering in the Amarna Letters. Add in about 1,000 Levites, then women and children, and the population count becomes about 20,000 Israelites.[241] Around this time, Canaan had about 50,000 people, and evidence shows a sudden C13 increase of about 20,000 non-pig-eating inhabitants! The

---

[241]   See Kitchen 264-5—a hands-on, gloves off, book. Earliest writing didn't have vowels, and the meaning of 'lp included 'Elep (1,000 [eg Gen.20:16]; small team/clan [Jg.6:15]); and 'Alup (leader/officer [Gen.36:15]). Occasionally context is unclear as to which of these three meanings was meant—perhaps the wall killed 27 *officers*, not 27 *thousand*, in 1 Kg.20:30. Traditional ideas might be honest inflations through misunderstandings of Hebrew terms, and carrying the resultant counts into areas then unmapped by archaeology. This figure—and linked in to Ex.38:26—is calculated by Humphreys: www.xs4all.nl/~kielo/ColinHumphreysNumbers1.pdf. I am not fully convinced, and Ron E Allen's *Numbers* (EBC), should be considered.

numbers fit, using better translation of the Hebrew data which I expect that major Bible versions will soon, tentatively footnote, prior to going the whole hog.

<u>An awestruck man—a numinous name</u>

The Sinaitic Covenant would be sandwiched between the Exodus and the Entrance. Yahweh was committed to helping the descendants of the patriarchs and getting them into their covenant land (Ex.2:24; 6:4). Looking back, we can see that both the Abrahamic and Sinaitic covenants were steps in fulfilling the protoeuangelion (Gen.3:15). A big new feature would be a relational upgrade, bringing back something of Eden. This was signalled by a name once used by Eve, God's only true name.

One puzzle is Ex.6:3: "I appeared to Abraham, to Isaac, and to Jacob as El-Shaddai—'God Almighty'—but I did not reveal my name, Yahweh, to them" (NLT).[242] It's a mistake to think that it wasn't known before. We read it many times in *Genesis*, not least in Gen.12:8 which says that Abraham called on Yahweh?—but under what name? Many conservative Christians assume that Moses simply wrote this name back into the earlier stories. Alternatively, many quasi-Christians assume that centuries after an alleged Moses, people wrote (or rewrote/ redacted) the Bible to incorporate their take on religion under the motif, *Yahweh*. This latter idea is often called JEDP, where J goes back to a way of calling God either *Jehovah* or *Jahveh*. The EDP bits stand for *Elohim* (God), Deuteronomist, and Priestly, respectively. Some juggle these four letters around, and those who hold this literary theory often multiply these letters that they use for sources real or postulated. It's a hurly-burly hypothesis, and I do not assume that true Christians can't hold it.

From the fact that God's name features in pre-Mosaic personal names (theophoric names), I take it that God's name *was* known before Moses.[243] For example, the name *Judah* has a YaHweh component, the YH in

---

[242] Versions that put God's name as *Adonai, HaShem* (The Name), or even the LORD, fall below some earlier versions such as Tyndale, Great, Geneva, Bishops, and KJV. *Almighty* might not be best for *Shaddai*.

[243] I do not hold that Moses invented these theophoric names.

YeHuDaH (*yehûdâ*), which if versions nowadays didn't mind treading on traditional toes, they might translate as *Yudah*, since English has switched many Latin links from *J* to *Y*. "...[Leah] conceived and gave birth to a son, and said, 'Now I shall praise [(h)odeh] Yahweh!' Accordingly, she named him [Yehudah]. Then she had no more children" (NJB: Gen.29:35)—she ended on a note of praise. Yeshua, the lion of the tribe of Yudah, also held a Yahweh name.

So how should we interpret Ex.6:3? I think it helps to understand that the Hebrew *yâda'* (know) can carry the idea of intimacy: Gen.4:25— "Adam knew his wife intimately again" (CEB); "Adam again had sexual relations with his wife" (ERV); "Adam made love to his wife again" (NIV). The bigger picture sees *Genesis* as expressing relational levels. Much compressed, in early *Genesis*, the terms *God* (Elohim), *Yahweh-God*, *Yahweh*, and *Elohim* represent different levels of relationship. These levels are like a hill.

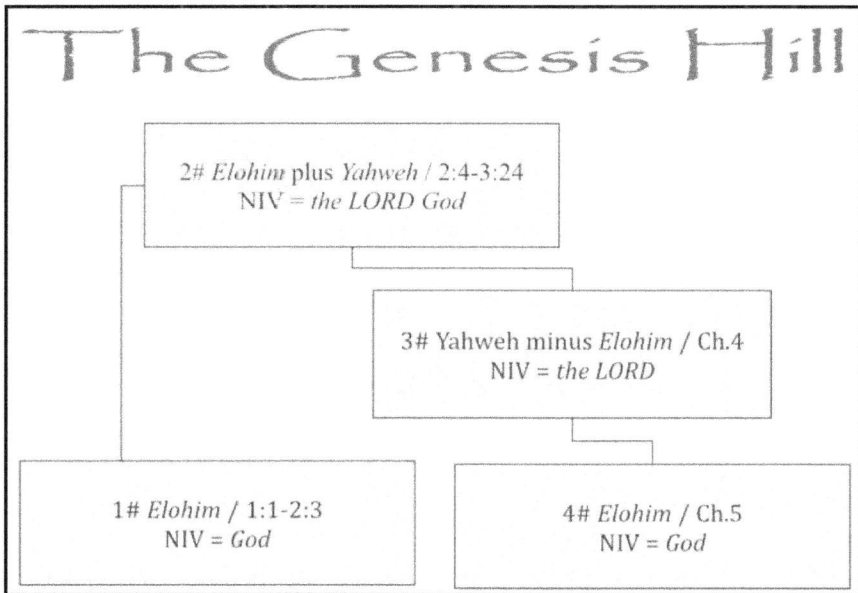

The Genesis Hill

2# *Elohim* plus *Yahweh* / 2:4-3:24
NIV = *the LORD God*

3# Yahweh minus *Elohim* / Ch.4
NIV = *the LORD*

1# *Elohim* / 1:1-2:3
NIV = *God*

4# *Elohim* / Ch.5
NIV = *God*

Stage 1 begins with a common humanity, a common creator (9:6). C S Lewis' *The Abolition of Man*, shows how ethics has been common across the global since ancient days, and that it is not a human (evolutionary) construct, even though variations exist. For example, cannibals consider murder objectively wrong, but believe that people who aren't in their tribe are cattle, not cousins, so are game to eat.

Try and picture human society in which murder and betrayal were virtues, or evolutionary ethics where self-sacrifice refused to go beyond instinct. And why ought I follow an instinct to risk my life for the less fit, if survival of the fittest is the ethical law? Whence comes the gut feeling that I ought to care for others enough to die for them if needs be? Ethics is objective. It is only our perceptions of right and wrong are somewhat subjective and socially warped, undeveloped, and atrophied. H D Lewis called conscience, God's indirect voice, highlighting its fallibility in hearing God's voice. Man has fallen into sin's barrenness, yet most being outside the moral void at least sense their common humanity. Common creation is the creation's default setting. God is.

Stage 2 shows a special relationship with the creator by name. It recaps creation, adding in colour to the personal, focusing on Yahweh and humanity. From the commonality like a handful of earth, mankind is given a priestly focus, the arboreal temple of Eden. It was *Genesis'* high point. God is Yahweh.

Stage 3 reflects man, after the Fall, forgetting Yahweh as Creator (*Elohim*). To the Snake, lacking relationship, he was simply *Elohim*. The Snake got Eve talking that way, taking special covenant relationship out of the picture. She came to fear Yahweh's approach. Her gratitude at the Yahweh-level regarding Abel (4:1) would drop to gratitude at the Elohim-level regarding Seth (25)—her spiritual level fell. The special relationship continued on Yahweh's side, but he wasn't talked about much. There was day, there was night, and there was the first murder. Some people attempted revival (26): Yahweh is.

But with Stage 4, things more or less fell back into common humanity. Chapter 5 is Elohistic, until Noah's father prophesied that his son Noah would revive something of Yahweh among the people (29). But by then the rot had set in. The story of Noah reminds us of how deep spiritual rebelliousness was. Thereafter in *Genesis* one finds mention of *Yahweh* **or** *Elohim*, but never the lost connection *Yahweh-Elohim*—the closest was Abram speaking to Yahweh as *lord*—*Adonai Yahweh* (Gen.15:2,8). Abraham could give Yahweh-names to places (22:14), but he never knew the fullness of the name such as Moses would within the great deliverance and national covenant of exodus. At least God is.

The Patriarchs had mostly known God at an *El Shaddai* level (Gen.17:1), meaning that God was their sufficient and special support. Yahweh had looked after them in *El Shaddai* mode. He preserved them, gave them a certain amount of social upgrade, and they became tribal and later national. Thus, when Moses asked to know what the relationship would be, he was told that it would be a Yahweh one (Ex.6:4). More than an unconnected name, it was about a new personal *Yahweh* relationship, superseding the *El Shaddai* level. It would be a fully-fledged ethnic covenant with Moses as its mediator, and Yahweh at its centre—think sacred tent/temple. The spiritually dark nations, some perhaps with dim memories of Yahweh times, would at best know him at the level of common humanity, *Elohim*.

Outsiders had a muddled and imperfect sense of what he was like, then gave his facets different names and called them deities. These elohim could be idols, misrepresentations, in contrast Yahweh was creator (Ps.96:5). To worship a 3D picture (idol) of a false and limited representation of God, was by and large a sad waste of time. Playing with jigsaw pieces without getting the true picture, so to speak, leaves one puzzled but can intrigue. They were a bit like Jesus' parables, but darkened by pagan darkness. Such spiritual confusion was commonplace outside of Ethnic-Israel. Even Jews needed their prophets to laugh such ideas out of their heads (eg Is.44:19), when they were tempted to believe that Yahwism didn't pay.[244] And of course they were right: it *didn't* really pay unless one loved Yahweh. Sinaitic Covenant upgraded relationship from the Abrahamic.

A new vision

As said, when God revealed his plan of deliverance to Moses, he spoke of this deeper Yahweh relationship: covenants are relationships. And it involved the whole people being in their own land, not just a large immediate family of a covenant holder. It was this shift to

---

[244]   To ancient Israelites & Jews, squeezing into the pagan mould offered the benefits of joining the crowd, even as going the sub-pagan route of Westernism today offers those benefits of social equality: why put Christ before censure & career?

nationhood, thus to national identity, which the Sinaitic Covenant addressed through Moses. This covenant was very deeply regulated, revolving around core stipulations for God's new kingdom, which were elsewhere worked out in details covering many aspects of life. A framework of core priesthood was set up, with masses of detail about structures and sacrifices, with deep symbolism for the following age. The relationship Yahweh had with Israel was intended to be intimate. This can be seen in key analogies between himself to Israel of father to son, and husband to wife (or wives)—highly personal terms.

Law, is a somewhat term misleading. Torah spoke of obedient family guidelines to enrich their relationship.[245] Their covenant was not a legal contract, nor a contract of legality, and included ingredients of how human beings around the world ought to live—moral imperatives. The many symbolic things to do or not to do, hinted at a deeper level of God's plans for them and for the future, teachings about spiritual norms available within covenant (as Eden), and of spiritual abnorms lurking outside covenant (as the Fall). Covenantally all other peoples were in the spiritual abnorm, out of sync; Ethnic-Israel alone was in the spiritual norm (clean), and its inner core was holy (*supranorm*). Yet that norm was never the ideal, simply the shadow of the ideal. Ethnic-Israel only saw a bit of God's glory/design, as if seeing the back side of his plan, rather than the front—shadow rather than shine (Ex.33:23). Paul pictured Sinai as hidden truth now unhidden from those who turn to messiah (2 Cor.3:16).

The vision beyond the vision

God's true norm is nowadays open to all, and doesn't come with Sinai's trimmings. The messianic kingdom has superseded Sinai's kingdom. The norm now is a holiness that even Sinai's high priests lacked. The high priests worshipped within the tabernacle or temple. Nowadays at the simplest level, Christians worship simply by being living tabernacles/temples: "you should know that your body is a temple for the Holy Spirit who is in you. You have received the Holy Spirit from God. So you do not belong to yourselves..." (NCV: 1 Cor.6:19).

---

[245]   Alternative terms include commandments/instruction/torah/teachings.

Here the Greek *naos* carries the idea of the most holy part of the temple, the shrine, the inner sanctum. Paul underlined that in this relationship, even our sexuality is to align to ultimate standards for humanity. To what extent the sexuality laws in *Leviticus* were global norms, is moot. Certainly they offered physical and psychological wellbeing, but arguably the focus was a spiritually symbolic rationale, a metanarrative behind the total package. Yahweh's commitment was that "...if you obey me fully and keep my covenant, then out of all the nations you will be my treasured possession. Although the whole earth is mine, you will be for me a kingdom of priests and a holy nation" (NIV: Ex.19:5-6). Today's messianic covenant is global.

Son of Nun, leader into land

With a new covenant, and an ethnic-national one at that, the population had to choose. Indeed Joshua, shortly before leaving the stage, checked whether they really wished to reaffirm that covenant (Jos.24).[246] The very name *Joshua* is also familiar in another form, *Jesus* (Gk. *Yēsous*). Indeed, the exactitude has caused a few translational problems, indicated below.

Text	Latin	Luther	KJV	RV	NKJV	NIV
Lk.3:29[247]	Jesus	Jose	Jose	Jesus	Jose	Joshua
Ac.7:45	Jesus	Joshua	Jesus	Joshua	Joshua	Joshua
Heb.4:8	Jesus	Joshua	Jesus	Joshua	Joshua	Joshua

The Hebrew *hôšea* means *salvation*. The son of Nun/servant of Moses, once bore this name (Hoshea, Nb.13:16) but became known as *Ye hôšua'* (= 'Yahweh is saviour/deliverer'). His name is usually put as *Joshua* in Bible versions, but is the same as *Jesus*. In Aramaic, spoken later by the Jews, *Yehoshua* was shortened to *Yešu'* (see Neh.3:19 = *Yeshua*). The Greek *Iēsous*, with the capital iota pronounced as a Y, then varied a bit after 1066 when the Norman *J* began to replace the beginning *I* and *Y* in words. By 1671 the KJV had updated its orthography to *Jesus*,

---

[246]   Peter J Gentry called this check a making of a covenant to keep the earlier covenant, hence *karat*/cut.

[247]   The MT/NU texts are the same for *Acts* and *Hebrews*, but for *Luke*, the MT has *Jōsē*, and the NU has *Iēsou*. As appropriate I've updated to current names.

and *Jehovah*. You might have noted that nowadays, a J or v might be replaced by a Y or w: living language is changeable. Gone are the Genevan days when messiah's name was "Iesvs: for hee shall saue his people" (Mt.1:21).

Technicalities aside, *Jesus* says "Yahweh is saviour" from the common Aramaic of C1 Palestine. Arguably "Jesus is lord" implies that "Jesus is Yahweh" and that "Yahweh is lord". But beware dumbing down to convenience terms. We should see Yahweh as the eternal society (the trinity), with each member playing their part towards our well-being. That the Second Person became human and then bore the name *Jesus*, highlights the pivotal salvation event of his birth, life, death, and resurrection to glory. It is only shorthand (usually best avoided) that speaks of *Jesus* pre-existing the incarnation, and always the biblical contexts of his deity flag up that he is not God alone—whatever some songs tout. I am human but not humanity. God's son is God (in substance) but not all there is to God. We thank God for the first Joshua, and still more for the true Joshua. If the first Joshua had given them true rest, God would not have spoken later about another day (Heb.4:8). The Christian journey is about expanding into true Canaan.

Covenant Commitment

We've looked at an Adamic, an Abrahamic, and a Sinaitic *covenant*. To understand more fully the relational side of things, let's now compare and contrast covenant and contract. And bear in mind that although God can squeeze his will into human conventions, he can also squeeze human conventions into his will. Covenant can thus be an idea shaped by and used by God. The idea *covenant*, like Ancient Near Eastern treaties, was presented in the ideal of eternal language, but in reality allowed annulment if gross disloyalty occurred. Using the marriage picture, Jr.3:8 indicates that she who deserved divorce, could instead become a good wife: patiently, graciously, God covers a multitude of violations. Marriage can *contain* contractual legalities but isn't a contract—think covenant, think marriage.

Covenant	Contract
describes the relationship	describes the transaction
is for relationship	is for items
is person-orientated	is thing-orientated
demands loyalty	demands performance
has no fixed end	has a fixed end

Every covenant, whether it says so or not, is conditional on loyalty, but not on performance. Even that with Adam indicates that if ever the human race totally failed to appreciate the Imago Dei, all bets would be off—man would have abolished man. C S Lewis wrote about *The Abolition of Man*, the sub-pagan trend of subjectivism so deeply infecting the West. Yet the *Imago* has a habit of bouncing back to the *Dei*—we have an internal witness to God, a God-shaped void, a moral perception. That said, one day Christ will return, the Adamic Covenant will be annulled for gross violation, and Redeemed Adam will fly free.

Dating witnesses

Covenants could come in many shapes and sizes. Apache leader Geronimo, spoke of having "placed a large stone on [a] blanket before [covenant parties, making a treaty by that stone, which] was to last until the stone should crumble to dust" (Barrett 1906:1245-6). That idea was nothing new. There had long been symbolism in having a neutral third-party witness. Laban and Jacob used rocks too, knowing that God was the invisible witness (Gen.31:48,50). C14 BC Šuppiluliuma and Niqmandu evoked their gods as witnesses: "may a thousand gods know it: the god of Hebat, the god of Arinna..." (Martens 76). There have been many forms of witness, and perhaps the more parochial were the less ornate, like a gold ring. These things can sound pretty random, but it's good to see that covenants had formal structure. For example...

Phase 5	Sinai	Phase 6	Phase 6
Hittite	**Ex-Lv.; Dt.; Jos.24**	**Sefire**	**Assyria**
Suzerain Title	Suzerain Title	Suzerain Title	Suzerain Title
Historical Prologue	Hist. Prologue	Witnesses	Witnesses
Stipulations	Stipulations	Curses	Stipulations
Deposit/Reading	Dep/Reading	Stipulations	Curses
Witnesses	Witnesses		
Curses	Blessings		
Blessings	Curses		

Hittite-based documents could have structural variations, but "the minor variations of order in the Sinai covenant and renewals are of no consequence; the main order and overall content is what is really significant" (Kitchen 288). Of note between these phases is that the historical prologue, stipulations, and integral facility for storing and reading the covenant, are absent from Phase 6. Sinai is a special blend of Law (intranational relationships), Treaty (international nonaggression pacts between two groups, non-incursion), and Covenant (international bonding between two groups, eg deity and people, cohesion). In this confluence, the main framework fits Phase 5 treaties, but the stipulations, the imbalance of more curse than blessing, and the interim epilogues go back to older practice of law codes rather than to treaty framework. Dating to Phase 5 helps us affirm the doctrine of deific inspiration of Scripture, linking the format to the historical Moses.

Covenant divisions

Covenants divided into two main types. Some were between two more or less equal powers, or indeed friends, such as David and Jonathan's covenant alliance.[248] Jonathan, seeking Yahweh's kingdom to come, wished the true anointed to reign. These are called parity covenants. Others were granted or imposed by a greater power and are called suzerain-vassal covenants. Suzerain-vassal covenants, or for short simply suzerain covenants, varied in familiarity. They could be formal, as between a superpower and its vassals, with little love

---

248   Academically the idea of homosexual liaison between them is a grasping for invisible straws. Jonathan backed God's election of David and swore commitment (love) to the king elect.

between. The superpower pledged support, so long as the vassal maintained loyalty and continued to pay tribute. This was a lord to servant covenant. Or if the superpower had a heart for the vassal power, it could be familial. Though the vassal still had obligations of loyalty and tribute, terms between each party would be more endearing, such as parent to child, expressing real care.

The Sinaitic Covenant had formal and informal emphases. Yahweh was father-lord of the covenant with his vassal-son. Most of my Bible versions overweight the idea of lordship. Once all the false *LORD*s are taken out from them—where they should never have been—you'll find relatively few mentions of Yahweh being lord—though he was. Sadly as biblical education wanes, these LORDs also help undermine trinitarianism. Too often folk make a simplistic jump to the idea that since Jesus is lord (a New Covenant emphasis), he must be the LORD of the Old Covenant, and many trinitarian audiences blithely sing that Jesus *alone is God*, thus in happy hour denying their faith under the guise of Hillsong worship.

This is another good reason why those Bible versions which make at least some show of God's name, deserve our thanks.[249] In the OT, there was no such confusion, though there was a temptation to merge Yahwism with neighbouring religions, to be squeezed into the world's mould. As with marriage, covenant with Yahweh involved "forsaking all others, [being] faithful only to him so long as...both shall live". For faithful Yahwists—even if persecuted within their own land—there was the incomparable joy of knowing Yahweh as lord, and as father to their religious identity. Covenant was central. And with messiah came a better covenant.

---

[249]   And rapprochement to Judaists should not abandon biblicality.

Book Conclusion

Covenant is a central biblical theme. Dispensationalism wrongly taught that so-called unconditional covenants would continue to last until Christ returns, since there were no conditions to violate. It acclaimed Abraham's, scotched Sinai's, and taught that God has a special salvation plan for Ethnic-Israel, or at least that part that nowadays we call Jews, or—since Christians are Jews—*ethnic*-Jews. No, Ethnic-Jews belong to the human family, and are neither worse nor better than others, though are blessed to have the OT spring-board. Since they aren't under the covenant of Sinai, human evangelism should be extended to them in the same way, and with the same priority, as for any other peoples.

To look at marriage is to look at covenant, and in turn to see what marriage is, and what it is not, that humanity has no permission to define it in its own image. Marriage is spoken of as lifelong until death—what dispensationalists could call an unconditional covenant. Nevertheless the Bible supports divorce, the annulment of covenant, on certain grounds. Covenants (unlike promise) divide not into unconditional and conditional types, but into those with implicit or explicit grounds for annulment. All require basic loyalty, and may be ended for gross disloyalty. Sinai—the ethnic focus of Abraham—long violated, was annulled by God when a global covenant began. So the residue of Ethnic-Israel, ethnic-Jews, are no longer in the Sinaitic covenant since they supersede it. Nor is the State of Israel *the Holy Land*: that glory has departed. The messianic church is that land. The secularised people and nation should be treated no better and no worse than any other secular people or nation—fairness should prevail without prophetic bias.

The keyword *Israel* is the name of the salvation plan that has unfolded through different phases. Jacob and his people became its foreshadowing, but then the name went to messiah, who in turn bestowed it on his faith community: it's the key to God's kingdom. Physical circumcision—dedication to God—symbolised an ethnic people, and foreshadowed God's true people, a faith community under messiah's lordship: they are the spiritual circumcision.

Those who argue that Sinai continues, use a number of key texts. In particular I have taken three of these to argue that they witness to spiritual Israel, God's Israel, the church of the new covenant. All godly Israelites/Jews will be saved only through Yeshua, whether saved ultimately without having been Christians, or firstly saved by knowing Jesus. Ethnically an Israelite-Jew, Paul had himself been saved in his mortal days through knowing Yeshua. Some godly remained within those hardened by God's design, excluded from messiah's kingdom for the greater good: not excluded from ultimate life, and in which individuals may repent into messianism, even as Rahab and Ruth became Yahwists.

It is important to understand the levels (or dimensions) of salvation. Nicodemus was already saved by Yahweh (Level 2) by having been born into God's ethnic kingdom, yet he could only enter God's spiritual kingdom and be saved by God in a deeper way (Level 3), through spiritual 'birth'. This birth is only available subsequent to and consequent on the cross of Christ, so even the likes of Abraham were never in God's messianic kingdom, howbeit they are ultimately saved and in their days were also saved at some level of spirituality by faith in Yahweh, even if not knowing him as Yahweh.

"I tell you the truth, of all who have ever lived, none is greater than John the Baptist. Yet even the least person in the Kingdom of Heaven is greater than he is!" (NLT: Mt.11:11). God's spiritual kingdom is now open to whosoever welcomes messiah, though welcome is limited to those informed about it: we know Yahweh through Yeshua. Those who 'hear' and 'heed' the good news become, metaphorically speaking, indwelt, and are new people with a new age genesis opening up new spiritual possibilities in this life. From heaven's perspective, those who wilfully reject it gain hell in this life.

Many people have a desire for and a knowledge of God, yet fall short of knowing him as family. Familial relationship is the unique beauty of the Christian level (Level 3), but the other world religions all bear witness of a lesser level of salvation, howbeit less than what was known under Sinai. They do not save as such, but true devotees can find a level of salvation (Level 1) in them. Ultimate salvation towers above all religions, and is procured by the death of Christ for any who truly desire God, irrespective of what religion they have had on earth.

This last point is also relevant to those who die in infancy, as well as to others who die outside the gospel. Ultimate life (Level 4) is dependent on individual faith-welcome. God shows no favouritism, no bias towards people who die in or before infancy, whether or not they have been conceived or born to a Christian parent, and/or have been baptised. Call it election or the luck or ill luck of the draw, but some are conceived with or without a true desire, with or without a genuine faith-welcome for God. God, who sees each heart, will welcome all who have welcomed him, and allow all others to go their own way, which by rejecting him is damnation by individual choice.

Damnation may well be bearable from their perspective, but not from heaven's perspective—subnature. In adult life, these people would never truly seek God as God, however religiously they might perform: no archbishop, atheist, ayatollah, buddha, patriarch, pope, or sannyasin, will necessarily be saved in life's ultimate sense. Ultimately the Good News is superfluous for ultimate life, but is the Best News we can ever have in the here and now. Desire for God won't spring up from bad seed; all good seed will one day flower in God's garden.

The good news opens up immediate *assurance* of ultimate life, and immediate *fellowship* with God as father. Christian salvation is deific, though can cost us dear. Grace is neither cheap to God nor to us, even though it is free and frees humanity into freedom. Christ is a dangerous lord and brother. What Ethnic-Israel modelled in shadow form, has become the norm in true light for Christians, and myth became fact in Christ. Sinaitic themes such as land, priesthood, worship, forgiveness, relationship, insight, are individualised for each believer within God's family. There are great blessings in the here and now within the meaning of life. We can grow into God's perspective. Let's preach the good news as really good news.

After death there awaits ultimate life. It is for those who truly desired God as God. This is no eternal camp fire sing-along surrounding some supreme egotist, or white clouds populated with little cherubs stroking golden harps. This is eternal enjoyment within God's creation, once we're freed from the limitations of mortal life, once our bodies are immortalised and able to travel throughout the universe at will. Exploration and marvel shall be ours, within the universal voice and face of our creator. Our unending joy will be to his praise when we see as we are seen. Or it will be better.

This all comes from the fulfilment of salvation history, hinted at in Eden, and slowly focused through covenants under the Israel theme. Spiritually salvation is unimportant in itself; its importance is in the life that it is the means to. Of special interest are studies in the covenants with Adam, Abraham, and then Moses—linked by Jacob—culminating in messiah, humanity's lord to the glory of God the father, and showing the true face of God that ancient Israel only briefly glimpsed.

The children of Israel could rejoice in the joy of the immediate, and could also know the joy of knowing that something deeper, something global, was in store, though they were not as such called to do anything to bring it about. Those most sensitive to Yahweh, his prophets, seriously tried to fathom what his plans were (1 Pt.1:10). And as I've said (page 76), Mt 5:17-20 and Jhn.19:30 show the answer to their search. Namely, that the Sinaitic has given way to messiah's covenant, messiah's kingdom. "...whenever anyone turns to the lord, the veil is taken away" (NIV: 2 Cor.3:16). Commitment to Christ includes a knowledge of forgiveness from sins, the deepest spiritual blindness being over and done with, new life with God's spirit, holiness, and distanciation from the perverseness of surrounding cultures (Ac.2:38-40). All who welcome God's son become children of God. His son died for us. His spirit is committed to living with us, guiding us.

Glossary

Christian religion	A direct covenant upgrade, whether from Level 1 or 2, to Level 3 Golgotha
Ethic-Israel/Jew	Belonging ethnically to Jacob-Israel
Global-Israel/Jew	Belonging spiritually to Yeshua-Israel
Inexclusivism	The idea that Level 4 life is inclusivist, but Level 3 life is exclusivist
Level 1/Pre-Alpha (salvation & life)	The common life under Adam: Level 1 life
Level 2/Alpha (salvation & life)	The clean/kosher life under Sinai: Level 2 life
Level 3/Omega (salvation & life)	The born anew life, eternal life before death: Level 3 life
Level 4/Post-Omega (salvation & life)	Being with God beyond mortal death: Level 4 life
Sinaitic covenant	The covenant Moses mediated on Sinai: Level 2 life
Sinaitic people	Those under Moses during that covenant: Level 2 life
Sinaitic religion	A direct covenant upgrade from Level 1 to Level 2 Sinai
Ultimate life	A direct upgrade after death, whether from Level 1, Level 2, or Level 3 life
World religions (excluding Christianity)	Enriching Level 1 life
Yeshuic/Golgothic covenant	The covenant Yeshua mediated on Golgotha: Level 4 life

Works Cited:

Jay Adams' Marriage, Divorce and Remarriage: 1980

Tokunboh Adeyemo's *Africa Bible Commentary*: 2006

Pat Alexander's *Lion Handbook: The World's Religions*: 1994

J N D Anderson's *Christianity and Comparative Religion*: 1970

David Aune's *Revelation 6–16* (WBC): 1998

Glenn Balfour's *A Step-by-Step Introduction to NT Greek*: 2005

C K Barrett's *The First Epistle to the Corinthians*: 1986

S M Barrett's *Geronimo's Story of His Life*: 1906

Richard Bauckham's *The Theology of the Book of Revelation*: 2001

G K Beale's *The Book of Revelation*: 1999

G K Beale's *The Temple and the Church's Mission*: 2004

Beale & Carson's *Commentary on the NT Use of the OT*: 2009

Louis Berkhof's *History of Christian Doctrines*: 1985

Darrell Bock's *Luke* (NIVAC): 1996

Boëthius' *The Consolation of Philosophy* [trans. V E Watts]: 1969

Colin Brown's *New International Dictionary of NT Theology*: 1975

George Buttrick's *The Interpreter's Bible*: 1952-7

John Calvin's *Institutes*

D A Carson's *The Gospel According to John*: 1991

D A Carson's *The Gagging of God*: 1996

D A Carson's *New Bible Commentary*: 1997

D A Carson's *Matthew* (EBC): 2010

Colin Chapman's *The Case for Christianity*: 1984

Brenda Cox' *Fashionable Goodness: Christianity in Jane Austen's England*: 2022

C E B Cranfield's *Romans* (ICC): 2004

David van Daalen's *A Guide to Revelation*: 1986

William Dumbrell's *Covenant and Creation* 1983

William Dumbrell's *The Faith of Israel*: 2003

Edwards and Stott's *Essentials: A Liberal-Evangelical Dialogue*: 1988

Walter Elwell's *Evangelical Dictionary of Theology*: 1985

Anthony Flew's *There is a God*: 2007

Richard France's *Matthew* (TNTC): 1985

David E Garland's *1 Corinthians* (BECNT): 2015

Raphael Gasson's *The Challenging Counterfeit*: 1972

Kenneth Grahame's *The Wind in the Willows*: 1992

Wayne Grudem's *Systematic Theology*: 1994
Donald Guthrie's *New Testament Theology*: 1981
Donald Guthrie's *Hebrews* (TNTC): 1986
William Hasker's *Metaphysics: Constructing a World View*: 1983
Arthur F Holmes' *Ethics: Approaching Moral Decisions*: 2007
E C Hoskyns' *The Fourth Gospel*: 1954
Reidar Hvalvik: *Journal for the Study of the NT*: 1990
Eric Ives' *God in History*: 1979
Karen Jobes' *1 Peter* (BECNT): 2005
Johnston & Walker's *The Land of Promise*: 2000
William K Kay's *George Jeffreys: Pentecostal Apostle and Revivalist*: 2017
Craig Keener's *Commentary on the Gospel of Matthew*: 1999
Kenneth Kitchen's *On the Reliability of the Old Testament*: 2003
Andreas Köstenberger's *John* (BECNT): 2004
Hans Küng's *The Church*: 1986
George Ladd's *A Commentary on the Revelation of John*: 1972
C S Lewis' *English Literature in the C16*: 1954
C S Lewis' *Miracles*: 1960
C S Lewis' *The Problem of Pain*: 1972
C S Lewis' *Fern-Seed and Elephants*: 1975
C S Lewis' *A Grief Observed*: 1985
C S Lewis' *Mere Christianity*: 2002
Richard Longenecker's *Galatians* (WBC): 1990
Alister McGrath's *C S Lewis: A Life: Eccentric Genius, Reluctant Prophet*: 2013
Howard Marshall's *Acts* (TNTC): 1992A
Howard Marshall's New *Testament Interpretation*: 1992B
Howard Marshall's *New Testament Theology*: 2004
Elmer Martens' *God's Design*: 1994
Thomas Martin's *Reading the Classics with C S Lewis*: 2000
Douglas Moo's *James* (TNTC): 1990
Douglas Moo's *Galatians* (BECNT): 2013
Leon Morris' *Romans* (TNTC): 1988
Leon Morris' *Revelation* (TNTC): 1995
Alec Motyer's *The Prophecy of Isaiah*: 1993
Alec Motyer's *Isaiah* (TOTC): 2005
Chawkat Moucarry's *Faith to Faith: Christianity and Islam*: 2001

Robert Mounce's *Revelation* (NICNT): 1998

David Petts' *The Holy Spirit: An Introduction*: 1998

Roth and Wigoder's *Encyclopaedia Judaica*: 1971

John Sanders' *No Other Name*: 1994

Stephen Smalley's *The Revelation to John*: 2005

Jonathan Smith's *Harper-Collins' Dictionary of Religion*: 1996

Soderlund and Wright's *Romans and the People of God*: 1999

Robert H Stein's *Mark* (BECNT): 2014

Scorgie, Strauss, & Voth's *The Challenge of Bible Translation*: 2003

Willem VanGemeren's *NIDOTTE*: 2001

John White's *The Golden Cow*: 1979

Hans Wolff's *Joel and Amos* (HERM): 1977

N T Wright's *Colossians & Philemon* (TNTC): 1986

N T Wright's *The Climax of the Covenant*: 1991

Mosab Hassan Yousef's *Son of Hamas*: 2010

Books by this Author

Theology

Israel's Gone Global

Israel's Gone Global traces salvation through the term, Israel. Was the covenant with the people-nation of Yakob-Yisrael, crossed out? How eternal is covenant? To examine that, we examine marriage. Can a covenant partner be truly divorced? Has Yeshua-Yisrael mediated a spiritual covenant with a spiritual Israel? Is evangelism of ethnic-Jews needless, a priority, or neither?

No one could have everlasting life but for the cross, but has it always been globally accessible? Might any who die as Atheists, Hindus, or Islamists, make heaven? And is eternal life joyful? Is everlasting life fun?

Tackling the question of people who die in infancy (or as adults who never heard the gospel), we consider whether it is fair if only those who don't die in infancy get a chance of eternal damnation (if infant universalism), or alone get a chance of eternal heaven (if infant damnation). Does predilectionism make best sense of biblical revelation?

Opportunities to enjoy eternal life spring from the new covenant—reasons to rejoice. But what about salvation history before that covenant?

∞

Singing's Gone Global

Singing's Gone Global, briefly explores the background of singing, before and into ancient Israel. It examines the impact songs have on those who sing, and on those who listen, touching on spiritual warfare. It looks at how nonsense songs neither make sense to evangelism, nor to the evangelised, and asks, "Is there a mûmak in the room?"

Oddly some songwriters simply misunderstand prayer. Part two covers the basics of the trinity, focusing on the spirit in order to understand types of prayer (eg request, gratitude, adoration, chat), leading in turn to a better understanding of our heavenly father, our brother, our helper, and ourselves in Christ's likeness.

Next we look at some common problems. Part three focuses on problems such as buddyism, decontextualising, misvisualisation, and unitarianism. Diagnosis can help Christ's 'bride' to recover from suboptimal and unbiblical songs (Eph.5:18-30).

Giving a Problem Avoidance Grade (PAG)—an A+ to Unsatisfactory scale—in part four we examine specific songs. Weapons forged (Part three), the mûmakil can be attacked, seeking to save and be saved.

Subsequently the book concludes by showing how Christmas carols may be tweaked to better serve our weary world, rejoicing that joy to the world has come.

∞

The Word's Gone Global

The Word's Gone Global, examines Bible text (trusted by early Islam) and introduces textual critique. It looks at the Eastern Orthodox Bible and the Latin Vulgate. Did the Reformation improve text and translation? Were Wycliffe, Tyndale, and Martin, helpful?

Why did the New International Version begin, and why does it enrage? Why did complementarians Don Carson and Wayne Grudem, clash? Is marketing hype between formal and functional equivalence, meaningless? Which version or versions should you regularly read?

In English-speaking circles, Broughton wished to burn Bancroft's King James Version, yet many KJV proponents—think Gail Riplinger and Peter Ruckman—wish to burn all alternatives. More heat than light?

Grade Charts cover 30+ English versions on issues such as God's name, God's son's deity, marriage, gender terms, anti-polytheism, and various issues in John's Gospel. No, Tyndale was not 'born again'. No, John was not antisemitic. No, he did not disagree with the other Gospels.

∞

Prayer's Gone Global

Prayer's Gone Global, begins with ancient civilisations and prayer (the Common Level). Then it narrows into Ancient Israel and prayer (the Sinai Level). Then it deepens and widens into Global-Israel and prayer (the Christian Level). Deity is revealed as trinity: Sabellians mislead.

Relating to the trinity includes the Holy Spirit. We should of course work with him, but should we worship him, complain to him, chat with him? Above the spirit stands the often forgotten father—oh let Jesusism retire.

Authority is another issue. Are we authorised to decree and declare? Is binding and loosing actually prayer, or is it evangelism? Is it biblical never to command miracles? Do we miss out on the supernatural which Jesus modelled for us, too fearful of strange fire to offer holy fire?

You can freshen up your prayer life—ride the blessed camel, not the gnats. Listen to Saint Anselm pray, and C S Lewis and 'Malcolm' discuss prayer, and be blessed.

∞

Revelation's Gone Global

Revelation's Gone Global, is a telling of John's future, as if by a then contemporary named Sonafets speaking to his church about how John's apocalyptic scroll related to their days, and about what was still future to John.

Encouragement is a big theme. Roman persecution was an unpredictable beast which ferociously lashed out here and there— what church or Christian was safe? But God stood behind the scenes, allowing but limiting their enemy, and messiah walked among the churches, lights to the world.

Victory lay neither with Rome nor demons, but with God, and with the warrior lamb who had been slain. Victory was guaranteed, and would finally be enjoyed.

Exhortation was given to believers, to play their part while on the mortal stage. They were to walk in the light, and not to let the show down by straying.

Angels of power, actively working out God's will, far exceed the puny forces against God and his church. His wrath was not pleasant, but could be redemptive until the new age begins.

C S Lewis' essay, The World's Last Night, is briefly examined to enjoin a calm awareness of the ongoing battle we are in, and the brightness to come when the king returns.

∞

The Father's Gone Global

Focusing from God as father, to the specific person of God the father, The Father's Gone Global looks at the biblical parent/child pattern from Genesis, through Sinai, and into the Church.

Abba as a new covenant word expresses deep filial affection even under deep anguish in our Gethsemane battles. Coming through God's belovèd son, it speaks into the church and into our lives.

Though to many the 'forgotten father', human parents/fathers should 'put on' God the father, and his children should 'put on' his son. We forget him to our cost.

Human applications aside, what is the Eternal Society? Is filial relationship modelled by God the son incarnate? Are we to be always obedient to our father and guided by the spirit?

Eschatologically the father will be supreme, but even now he is the one to whom the son points. Christian life should relate to God our father, God our brother, and God our helper, prioritising the father.

Renewal of the church is vital for our confused world, but renewal which downplays the father falls short of the good news which Christ created and the spirit circulates. May this book play its part.

∞

Salvation Now and Life Beyond

Salvation Now, divides the doctrine of salvation into the four main levels of common humanity, the old covenant, the new covenant, and life beyond.

A big weight is put on the term, Israel, as God's master plan. This too has four levels, meaning a man, a people, a new man, and a new people, respectively.

Various ideas of what Christianity, the new covenant for the new people, is good for, and how we get into it and best enjoy it, are examined, and a faith-based inexclusivism is suggested.

Everlasting life is seen as the ultimate goal of salvation, universal meaningfulness and love beyond all fears and pains.

∞

Revisiting

Revisiting The Challenging Counterfeit

Revisiting The Challenging Counterfeit, is an extended review of Raphael Gasson's 'The Challenging Counterfeit' (1966). Raphael was an ethnic-Jew whose spiritual journey included many years as a Christian Spiritualist minister.

Today, when psychic phenomena captures the imagination and the bank accounts of popular media, it is useful to unearth the witness of one who had well worn the T-shirt of a medium with pride, only to bury it in unholy ground as a thing of shame and of sorrow and of wasted time.

Challengingly, his book exposes what true Spiritualism is. He had nothing but high praise for Spiritualists, and deep condemnation for Spiritualism. For he had discovered true Spiritualism to be itself a fake of true Spirituality, a mere Counterfeit that, in deposing death in the mind, enthroned it in the soul.

Counterfeit phenomena covered include apparitions, Rescue Work and haunted houses, materialisation of pets, psychic healing, Lyceums, clairvoyance, and OOBEs—to name but a few. This book surveys his exposé of Spiritualism's offer of fascinating fish bait, false food falling short of real food for the soul. Though it takes issue with

Raphael on a number of points, his core insights are powerful and timely, helping us to avoid—or escape from—a Challenging Counterfeit, and to discover true spiritual currency.

∞

Revisiting The Pilgrim's Progress

Revisiting The Pilgrim's Progress, is a re-dreaming of John Bunyan's most famous dream. An ex-serviceman and ex-jailbird, he found fortune, freedom, and fans worldwide.

This dream journey is substantially Bunyan's from this world, and into that which is to come. It is not a fun story, but it has lots of danger, and joy, and reflection on some big life themes.

Profoundly, sinners who become pilgrims become saints. But that can make life more difficult. One big question is, Is it worth it? One big temptation is, Turn back or turn aside. And if you see others do so, that makes it harder not to. Bunyan was tempted. And he discovered that not deserting, can lead to despair. But he also discovered a key to liberty.

Pre-eminently, it is a story of grace which many follow. Grace begins the journey, helps along the way, and brings the story to a happily ever after. Are all fairy stories based on heaven?

∞

Fantasy

The Simbolinian Files

From Simboliniad, a crystal planet long gone, came the vampire race, the wapierze, the lodynamic shapeshifters seeking blood. Most oppose Usen, King of the Light, so side with the Necros. Seldom do the Guardians intervene. These files, secretly secured from various insider sources, reveal something of what they have done, and will do.

∞

Vampire Redemption

Artificial intelligence, created by superpowers to save man, questions man's worth, and becomes The Beast. Escaping into the wild, many discover a wilderness infested by zombies and diabolical spirits. Who will help? Father Doyle? He's tied up with the mysterious Lilith.

Tariq? He's tied up with Wilma. Can the bigoted old exorcist deliver him from evil?

Radical problems can require radical solutions. But does man really need hobs, elves, and the more ancient of days? In the surrounding shadows, vampires and demons form an alliance, raising the stakes against Whitby and Tyneside. Powerful vampires live shrouded within Whitby, speaking of life beyond this galaxy. Is salvation in the stars? Is Sunniva, the despised woman of Alban, worth dying for? Big questions, needing big answers. Not even Guardian Odin can foretell man's fate and, as silent stars go by, one little town must awake from its dreams.

Though The Beast slumbers purposeless and undisturbed, in the far west a global giant slowly opens its yellow eyes and threatens to smother the earth in fire and ice. There is one chance only.

∞

Vampire Extraction

Bitterly long their imprisoned spirits lay, fast bound to Earth's drowsy decay. To the Simbolinian race, there was no hell on Earth, for Earth was hell, and Usen the cosmic jailer. Was it so surprising that as vampires they stalked Usen's children for blood? Most chose the Kingdom of Night, wary of both the Kingdom of Necros and the Kingdom of Dawn.

As queen of the Night, Lilith's story streams through the summer sands of Sumer, and through the green woods of Sherwood. It flags up both dishonour and joy, and cuts across the paths of Ulrica the Saxon and Robin the Hood, as tyrannies rise and fall in merry England. Bigotry seldom has a good word to say about Usen, nor about mercy. Reluctantly, Lilith examines what it means to show mercy, to show weakness. Wulfgar had enslaved Ulrica: is it mercy to let her burn; should mercy have spared Lona? Could Hamashiach turn daughter into sister? Could Count Dracula be turned from his madness? Has Draven really betrayed his mother? Life has many questions.

Tales picture ideas, letting us walk through the eyes of others to better see ourselves. This story exposes subplots behind common history. How these chronicles came to be written up is, in the spirit confidentiality, not for the public eye. What truth is within you must judge. Discrimination is a gift from Beyond, from which the words still echo: mercy is better than sacrifice. Indeed mercy can be sacrifice. Judge well.

∞

Vampire Count

Vampires were not always earthbound, nor are all evil, but being victims of Usen's Eighth Law, his Children became their fair game. Yet the Night Kingdom was divided: some veered to the Necros; some to the Dawn. Who was wrong; who was right?

Long ago one incited his people to racial violence against elven and human kinds. Ever he strove to be king of the Night, and unto Necuratu the Dark Lord he gave the dragon shape. He made war upon the ancient Middle East, even the Nephilim War. Against him the Light raised flood and division.

At last his own people, paying the price of his rampage, bound him in deep sleep. Yet the millennia seemed meaningless to him: even the rising of Hamashiach hardly disturbed his dreams. At last awoken, he and his brides stalked the hills of Transylvania. Only the fear of Lilith—and after her unforgivable sin, Queen Rangda—chained their bloodlust.

Dracula sought escape and autonomy. By cunning and devious means, he immigrated to London via Whitby. Pursuit followed swiftly, with a shadowminder helping a circle of human headhunters, though they sought the death of all vampires.

∞

Vampire Grail

Wulfgar is a vampire, a thelodynamic creature from another galaxy, now locked into our world by one called the Cosmic Jailer. He hides a tormenting secret from his queen, Lilith, which the Necros use as blackmail. She will only go so far with the Necros against Hamashiach—Wulfgar must go further.

Unknown to the Darkness, to bury Hamashiach is to plant the Light. From the buried seed springs life, and humanity must reimagine itself. Longinus turns to The Way, the nexus of the Seventh Age. His spear goes on a special mission to the island of Briton, where Wulfgar lives again.

Logres is centred on Avalon, but raises up Arthur, a man of mixed race, to carry its flag and to protect against the Saxons. But its main enemy is the Darkness, which ever seeks to extinguish the Light it hates and fears.

Finally, it seems as if the Darkness has won, and the dark ages descend. But does the Light not shine in the Darkness? Must Wulfgar remain in the Night?

∞

Vampire Shadows

Dark vampires, hidden within the ancient empire of Khem, fall out with the king who, stirred up by the Necros, enslaves the Sheep People. But Iahveh, the shepherd-divinity, is stirred up, and stirs up a hidden hero to force a way out.

Apprehensively the two vampire-magicians join the Sheep of Iahveh, on their long and deadly trek in search of a promised land. Can any survive?

Warily they ask deep questions. Is Usen evil, as prejudice says? Is he possibly a good jailer? Are his unusual regulations, meaningful? They risk ending up in death.

Neverendingly the Sheep's sorry story drags out in interminable peregrination. Weary of wandering, most would settle for some green pastures and untroubled waters. But as they well know, that would take a miracle.

www.ingramcontent.com/pod-product-compliance
Lightning Source LLC
Chambersburg PA
CBHW061427040426
42450CB00007B/935